Italo Pardo has produced a thoughtful a
life of Naples, a city in which the ethics of work, family and neighbourhood
exist in complex relationship with the teachings of the Church and, crucial
to key processes of democracy, with the power and limitations of law,
bureaucracy and government. Dr Pardo identifies the importance of strong
continuous interaction between material and non-material aspects in the
entrepreneurial strategies of ordinary Neapolitans and shows the ways in
which different ethical systems are negotiated in everyday life. Success is
measured not only by material gain, but also by satisfying spiritual obligations and meeting the claims of intimate loyalties. This is one of the very few
ethnographic studies of a European city; it questions old assumptions and
raises fresh issues in the field of urban studies demonstrating the significance
of empirical analysis to mainstream debates in social theory.

Cambridge Studies in Social and Cultural Anthropology

104

MANAGING EXISTENCE IN NAPLES

Cambridge Studies in Social and Cultural Anthropology

The monograph series Cambridge Studies in Social and Cultural Anthropology publishes analytical ethnographies, comparative works and contributions to theory. All combine an expert and critical command of ethnography and a sophisticated engagement with current theoretical debates.

A list of books in the series will be found at the end of the volume.

MANAGING EXISTENCE IN NAPLES

Morality, action and structure

ITALO PARDO
University of Kent at Canterbury

CAMBRIDGE
UNIVERSITY PRESS

Published by the Press Syndicate of the University of Cambridge
The Pitt Building, Trumpington Street, Cambridge CB2 1RP
40 West 20th Street, New York, NY 10011-4211, USA
10 Stamford Road, Oakleigh, Melbourne 3166, Australia

First published 1996

A catalogue record for this book is available from the British Library

Library of Congress cataloguing in publication data

Pardo, Italo.
  Managing existence in Naples: morality, action, and structure /
Italo Pardo.
      p.   cm. – (Cambridge studies in social and cultural
anthropology)
  Includes bibliographical references and index.
  ISBN 0 521 56227 9 (hardcover)
  1. Naples (Italy) – Moral conditions.   2. Ethics – Italy – Naples.
3. Entrepreneurship – Italy – Naples.   4. Bureaucracy – Italy – Naples.
I. Title.   II. Series.
HN488.N3P37   1996
306′.0945′73–dc20   95-48163   CIP

ISBN 0 521 56227 9 hardback
ISBN 0 521 56665 7 paperback

Transferred to digital printing 2003

SE

To my parents

Contents

Preface

This book is an attempt to communicate a view of life and culture in Naples that has emerged over years of field research. The original fieldwork in a neighbourhood of the centre was conducted over twenty months between 1984 and 1986. In 1988 I was awarded a Ph.D. in social anthropology from the University of London. Since then I have periodically visited Naples and have carried out further extended fieldwork in 1990/1 and 1992/3. This supplementary field research has allowed me to update the material and, above all, to place the micro-level analysis in a broader sociological context. The result is a substantial revision and expansion of my doctoral dissertation.

Because our anthropological knowledge of urban Europe remains quite limited, Naples confronts the observer with a difficult decision – whether to dismiss it as a chaotic and anarchic place doomed to suicidal extinction through resignation to deprivation, marginality and ruin or to ask whether there is a rationale for its appearance that might explain things differently. If my initial work on belief and thought (1978–83) had left me with a mixture of irritation and intellectual curiosity, my instinct as an anthropologist definitely pointed in the direction of further research. Knowing that superimposing categorical distinctions on the empirical situation may give a neat look to our production but is misleading, I eventually decided to invest some effort in trying to come to terms with the messiness of real people's managing their existence. That this investment might pay off in terms of scholarship became a reasonable possibility only much later.

The analysis offered here moves beyond the opposition of morality (and spirituality) to rationality and to self-interest. Focusing on the micro-level sheds new light on the way social morality and individual choice are merged into action. Through detailed examination of how people negotiate their lives in a complex and changing environment, the discussion identifies the deep-rooted significance of strong continuous interaction between material and non-material aspects, between the symbolism of personal identity and the ethics of entrepreneurial management of existence. This interaction profoundly informs the actors' sense of the relationship between action and results in all spheres of their lives, with an emphasis on the role of the significant others (living and dead, through belief in a relationship of mutual influence) in the individual's entitlement to feeling worthy and therefore fulfilled in the broad sense – non-materially as well as materially – and in the long term.

Treated quite unsympathetically by Marxist orthodoxy, the rationality underlying this complex situation has been subjected to the corrupt practices of a long series of centre-right governments. The fact that so much in Italy happens in the blurred and variegated domain between the formal and the informal, often in defiance of the law, certainly complicates the relationship between ordinary people's motivations and expectations and their rulers' views and policies. The civic choices made by most Neapolitans at this critical historical juncture underline the problematic character of political representation and trust. Recent events indicate that such choices are strongly oriented to stability and that there is an equally strong desire to vote the inefficient and the corrupt out of power. Having long learned that a new broom does not necessarily sweep clean, people do not expect miraculous undoing of the damage done by years of political greed and shortsightedness. What they expect is the systematic improvement of a city which they still have the privilege of feeling as a whole entity about them. Rhetoric quite apart, what they definitely deserve is the kind of encouragement that can be provided by a responsible political representation prepared to understand constructively citizens' values and actions. Time will tell whether it is bitter irony to feel that, should such a basic condition of modern democracy and civil society be finally met, Naples could well come closer than ever to fulfilling its historical role in Europe.

In the following pages I seek to show that, even in Western urban studies, empirical investigation of the individual dimension need not be limited to the important task of interpreting the micro-level. A major objective of this study is to encourage the serious questioning of existing models of bureaucracy and relations of power, of overly structured analyses of social relations, and of the class-analysis approach to contemporary society. Drawing on a critical reading of modern social theory, the discussion builds towards a demonstration of how confronting the individual in society allows controlled speculation on the processual relationship between agency and structure. I shall argue that, because this level of analysis carefully avoids a deterministic view of culture, organization and power, it brings to light important processes in the (re)consolidation of democracy.

Over the years I have contracted many debts of gratitude. While I was in the field I found stimulating response in Antonino Colajanni. Sandra Wallman and Jeremy Boissevain commented on my doctoral dissertation. The construction of my argument has greatly benefited at different stages from thought-provoking discussion with Rosemary Harris and Jonathan Parry. Nevill Colclough reacted encouragingly to parts of the final draft. My colleague and companion, Giuliana Prato, has provided assistance in the field and criticism and feedback throughout the lengthy process of writing up the material. I have presented parts of it in seminars at University College London, at the University of Rome, at the University of Cambridge, and at the University of Kent. On all these occasions I have benefited from helpful comments. Barbara Metzger has helped immensely in fine-tuning style and clarity. Finally, I am grateful to anonymous readers for Cambridge University Press for having pointed out various weaknesses in an earlier draft and to Jessica Kuper, whose cooperation and encouragement have exceeded her editorial duty.

Many Neapolitans have generously cooperated in my task. I acknowledge the help given by specific individuals at the appropriate places in the text. My research would not have been possible without the cooperation of the people of the neighbourhood in which I lived and worked. Regrettably, they will have to remain unnamed (or given pseudonyms), as will the area itself, in fulfilment of the promise of confidentiality on which their cooperation depended. Of course, I am well aware that no precaution can lighten my sense of responsibility. There seems, indeed, to be no cure for the ethical dilemma posed by in-depth research. Above all, given my obvious academic obligations, the problem of making my research harmless to the people who have helped and trusted me has been made particularly serious by the illicit element of life in central Naples. This makes my debt to them most certainly unrepayable.

The doctoral research was supported by the Italian Ministero della Pubblica Istruzione, the Folklore Fund (University College London), and the Radcliffe-Brown Memorial Fund (Royal Anthropological Institute). Further field research and writing have been supported by the British Academy. I am grateful to these bodies.

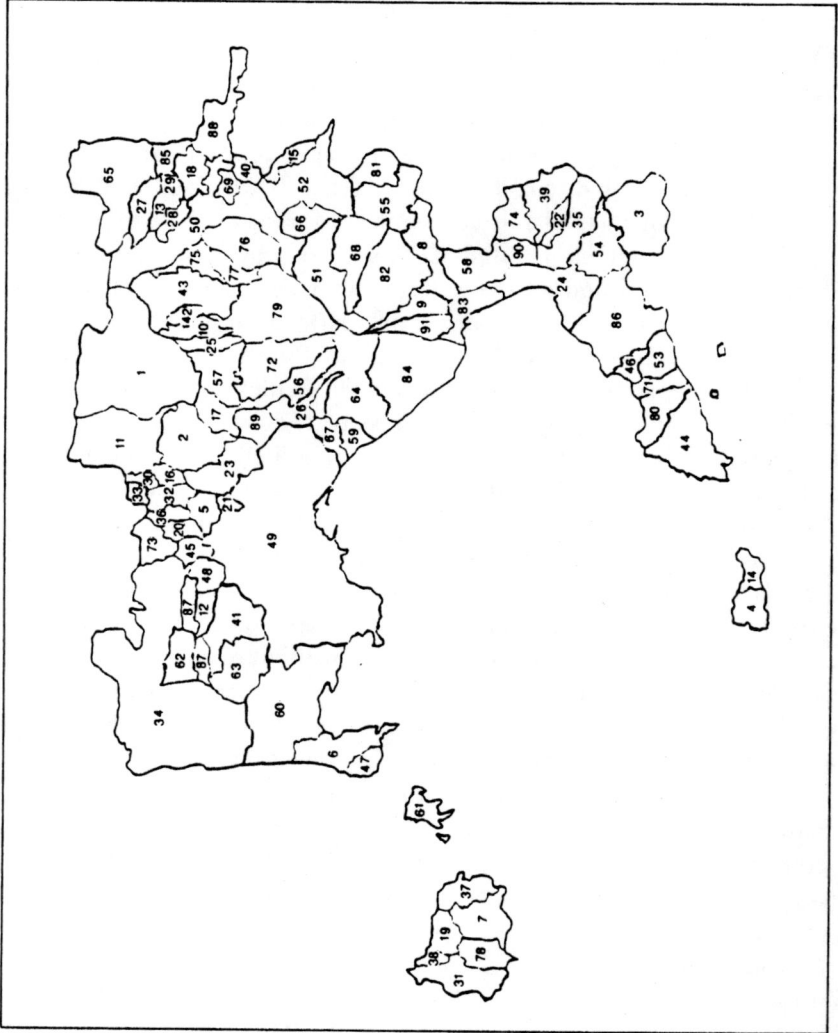

Map 1   The province of Naples
Source: Comune di Napoli, Annuario Statistico

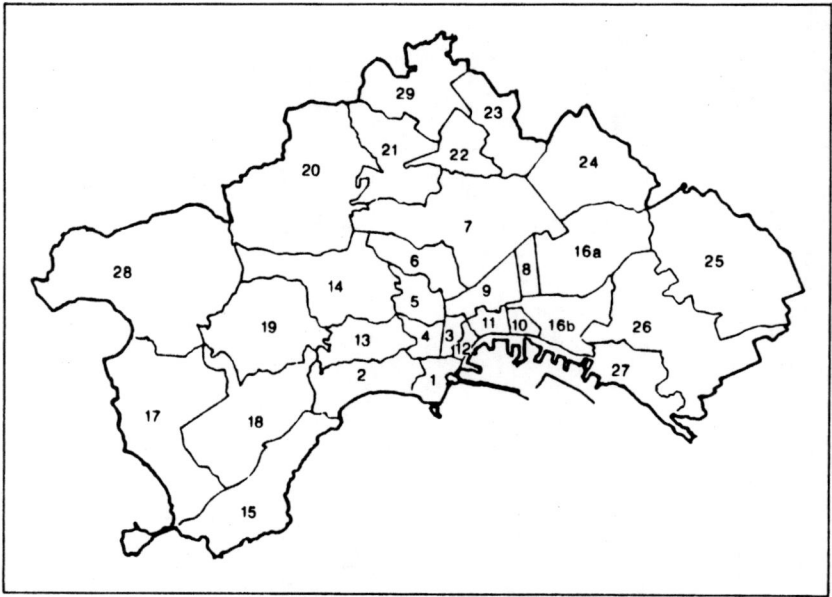

Map 2   The districts of Naples
Source: Comune di Napoli, Annuario Statistico

Key

01 S. Ferdinando	11 Pendino	20 Chiaiano
02 Chiaia	12 Porto	21 Piscinola
03 S. Giuseppe	13 Vomero	22 Miano
04 Montecalvario	14 Arenella	23 Secondigliano
05 Avvocata	15 Posillipo	24 S. Pietro a Patierno
06 Stella	16a Poggioreale	25 Ponticelli
07 S. Carlo all'Arena	16b Zona Industriale	26 Barra
08 Vicaria	17 Bagnoli	27 S. Giovanni a Teduccio
09 San Lorenzo	18 Fuorigrotta	28 Pianura
10 Mercato	19 Soccavo	29 Scampia

1

Issues of anthropological research in urban Europe

In the congested midmorning traffic of the busy centre of Naples, a man speeds on a moped bearing stickers of the Volto Santo (Holy Face of Christ) and of the Naples football team's mascot. Various logos adorn the expensive helmet which, instead of being worn as prescribed by law, hangs from the back of the moped. Probably in his early forties, the man wears fashionable jeans, shirt and trainers. Suddenly he brakes to shout and exuberantly gesture a respectful greeting to a *dottore*[1] who is negotiating his way along the sidewalk among cars half-parked on the pavement, other pedestrians and street-vendors' improvised stalls and show-rugs. Without stopping, the *dottore* acknowledges the greeting, waving his briefcase-free hand. Under the wisely inattentive eye of a bored, perhaps stressed *vigile* (pl. *vigili*, watchman),[2] the man U-turns in the one-way street and, having quickly parked and locked the moped, approaches the *dottore*. The minor disturbance is speedily absorbed by the apparently chaotic but in fact virtually self-regulating stream of traffic. Speaking gently, touching the *dottore*'s arm, the man coaxes him towards a fashionable bar nearby. A quick coffee, a concerned chat, and the brief encounter is over; the moped-rider joins his mates standing by, and the professional enters a building.

The *dottore* and the moped-rider are a council bureaucrat and a council manual worker. They meet near the *comune* (town hall), but similar encounters can easily be observed near any public building or central place of leisure. Perhaps this has been a transaction or an image-boosting, satisfaction-giving event. The actors here are matter-of-fact, natural, but others may (though it is unusual nowadays) stress hierarchy. Depending on the political situation, the traffic may be more ordered and the *vigile* more self-conscious, overzealously aware of an opportunely renewed sense of duty. The obstacles to be avoided may be less obvious, less physically

1

demanding, but they could include uncollected rubbish, perennial street repairs or protesters demanding services, benefits or jobs. The episode, nevertheless, vividly exemplifies a kind of behaviour which is most usual in Naples, whatever the actors' social positions and employment statuses. It is also a good introduction to the challenging tangle of appearance and reality that confronts the observer. Throughout the centuries this compelling city has inspired richly imaginative forms of art and, most ambivalently, romantic rapture and contempt. Notoriously, Naples is *la nobilissima, la corrotta* (the noblest and most corrupt) – stereotypically paradoxical.[3]

It is probably true that to understand life in Naples we cannot avoid penetrating the life and culture of its ordinary citizens; particularly the *popolino* (populace, used as a plural) who make up the majority of the inner city's population. The Naples *popolino*, who nowadays use the word to describe themselves as ordinary people, have been addressed in the most diversified literature, from the comparative Victorian concern of White-Mario (1978 [1876]) and the realistically emotional pleading of Serao (1973 [1884]) to the stigmatizing remarks of Croce (1967 [1944]), and more recent detailed journalism and studies by sociologists, political scientists, and folklorists (e.g. Luongo and Oliva 1959; Guadagno and De Masi 1969; Allum 1973; Laino 1984; CENSIS 1984; Lay 1981; Mazzacane et al. 1978). A view of them as *misera plebs* may be true to certain aspects of their desperate postwar condition, contentiously rendered by playwriters and novelists (e.g. De Filippo 1973 [1945]; Lewis 1978; Malaparte 1952; Burns 1948), but it certainly does not suit them today. It is nevertheless reiterated not only in certain sectors of the media but also in recent works such as that of Thomas Belmonte, published in 1979 and reprinted in 1989 with addenda which endorse the original argument.

Belmonte reports on aspects of life among the *popolino*, concluding that they 'inhabit a world connected and apart from the main, a dense and crowded urban world, . . . where the moral order is exposed as a fraud which conceals the historical ascendancy of cunning and force. Cunning and force, the *materia prima* of life in the poor quarters' (p. 143).[4] Thus, recalling the account of the rural South given by his predecessor Banfield (1958),[5] Belmonte portrays the inhabitants of the neighbourhood of the centre where he worked as an underclass – a grasping and backward lumpenproletariat that, dragged down by its culture and beliefs, is irremediably caught into negative reciprocity and resigned to marginality and deprivation (see pp. 137–44). From such a viewpoint, these people's actions and aspirations appear strictly short-term, self-oriented and endogenous. We are told that, socially segregated into a sort of Tönniesian *communitas*, they, when not in jail, spend their lives attempting to take advantage of each other and especially of 'outsiders' (see esp. ch. 2 and the addenda).[6] Their sense of localness, Belmonte goes on to suggest, is based on a strong opposition to an 'outside' political and social environment on which they have no influence (see his conclusions and also, e.g., pp. 131–2) and to a state with which they have characteristically negative relations and by whose representatives they feel cheated and exploited through vertical networks of dependence.

Anthropologists are traditionally aware that narrow empiricism is as misleading as unjustified abstraction (Leach 1977: xviii). If micro-level evidence is to have theoretical value, more than simply being detailed and accurate, it must be set in the broader historical and sociological context.[7] In a way, the multifaceted character of urban life in contemporary Europe further complicates the dilemma of tenable theoretical speculation. It seems to me, however, that understanding life in cities is made particularly difficult by a simplistic approach and conceptual superimposition which obscure a complex situation. Situating the analysis between the poles of subjectivity and objectivity is a challenging task, especially when we happen to be addressing issues that are close to us.[8] Of course we cannot disengage ourselves from our personal experiences and, indeed, personalities. However, as a Neapolitan who has done research in Naples for more than a decade I have found that this need not sharpen the opposition between us as ethnographers ('who know better') and them as 'the observed' or inhibit our sense of the problematic in the relationship between 'surface appearance' and 'underlying reality' (Davis 1992: 24–5). On the contrary, controlled use of the complications and contradictions that make up this resource may help us to fulfil a basic requirement of 'understanding' – achieving an empathic grasp of the situation through prolonged interactive involvement in the flow of local life (Pálsson 1992: 35).

In the specific case of Naples, this requirement must be fulfilled if we are to penetrate a situation which, because it does not conform to abstract models of 'how it ought to be', is usually described as hopeless or, from the establishment's viewpoint, uncontrollable. During the research it became obvious that it would be parochial, if not politically expedient, to assume that the *popolino* lacked moral, spiritual and material resources because they lived in a part of the city that, because it is central and historic, was the object of endless political debate but remained afflicted by more than its fair share of the problems that make life difficult in the urban West.

Certainly, the objective difficulty of their lives did not mean that they could not benefit from an understanding of the importance, and the potential, of certain features of their economic and cultural life that defy standard definitions.

In this book I use ethnographic material to take a fresh look at the dilemmas of local ordinary life, beyond stereotypes and condescension. My main motivation is to see what new insights an anthropological approach to the study of this major European city can bring to a central issue of modern social theory (Giddens 1979; Abrams 1982), the relationship between individual agency and 'the system' in the areas of culture, organization and power. In-depth study of actors' values in relation to their spiritual and material lives is, I believe, a fundamental condition for understanding human beings in society. In the contextual situation examined throughout the book, I investigate in detail the way in which people negotiate, over time, the terms – formally absolute but in fact ambiguous and flexible – of morality and of bureaucratic rule of the market and civil society. Moving beyond strong perspectivism about 'rational conduct',[9] the discussion offers an empirical demonstration of the inadequacy of current concepts of purposeful action, social relations, and political organization.

The broad aim of this exercise is to see what contribution our understanding of power and social relations and of the agency/structure relationship in Naples brings to the theory of the organization of society in modern democracy. It seems to me legitimate to hope that knowledge of what is actually going on in Naples at what appears to be a critical phase for Italian democracy may stimulate a better comparative understanding of phenomena that are central to the political and economic mainstream in European society.

The methodology of research round the corner
Despite the pre-eminence of the city as a model of associated life, anthropologists have largely neglected to address urban Europe.[10] John Davis is probably right when he points to professional insecurity as a possible explanation (1977: 7; see also Boissevain 1975 and Crump 1975). A rather strong possibility is that the detailed and prolonged study of the urban situation has been discouraged by a tendency towards doing research to order[11] and by the argument that the participant-observer's holistic approach is inapplicable to the study of the city.

In my case, six months of preliminary research helped me to cope with a large amount of documentary information[12] and to establish the indispensable contacts.[13] Then I spent fourteen months in a neighbourhood of the centre. During this period of constant and intimate immersion in 'the field', I employed a reasonable degree of participation in everyday life, family celebrations and situations of socialization in the area and outside it. Otherwise, I tried to share in what was possible to share, as in the case of religious rituals, ritual games, various kinds of problem-solving and events occurring in workshops, offices and institutions. I collected case-studies of significant individuals over several months, through the construction of genealogies, godparenthood maps, work histories, and maps of their universes.[14] The combination of these strategies has been crucial to penetrating actors' self-perceptions and world-views and to making intelligible the meanings, rules and logic of the situation, including the unsaid, the unconceptualized and their connections with broader social processes. On a different level, it has illuminated the way in which local people interact with the socio-economic, political and cultural life of the city and the country.

I originally selected three typical *quartieri* (sing. *quartiere*, quarter, as Italians call their neighbourhoods) of the centre.[15] The three quarters are densely populated conglomerations of narrow, cobbled alleys called *vicoli* (sing. *vicolo*) and century-old buildings, weathered by time and shattered by earthquakes. Some of these buildings are hospitals or civic institutions. Street markets and other business activities, legal and illegal, are characteristically part of the bustling life of these quarters, and so is crime. Each quarter includes one or more churches and, inhabited by a predominantly non-industrial population of *popolino* and petty-bourgeois origins, embodies a scaled-down version of the historical coresidence of people of various socio-economic positions (see, e.g., Galasso 1978:141; De Seta 1988:285).[16] Later I shall argue the difficulty of looking at this contemporary urban setting from a class perspective. For now I shall only indicate that, given this difficulty, it is for the sake of simplicity that I use such terms as *popolino* and bourgeois and that I deliberately do so because of their generality.

I eventually settled in the quarter that seemed likely to give me the most cooperation. It is part of San Lorenzo district (see Map 2), and, although there is no break from the surrounding urban environment, its boundaries are traditionally identified with certain major streets and squares. The area is about a mile square and is inhabited by a little less than three thousand people. It is quite central; for one reason or another many Neapolitans have to cross it, some with contempt for its low status and others with interested pleasure. It is here that many of the local people's contacts and activities – though definitely not all and not always the most important – form, develop and have significance.

One autumn morning, on my arrival in Naples to begin fieldwork, I met Lino, a stall-keeper in the local street market who was then in his thirties, and his wife, Luisa. Having enquired at length on the purpose of my research, the couple promised their cooperation. They shared with most locals a strong sense of belonging and an explicit concern about the improvement of the quarter and of its inhabitants' reputation.[17] The Neapolitan *popolino* had been grossly misrepresented, Lino said, and he hoped that, because I appeared to be genuinely interested in learning about their lives, culture and motivations, my study 'could help to set things right'. At first, thinking of Whyte's (1955) experience, I felt that, with some luck, Lino might become for me a 'Doc' – a favourite informant who would help me to orient myself in local life. However, he became something more. I have enjoyed relations of 'vivid human interaction' (Firth 1984: vii) with many locals, but without such a close relationship with a person like Lino my pursuit of intimacy and depth would probably have had far less success. Lino opened up for me much of local life. What I learned from him provided a stimulating background for the information I obtained from others.

As I began to travel to the quarter every day, it was instrumental that Lino, Luisa and other early contacts began to explain my task and introduce me to their peers starting, they proposed, with those they knew would cooperate, whether they liked them or not. Of course, they also agreed, residing there would be a crucial asset but, they warned, finding accommodation would not be easy. Decay apart, shortage of accommodation available for rent in central Naples is explained by insufficient public housing and the use of housing for commercial activities. Moreover, while access to property is widely seen as an opportunity to improve personal status, a strong emphasis is put on the moral and spiritual themes that here as elsewhere make a house (and in many cases a shop or other premises) more than a commodity (Pardo 1992); accordingly, when people move they may keep their former apartments because they feel sentimentally attached to them as loci of stability and well-being.[18] It was only four months after starting fieldwork that I acquired lodgings in a shared flat (with an old widow and a middle-aged couple) near the market. Although the previous student-tenants had moved months earlier, my *popolino* contacts gave me this important information and produced me as a candidate to Gino, the landlord, only when they had begun to regard me with less suspicion. Explained only in part by the fact that many here deal below the strictly legal line, this behaviour exemplifies the way in which the *popolino* establish control over personal relations, and over access to properties. Gino, a part-time university student and semiprofessional occasional labourer now in his late thirties, had known my accommodation requirements since we met, months previously, but he offered me a contract only when I clearly enjoyed local approval and backing. Soon I learned that, in accordance with the symbolism of liminality attached to some local buildings, the place was believed to be haunted by spirits such as the Monacello (Little Monk),[19] the results of particularly unaccomplished lives which, in turn, engender unaccomplished deaths. Probably a factor in making the accommodation available to me, this abnormality was gradually domesticated as with time and the help of Mario, a local manual worker who claims spiritual powers, my apartment was checked and found free of evil spirits.

Taking up local residence positively affected the relationship between penetration and acceptance, giving new impetus to the fieldwork. Most people's wish to deal with me publicly became sufficiently negotiable to allow interviews to occur in the privacy of my lodgings or of their homes.[20] My network expanded quickly to include my neighbours and their relatives and I found it easier to participate in all sorts of events. I was invited to join conversations, meet new people[21] and offer my opinions,[22] finding that it was rarely wasteful not only to chat at a road-corner, outside a *basso* (pl. *bassi*, ground-floor dwelling room),[23] or on a doorstep but also to spend time at one's window or balcony. In warm weather, I found, a window is a vantage point from which to observe and be seen and contacted. This is an ordinary fact of a highly socialized, noisy and overcrowded life-style[24] that, at some expense of a privacy that here has a distinctly flexible meaning, helps to reduce the price in pain and loneliness that the individual, especially the entrepreneurial individual, must pay for individuality.

However, only through the experience of trial and error could I make the best of the familiarity acquired over the years with the *popolino* and their culture and form a useful idea of how to behave, what questions to ask, and how to ask them. It was difficult to determine the unspoken but agreed-upon significance of the various forms of expression which, depending on circumstances, obviously conveyed a contrary, complementary, or much watered-down version of their surface meanings. This complexity, set in a blend of baroque theatricality and ruthless irony, finds expression in hyperbolic body language and figures of speech. Equally, self-pity is often intermingled with an ability to laugh into perspective normal crises, embarrassment and sometimes more serious events through a balanced use of irreverence, humour and self-mockery[25] which also serves the purpose of 'normalizing' others, establishing individuality and independence and reducing distance. The deceptively simple picture of local life thus conjured up provided a constant reminder that nothing should be taken for granted about the significance of events, and that actors' motives and self-representations could indeed be easily misinterpreted. The *popolino* themselves say that one should always distinguish the truth from its representation, which is, after all, a necessary condition for our analysis of the situation if it is to avoid the mediocrity that inevitably goes with the a priori logic of determinisms.

I was given examples of and introduced to people who were 'downtrodden and without *maniglie*' (sing. *maniglia*, handles, useful contacts), and who 'coped only with difficulty'. However, many entries in my notebooks have to do with the intriguing contrast between the representation many *popolino* initially provided of themselves as poor, disadvantaged and exploited and their actual ability to manage their existence relatively successfully.[26] For instance, Lino, who in his culture and origins belongs and describes himself as belonging to the *popolino*, is like many others in having managed to obtain a steady public-sector job; he also performs other work activities, some paid and some not, has developed useful contacts and the power to help others, and is well integrated into the life of the rest of the city at various levels. I could make some early guesses about local people's networks, but their actual breadth, diversification and value fully emerged in a systematic way only later, when the universes of a number of individuals were mapped. By then I had formed an idea of the complex economics of social exchange underlying apparently insignificant situations in the daily routine and of the results that sprang in time from such situations, including new alliances and the expansion of personal resource systems. I had also observed people's various work activities, spanning throughout the city and outside, and had witnessed their dealings with the establishment by accompanying them on their errands in the bureaucracy, the educational system, the law, the trade unions, etc. More immediately, value judgements aside, I could not ignore the market value of the furniture and status symbols (such as television sets, hi-fis, VCRs, cars, jewellery and clothes) that adorned the homes and persons of many locals, or their investments in prestigious tasks such as family celebrations, leisure and private education and, when necessary, in contacts and favours. Equally, in agreement with a national pattern (De Mauro 1993), many *popolino* soon proved that their low level of formal instruction did not mean that they could speak only Neapolitan or unusually poor Italian or that they were particularly restricted in their views, information and ability to express criticism.[27]

As local people's trust increased, so did their interest and active cooperation.[28] The improved quality and quantity of relationships and information was a key factor in coming to terms with the intricate interplay between secrecy, embarrassment and gossip. This issue of trust took on a new identity during updating field trips. While some people cold-shouldered me on my visit two years later, in 1988, the majority appreciated that I had not completely disappeared, greeting me as 'an old friend' and indeed behaving more informally and warmly than ever before. This response, partly explained by my renewed commitment to keeping my promise of confidentiality, has made it easier for me to return to the field.

Theory and ethnography in urban research

On a theoretical level, anthropological enquiry in urban Europe has largely been frustrated by the disposition, mentioned earlier, to think of the city as a patchwork of socially, economically and culturally separated areas. Equally frustrating has been the tendency to reject in-depth study of the micro-level in favour of 'grand theory'. This tendency has been basically informed by a view of ordinary individuals as powerless puppets of exploitative and ineluctable powers and by the conception of social relations in terms of production and consumption, corresponding to the categories of dominance and class conflict.

Anthropologists have traditionally pointed to the political and socioeconomic changes brought about by actors' everyday choices in their goal pursuits and enhancement of personal power. More than simply affecting an individual's position, these choices are part of what Abrams has called the 'problematic of structuring' (1982: esp. xv–xviii), the power of the ordinary individual to *negotiate and influence social structure over time*. Believing that social theory has nothing to gain from privileging either agency or structure, I shall address the process of mutual influence of purposeful individual action (and morality) and society, focusing on the significance of different resources and domains of existence.

A sophisticated understanding of contemporary human beings in society must take very seriously the interplay between religion and civil society, thought and action, non-material and material life, belief and choice, value and transaction and people's own sense of right and wrong, good and evil. Our interpretation ought to be fully aware that these are not simply various aspects of life which fall into different analytical pigeon-holes. They are aspects whose meanings, relations and significance are redefined as information and experience are transmitted from generation to generation. For a real setting to be penetrated in its various levels of complexity and depth all these aspects need to be studied processually, not only in relation to self and to others but also in relation to the broader social and moral order in which individuals feel they belong. The crucial question, then, is what role this level of understanding is allowed to play in our analysis, and this emphasizes the importance of adopting a sufficiently pluralist theoretical framework.

A central part of the argument of this book is an expansion of a point which I first made in a coherent way in a shorter work (1992). There I observed that highly valued material assets are often transacted with stress on meanings – e.g., sentiment, self-representation, own moral image among significant others – beyond basic material need and strictly monetary value.[29] I stated that of course money is important for the *popolino*, as it is for the bourgeoisie, and financial well-being does constitute a basic aspect of their idea of success. Nevertheless, the distinction between good and evil is not strictly blurred by money, nor is competition exclusively determined by it. Demanding careful differentiation – not opposition – of moral meaning and material interest, throughout the fieldwork people's purposive actions, their modes of exchange and entrepreneurship, have consistently indicated that non-material aspects of existence play a tangible, important and rational role in the quality of actors' lives, and this includes aspects of their culture that have been described as evidence of superstition and subalternity.

The definition of purposive action which I propose here addresses the difficulty of drawing the line between social norms and rational conduct, financially oriented or not, and between identity and interest (Lukes 1991b; Runciman 1991; Offe 1991). Recognizing the role of the moral, spiritual and emotional in these people's rationality, I suggest, does not necessarily imply indulging in a value-laden exaggeration of the 'non-tangible' at the expense of the 'tangible'. From a Weberian angle, it means recognizing culture 'as an irreducible dimension of action which elevates man above the pure necessities of the material world' (Stauth 1992:219). But it also means recognizing the limitations of the perspectivist view, implicit in Weber's distinction between formal and substantive rationality (Brubaker 1991:4), that what is rational from one viewpoint may be irrational from another and vice versa.[30] I do not wish to argue for a (probably impossible) perspective neutrality. Broadly in agreement with Runciman's (1991) point, I would rather suggest that the profound implications of the above outlined themes for both actors and society make the concept of irrationality explanatorily redundant.

The early chapters address the relation of moral values and cultural resources to purpose in making a living. The diverse work activities of local people, it emerges, belong to ordered but multifaceted processes which develop and have significance well beyond formal unemployment and formal employment. Some of these activities may be expressions of an entrepreneurial spirit and cooperative attitude which do not always agree with some Western ideal. However, it is difficult to see why they should be classified as colourful examples of an *arte di arrangiarsi* (art of living by one's wits)[31] and, therefore, as evidence of marginality. Whatever may be thought of the significance of categorizing work activities in the contemporary West, I was initially stimulated by the debate on 'work' and 'employment' and 'formal' and 'informal' activities (see, e.g., Gershuny and Pahl 1979; Wallman 1979; Pahl 1984; see also Redclift and Mingione 1985). However, as the research progressed it became obvious that the issue of making a living belonged to a much broader analytical framework (Chapter 2).

Resources such as time, information, identity and contacts (Wallman 1984) are important, but account for only one aspect of the non-material domain of action. On a more complex level, the practical and moral significance of modes of behaviour and thought draws on *strong continuous interaction* between tangible aspects of existence and symbolic, moral and spiritual ones and, most important, between body and soul and between the world of the living and that of the dead.[32] This interaction marks people's ability to explain their own lives, negotiate 'risky' choices (in Heath's (1976) sense), and construct a sense of fulfilment and self-worth. Having a fulfilled life means feeling that one has accomplished or is accomplishing one's tasks in life, is satisfactorily improving one's personhood and enjoying the affection and support of the various important figures – living and dead – in one's universe (Chapters 3 and 5). Particularly as members of the household intended as a collective enterprise, actors show strong motivation to act in ways that give them reason to feel that they are actively engaged in the negotiated achievement of the *real* (Davis 1992: 16–20) ultimate end (Stauth 1992: 226) of material *and* spiritual well-being. It is widely believed that an individual's existential position depends both on his own deeds and behaviour towards the significant others and on his relationship with them after death, particularly during the (indefinite (Pardo 1989)) period of time the dead are expected to spend in purgatory. Defying explanation in terms of relatively short-term moves (Bourdieu

1977), action belongs thus to a future-oriented plan of fulfilment and well-being that at once accounts for and transcends the significance of immediate results.

The concept of strong continuous interaction raises questions about traditionally received notions of exchange, interest and entrepreneurship. For Fredrik Barth, 'the essence of entrepreneurial activity is to discover new possible channels and exploit them' (1963:12). This transactionalist view, focused on maximization of economic and political profit (Barth 1966; but see Kapferer 1976), underpins a body of anthropological literature that opposes normative to instrumental values (Bailey 1969; Boissevain 1974). From a different perspective (Bourdieu 1991) a similar argument suggests that actors' pursuit of self-interest is oriented to increasing both material and non-material (e.g., symbolic, political) capital and also to maximizing non-material (i.e., honour, prestige) profit. Moral and spiritual values, it is claimed, are functional to utility maximization, providing a veneer for instrumental motives. As it has been pointed out (Davis 1992: esp. pp. 73–4), there are serious problems with the argument that exchange (and indeed purposive action in general) basically obeys the 'clean' laws of economic behaviour. The concept of interaction is appropriately described as an attempt to transcend the marketistic model, requiring notions of value, utility and profit flexible and complex enough to include the non-monetary, non-prestigious and non-political and to account for both the individual and social significance of action.

Values other than those of industrialism and a certain moral and religious ethic give a strong meaning to the notion that exchange is a composite activity that encompasses more than the calculable and the quantifiable. They allow the management of self-interest to occur on what the *popolino* describe as more human bases. In this situation we may well observe a degree of domestication of the stigma placed in our society (as noted by Parry and Bloch 1989; see also Parry 1989) on the materialist aspect of personal motives, and of social, economic and political relations. However, it would be naïve to interpret people's grassroots tendency to mitigate constructively such an aspect as evidence that self and transactionable object in their lives are undifferentiated or intermingled (in the sense of Mauss 1966). Negotiated through morally and normatively consistent applications of value, the complex relationship between these categories that has characterized the West since Roman law (Weber 1978: ch. 8 esp. sect. 5, also pp. 82–5) simply does not make exchanges predominantly depersonalized and instrumental.[33] Of course it is important that, especially in cases of a more instrumental nature, (self-)interested action and disinterested action may well be performed and presented separately. And, of course, results may vary greatly and costs may be higher or lower than or equal to benefits, depending on what is invested, what is overtly transacted and what other assets different from those overtly transacted are included de facto in the transaction. However, we shall see that even in difficult situations, while tending to remain (self-)interested in monetary transactions most of my informants describe themselves as committed to a good moral image (of good-heartedness, in particular) and to 'feeling at peace with one's own conscience' (Chapter 2).

Given the principle of 'heterogeneity of morality' (Lukes 1991a: ch. 1), moral values and spiritual requirements are negotiable and changing, not rigidly normative. They may be differently located in this relationship between appearance and reality, but they deeply inform choices that are to a significant degree voluntary expressions of the self rather than mere forms of socially enforced behaviour. And they may well play other than an instrumental role in entrepreneurial spirit. My contention is that this role, often (though not necessarily always and not always completely) controlled by actors, affects in a characteristic way the fundamental difference between individual action – even when highly entrepreneurial and capital-oriented – and ruthless individualism,[34] and between strong orientation to personal betterment and antisocial opportunism (Pardo 1995b). Put bluntly, the significance of strong continuous interaction for local people's lives points to an approach that recognizes no ideological opposition between 'interest' and 'disinterest' (as defined by Jonathan Parry (1986: 466–9)). Committed to combining the two, such an approach exposes the mercenary, fatalist and subaltern character attributed to ordinary Neapolitans, particularly the *popolino*, as an example of the narrow understanding of the relationship between practical and economic life and moral and spiritual life that underlies so much materialist thinking.

The ethnography of 'special workers' such as prostitutes, moneylenders and *assistiti* (sing. *assistito*, assisted (by the good souls)) illustrates important aspects of the problem of self-worth in establishing a manageable relationship between transgression and order (Chapter 5). They embody conditions of moral and religious ambiguity and liminality which broaden options in terms of exchange, accumulation and management of capital, and entrepreneurship. But their analysis also suggests that the pursuit of respectability and material well-being is or may become crucial to generous and socially oriented action. Avoiding the pitfalls of the cynical approach, I must stress, does not mean arguing that this is an idyllic situation. Of course, not only do individuals act in terms of values that are important to them because they find support among their significant others (Boissevain 1974: 8) but also they may well choose to act (or refrain from acting) according to values that disagree with those traditionally adopted by their groups. This kind of choice observably affects crucial domains of life such as work, gender, education and social and political relations.

The distinction between kin and non-kin – and 'us' and 'them' – is here not so strongly discriminative as, for instance, it has been argued to be in Sicily in the 1960s (Boissevain 1966: 20). The study of social relations in such important domains as family, kinship and neighbourhood (Chapter 4) highlights the values of family (especially) and kinship as central to personal identity and career. There is reason to doubt, however, that this centrality, made obvious by the care and hard work local people invest in their households' welfare, and the importance of family relations in their existential well-being make them 'amoral familists' committed to the interests of their nuclear families at all costs and at the expense of others. Furthermore, because local people's resource options run contrary to a logic of social segregation, there is reason to doubt that kinship is inflexibly the primary resource in their universes. In agreement with a point made by Davis (1970) on Southerners, when they have sufficient information they may choose to engage in potentially profitable alliances and associative forms of action both within and outside the kinship system, with different motivations and different outcomes.

These alliances often involve a complex structure of favour exchanges (Chapter 6). Mainly interpreted as 'quasi-moral' *clientelismo* (clientelism, whereby, it is argued, favours are exchanged for votes), favour relations in Italy have been seen as evidence of an imperfect penetration of the state at the local level, particularly in the sense of insufficient services and structures and of institutional inadequacy. They have been seen also as evidence of the excessive presence of the state in the form of assistance (see, e.g., D'Antonio 1995a, b; see also De Giovanni 1983). Favour relations are not simply a matter of strong and weak, nor do they inevitably involve direct and certain reciprocation; much depends on the context. Case-material alerts us to the fact that in this contemporary urban situation ordinary people's access to services and benefits does not depend strictly on the 'intermediation' of patron-brokers who, 'organic to the power' (in Gramsci's (1971) sense), impose clientelism as the only option. The system of favours that characterizes Italian *sottogoverno* (subgovernment)[35] emerges as only one aspect of people's resources; and we cannot assume that because Neapolitans widely – and entrepreneurially – use it they are morally sympathetic to it, are subjugated to its rationale or see no alternative to it.

At this stage things are best put very simply: the processual analysis of strong continuous interaction among the *popolino* may help us to understand them in a new way. It gives a satisfactory account of the way in which individuals who originally have limited resources develop attitudes to life by which they achieve important long-term goals. Comparison between the careers, world-views and ideas of fulfilment of local *popolino* and those of the younger generation and of the petty bourgeois will be placed in the context of the recent history of Naples to call into question the idea that managing existence in a situation of 'imperfect competition' – in the sense of differences in power among individuals (Heath 1976) – is strictly a matter of gender, class membership, access to formal and/or criminal resources and formal location in the market. The hypothesis will be explored that, given certain contextual restrictions, interaction as defined here plays the determinant role not only in the dynamics of accumulation of capital and investment but, more generally, in the actors' careers and social mobility. Just as the position of the local bourgeoisie regarding work, consumption and education is not straightforwardly associated with pre-eminence, so that of their *popolino* neighbours does not involve particularly strong forms of submission and dependence. This important feature of the *popolino*'s identity is underlined by the combination of their culture of entrepreneurial management of contacts and favours with the basic independence of their financial and cultural positions from their positions in the sphere of formal employment. In brief, socio-economic constraints and inequality are not rigidly set and self-perpetuating. They have to reckon, instead, with two important processes fundamental to what Tocqueville described as the fragmentation of social class in modern democracy (1945): the pressure of cross-cutting, shifting alliances and interests (Saunders 1981; Lukes 1991a: e.g., ch. 16) and the increasing depolarization of social relations (Furbank 1985) – the individual construction of position in relation to other individuals.

Class and stratification analysis raises hotly debated issues. This book fully acknowledges the theoretical importance of investigating social inequality. But it also takes the view that neither inequality nor power can be explained in terms of class membership. The intellectual analysis of social organization and structure has been dominated by structural Marxists (Craib 1985). Only a few, such as Parkin (1979), have been willing to confront their paradigm, and even those few accept the concept of 'social closure' (i.e., the exclusion of the 'inferior' from access to the privileges and resources of the 'superior') as beyond dispute (see also Bourdieu 1984, 1991). The alternative view which emerges from empirical studies not based on this paradigm tends to be dismissed as the worthless product of exercises in narrow-mindedness. Neo-Marxist analysis has played an important role in pointing out the nature and implications of structural constraints and social inequality. Recent syntheses (e.g., Crompton 1993) claim, however, that modern society is still strongly stratified and that a modernized theory of class is crucial to our understanding of how social inequality is created and reproduced. In using microanalysis to challenge these assumptions, the final chapters aim at fundamentally restructuring received perceptions of social relations and relations of power in Naples.

Recent fieldwork in the corridors of power, particularly the study of the agency/structure relationship from the viewpoint of the socially superior, has stressed Martin's argument (1977: 166) that in capitalist society it is easy to exaggerate the power (or, in Gramsci's terms, hegemony) of any one group. In real life, power (e.g., Lukes 1974, 1991a; Harris 1986) and the processes of domination (Simmel 1964: pt 3, esp. pp. 181–3; Lenski 1987) are highly diversified. Domination constitutes only a special case of power relations (Weber 1978: 941–55); it cannot be assumed to be their prerequisite, naturally to the advantage of the 'socially better-off'. The analysis given here accepts that social relations may well be everywhere marked by an imbalance of power, tending sometimes to the extreme, that there are distinctions (and specific inequalities in means) among individuals and therefore restrictions (cultural, economic and political) on their action and access to resources, and that attempts to impose such restrictions may well be continually made. However, it also accepts that in capitalist democracy coercion is not a fundamental value (Martin 1977). In the context of the difficult process of redefinition of Italian democracy (Cotta 1992; Rusconi 1993), the multifaceted and flexible nature of urban culture and socio-economic relations highlighted by the Naples case gives us reason to ask an important question. We must ask (Chapter 7) whether we can safely assume that restrictions are part of a relationship between agency and structure determined by changing but basically unchallenged – because basically unchallengeable – instances of dominance established (and reproduced) by the socially superior,[36] or whether we should recognize that ordinary people are not inevitably constrained or manipulated into subaltern ideals and goals[37] and that their action over time helps to redefine relations of dependence and competition because it helps to modify both inequality and organization of the social system at the various levels of control, representation (Stankiewicz 1980; Cotta 1992) and value in the problematic relationship between bureaucracy and democracy (Beetham 1987; Smith 1987).

In addressing the agency/structure relationship in Naples – i.e., in a parliamentary democracy with a broad franchise – we cannot ignore the role played by the long-standing sterile policy of assistance in the chaotic appearance of this rationally organized democracy. It is important to recognize that the effects of political corruption and of the convenient representations of inefficiency and the instrumental biases of the system are a direct result of specific political interests; the very interests that, since the Unification of Italy in 1860, have determined industrialization and social relations in the South (Chapter 6). However, it would be inexcusably simplistic to overlook the power of action 'from below'.

Contemporary instances of *tangentopoli* (bribesville or kickback city; bribery and pursuit of personal interest through public office) throughout the country urge caution in explaining the combination of criminality, inefficiency and political corruption as an ineradicable Southern phenomenon. The choice of most Neapolitans to vote and keep the corrupt and clientelist-oriented out of power corroborates micro-level evidence that relations of clientelism and the corresponding politics have increasingly been resented by the people. As, for example, Communist administrators have found to their cost in the past, the way many ordinary people relate to the system is part of a sophisticated process in which individual action – as opposed not to society but to abstract communal ideals and formally organized action – has a strong underlying element of civic consciousness that denies reproduction of the existing system, including its 'people-oriented' parts. The cultural and practical aspects underlying such an opposition deserve attention for they point to the fact that ordinary citizens (including the *popolino*) have an important role to play in the negotiation of the new moral order in the city and, indeed, the country (Chapter 7).

We will find that important changes in the system have been paralleled, and to a large extent anticipated, by an observable improvement in actors' power – more obvious among the young (Chap. 3) – to do more than simply bend the rules. Within the framework established by actors' sense of their own worth, negotiations over values and ideas strengthen entrepreneurship, facilitating a degree of flexibility in local men's and women's dealings in problematic spheres of their universes, including spirits, villains and corrupt politicians and officials. We shall study how, saying 'Ajutat' ca Dio t'ajut" (God helps those who help themselves), the *popolino* display no resignation to the will of God or to the arrogance of the more powerful. Instead, they develop networks that, though not unlimited, cross-cut various levels and domains of urban life, use their experience of the socially better-off to their advantage and constantly improve their information on the system and their awareness of the resources available to them. Our analysis will have to account for the fact that most informants believe that their relations to the system are negotiable, and they act accordingly. Such a belief may not always be well founded but it plays an important role in individuals' active (though not necessarily intended) participation in the redefinition of the very logic of their dealings in the system, their choices and action being informed by their entrepreneurial spirit rather than by powerlessness and corruption. And, over time, the collective results of such participation do affect the tension between formal and substantive rationality. I shall contend that one observable outcome of this challenge posed by a relatively discerning and creative agency is that bureaucratic order and impersonal righteousness are defied to the potential advantage of civil society.

The Naples situation raises key questions about the relationship between objective conditions of restriction and inequality and actors' ability to negotiate these conditions. This book is committed to studying the significance of what I have called strong continuous interaction for ordinary people's changed understanding of their position in the democratic system. This is important because such a changed understanding appears to strengthen among them individual initiative and, increasingly, responsible citizenship.

2

Beyond unemployment: work, morality and entrepreneurship

Informal work activities have only recently attracted attention, despite their traditional significance in the lives of real people whether they are Londoners (Wallman 1984; Hobbs 1989), Neapolitans (Pinnarò and Pugliese 1985), or something else. My enquiry into what the officially unemployed in Naples[1] actually do and into their attitudes to work originally accepted the distinction between 'employment', including all types of formal and paid labour, and 'work', including also non-formal labour paid in cash or otherwise (Gershuny and Pahl 1979; Pahl 1984). This distinction accounts for the informal or reciprocal work activities (see also Wallace and Pahl 1985) which, according to Wallman (1979: 15), find space outside the formal structure or in its cracks. Pahl's (1980: 160) hypothesis of the revolutionary potential of informal work raises fascinating issues in the Naples situation, but it also poses problems. This form of labour, postulated as a separate 'mode of production' in the broader category of the informal sector, is seen to include, vaguely, 'black labour', small-scale undeclared production, and so on.

My perspective became more complex as the investigation of local people's attitudes to employment and work highlighted the arbitrary value that this distinction gives to the material and the monetary. The many formally unemployed *popolino* and petty bourgeois individuals whom I have met simply cannot be said to be participating in a 'casual economy' (Allum 1973; Becchi-Collidà 1984a) in which the Camorristi (sing. Camorrista, organized criminals) are powerful employers. Their culture of work is based on a blurring of boundaries, found in various degrees throughout Italy, between the categories of the modern organization of labour – between the formal and the informal, the legal and the illegal, and the material and the non-material. Among the *popolino* in particular, this

19

blurring of boundaries is not necessarily evidence of valuelessness or of a 'criminal culture'. It is informed by what I have called strong continuous interaction between different kinds of resources and domains of existence, the significance of which is emphasized by the balance that actors maintain between 'work' and 'success', on the one hand, and 'personal ability' and 'good-heartedness', on the other. It is in this framework that most ordinary locals pursue the ultimate end of material and spiritual fulfilment and stability for themselves and their families, in the process domesticating various forms of transgression and instrumentalism in their lives. To understand this, I suggest, we need to look beyond the formal categories of industrialism and the observable, material aspects of the Western concept of quality of life. Let us begin by examining more closely the semi-legal and illegal aspects of work and entrepreneurship.

Negotiated legitimacy? Semi-legal and illegal activities
Only a small proportion of the Neapolitans registered as unemployed are actually out of work. Many use contacts in the office (see, e.g., Miller 1981b) in the hope that, by gaining access to the lists, they will obtain benefits (assistance, housing, etc.) and, above all, a secure public-sector job. A large part of the formally unemployed perform informal work activities which, though not strictly legal, enjoy various degrees of negotiated legitimacy and the tacit (and sometimes overt) concurrence of the authorities.[2] These activities, appropriately described by locals as semi-legal, include unregistered employment in small workshops (sometimes unlicensed), trading in the name of figureheads or without a licence,[3] home labour, and a variety of tax-dodging enterprises.[4] Among these enterprises are tradesmanship,[5] small- and medium-scale moneylending, working as *rammar*'[i] (sing. *rammar*'[o]),[6] dealing in clandestine lotteries, organizing raffles, obtaining documents on other people's behalf,[7] selling smuggled cigarettes, pirated cassettes, videos, etc., petty organizing and management of gambling, provision of unlicensed private medical services,[8] colourful but monetarily rewarding activities such as selling goods and cleaning windscreens at traffic lights, working as unauthorized parking-wardens[9] and so on. Apart from such informal sources of income, the household budgets of the majority of my informants benefit not only from 'do-it-yourself' and household jobs done free by friends and relatives but also from 'savings' derived from tax evasion and manipulation of meters.[10]

Thus, ordinary people operate in the 'grey area' (Curi 1982) between 'legality' and 'illegality' without becoming or considering themselves 'real criminals'.[11] This, as I argue elsewhere at length (1995a), emphasizes both the contentious character of 'lawyers' law' (Weber 1978: 760) as a metaphor for social order (Starr and Collier 1989: 3 ff.) and the importance of understanding the relationship between control, norm and action (Moore 1978; Strathern 1985) in the specific social and cultural context (Hamnett 1977: 4; Saltman 1985).

The image of central Naples conveyed to us by the media as a stronghold of organized crime overestimates the situation at the expense of understanding. Broadly speaking, the relatively limited number of organized criminals who operate in the centre are relevant at two levels: they control the drug business, extortion and the clandestine lotteries, and they may also play a role in the ill-defined semi-legal arena, ranging from indirect and occasional influence to systematic long-term profiteering. Drug-dealing gradually became a major business in the 1970s (see, e.g., Arlacchi 1982; Figurato and Marolda 1981). *Capi-zona* (area managers) employ petty dealers who are mainly drug addicts, though non-addicted people, even boys,[12] may be involved. Extortion is widely imposed on trade and production, as well as on thieving, gambling, etc. Sometimes it takes the form of requests of money in aid of the families of convicts. It is seldom imposed on street-selling, but local bosses may shop free at local stalls, provoking the sarcasm of the outwardly 'honoured' keepers. Shopkeepers may be 'advised' to buy goods or services controlled by criminals, sometimes organized in 'cooperatives' of ex-convicts. The services on offer range from professional cleaning to management of business advertising,[13] shop furniture and decorations. Customers are 'overcharged' according to the size of the business.

Clandestine lotteries are a century-old business that has recently become more modern and efficient. Bets on football matches, national lotto and horse-races produce weekly profits on the order of millions of pounds. At the lowest level, they employ ordinary people like Antonio, a low-ranking clerk and stallholder now in his forties who, in cooperation with his social-services-employee wife, sells smuggled cigarettes, licit goods and tickets for the clandestine lotteries. Antonio demonstrates that he is successful in a characteristically emphatic way, wearing heavy gold necklaces and a large diamond ring on the long-nailed little finger of his right hand – a recognized symbol of the power of a man who can afford not to work manually and, in the past, of the power of a criminal. Categorizing Antonio by his appearance would, however, be unwise. He may well find satisfaction in such posing, and he may inspire strong jealousy in his peers but he surely does not inspire fear. He is described as a family man and an indefatigable worker ready to help others without tangible returns, not as a criminal. And he, like other petty dealers, believes that what he does is semi-legal partly because criminal control tends to remain unseen, partly because petty dealers are not normally prosecuted, and partly because such petty dealing very rarely leads to a criminal career.[14] At an intermediate level these lotteries, like drug-dealing, involve both full-time and part-time employees such as bookkeepers and accountants. Middle-range dealers are connected (through kinship or friendship) with but not necessarily themselves Camorristi. They keep 10 to 15 per cent of the weekly bets to manage the business locally and employ ticket-sellers who retain 5 to 7 per cent of the bets. Bets are placed on street-corners and in shops, stalls, public offices, factories, hospitals and private houses. A socially diversified crowd surrounds a local betting-stall especially on Saturday morning, when the last bets on lotto can be made just before the publication of results, and in the early afternoon, when winners are paid straight away,[15] giving an aura of efficiency to the business that increases its competitive edge over the state-managed lotteries.[16] The tickets are produced by clandestine or (sometimes) legal printers who extract tax-free profits from this and other side-jobs including counterfeit books and forged labels, headed stationery, and driving-licences.

The role of criminals in the local economy is much more difficult to assess when they become interested in legal or semi-legal activities. A vivid example is provided by the workshops which in central Naples produce mainly small crafts (sweets, artificial flowers, bijouterie, china, etc.) and clothing and leather objects, often fashionably labelled.[17] These workshops are often illegally used by legitimate firms for tax-free side-production.[18] The demand for these products is due in part to the fact that they are not necessarily of inferior quality and in part to the fact that many Neapolitans, regardless of status, try to buy goods (especially non-routine objects) informally and cheaply through relatives and friends who have contacts before going to a shop for them.

This is not simply a matter of a few independent workshops furnishing the market in a fragmented way. These small enterprises and their related cottage industries are often links in a chain which may involve national and foreign enterprises. Various persons furnish the raw materials and then market the products through stalls and shops, including high-street ones. Under certain circumstances this kind of production may assume especially large proportions. For example, when the Naples football team's 1987 first-division championship appeared probable but still uncertain, many stallholders and shopkeepers stocked various objects bearing the club's championship logo. As I observed in the cases of Lino and others, this risky choice was consistent with the actors' career strategies, and that it paid off encouraged them to behave similarly in anticipation of the team's 1989 European championship and, again, in 1990, when they repeated the 1987 success.

Apart from imposing protection, local criminals may invest money in temporary cooperation (often imposed) with ordinary entrepreneurs who run these workshops or local bars and clubs. They may also impose the leasing or purchase of equipment or transport and distribution from given firms and sometimes the employment of their protégés.[19] My informants often explained unusually successful local businesses and speedy money-making as money-laundering operations. Indeed, criminal intervention changes the nature of business in recognizable ways; considerably higher capital is invested, and profits multiply with inexplicable speed.

Ordinary people widely resent such criminal intervention in business, which they say they are forced to tolerate. Of course, some may have an interest in the licit and semi-licit job opportunities and increase in circulation of money that are the by-products of such money-laundering, as well as in the services provided, also indirectly, by local criminals. More generally, throughout Naples money-laundering is facilitated by the simple fact that, in the absence of overt violence, people tend to ignore criminal interests in enterprises until they are proved. This is illustrated by the case of Misso, a notorious drug dealer who has invested profitably in high-street shops and other legitimate businesses. Perversely, apart from financing neo-fascist terrorists (Gambino 1985; Calderoni 1985), Misso led for some time an organization of shopkeepers against extortion. Magistrates have prosecuted, throughout Naples and the region, this and similar businesses (also of much larger size) whose operations are valued at millions of pounds. For a long time, however, criminal interest has remained more often suspected than demonstrated, especially when politicians and the financial sector are involved.

The corrupting role of dirty money becomes objectively stronger and more widespread as this money is recycled through legitimate businesses whose criminal connections may be covert and indirect (Miller 1985: 400–1). Arlacchi (1987: 28) hypothesizes that what makes this phenomenon peculiarly Italian is the willingness of the official financial world to allow dirty money in legitimate business (but see D'Antonio 1995c: 68). Apart from obtaining lower costs and cheaper services and discouraging competition through corruption, intimidation and violence, these criminal entrepreneurs control larger quantities of money than honest ones, for whom accumulation and investment are slower and more costly because they must save or borrow to assemble capital and because they are forced to pay huge bribes to corrupt politicians.

There are many examples of this historically rooted relationship between the legal domain of society and the criminal one. Focusing, at this stage, on the relatively low-level graveyards affair (Miller 1981a), until recently a rare example of successful inquiry into dubious power connections in Italy, will be helpful because it was an important precursor to recent better-known and certainly more far-reaching investigations (in progress) and because the processes involved are very similar to those in high-level cases but more directly observable.[20] In the late 1970s, Social Democrat and Republican *assessori* (sing. *assessore*, councillors-in-power), Trombetta, a large and long-established firm of undertakers, and Trombetta's contacts among criminals and bankers set up a profitable criminal enterprise, the most important and pervasive aspect of which was construction in the council-owned cemeteries. Because Neapolitans largely practise second burial, the building and maintenance of niches and family chapels in which the exumed remains of the dead are placed[21] constitutes a profitable and inexhaustible business. Trombetta and its criminal allies established control through complacent council bureaucrats associated with the politicians whose election they had sponsored. Local building contractors were accustomed to having to bribe the politicians in control to speed up their permits. Now, however, the bribes became payable to Trombetta and its agents at unprecedented extortionate rates. Moreover, apart from enjoying exceedingly advantageous conditions in the building sector, the gang intimidated competing funeral directors into submission and often out of business. Soon it had established almost complete control over the funerary process, from the construction of coffins to the hiring of the funeral paraphernalia and the digging of the graves for first burials. The several convictions which resulted from the inquiry (Costagliola 1981) had only a temporary repressive effect.

This kind of relation between criminals and influential sectors of the establishment makes Neapolitan criminals (often well organized) seem omnipresent and overwhelming. There is reason to doubt, however, that criminal activities and values (the so-called Camorrista mentality) are sociologically determinant or – as some seem inclined to believe (Lamberti 1982; Nocifora 1982; Galasso 1978: 201) – that ordinary people's tolerance of criminals and involvement in not strictly legal dealings can be safely interpreted as evidence that criminality is socially pervasive. This point will become clearer as we examine the moral dichotomy between ordinary people and real criminals in its various aspects. For now I suggest that, as recent events throughout Italy show, criminals can be efficiently dealt with by good police work, even, up to a point, in defiance of dishonest or misguided political will (Pardo 1994b). Juridical and legal issues aside, I also suggest that ordinary people's resistance to becoming involved in real criminality belongs to the same culture that explains the blurring of boundaries earlier described. The opposition between *lavoro* (work) and *fatica* (toil) is a central aspect of this culture and a good starting point for the analysis of their careers.

'Work' vs. 'toil': the relationship between value and money

The *popolino*'s explanation of the distinction between work and toil does not overstress the monetary. Toil is labour which is unfulfilling and sacrificial. In some cases it signifies supramundane punishment that brings about secondary forms of expiating labour. In contrast, they associate work with personal ability and fulfilment, describing it in terms of meritorious independent labour and free enterprise. Thus intended, work is simultaneously an important means to the accomplishment of one's task in life and evidence of success.

A particularly negative meaning is given to dependent manual work to which no alternative exists. This is toil *par excellence*. The majority of local men and women of *popolino* origins have some direct experience of work in workshops, shops or stalls. They attach unambiguously positive meanings to such dependent employment when it is a source of extra income which allows flexibility and financial welfare under negotiable work conditions, but they describe it as unfair and precarious *faticà sott' 'o padron'* (toiling under a master) when it is one's only or main way of earning a living. This source of income, I was told, gives no satisfaction. It implies exploitative work conditions which one is in no position to negotiate, and it hardly contributes to fulfilment because it involves sacrifices which may well be justified by practical reason but are unrewarding in terms of value.

This second aspect appears to agree at least in part with some observers' argument that work in the informal sector is motivated strictly by need and brings no satisfaction (Pinnarò and Pugliese 1985).[22] From this perspective it is maintained that the *popolino* need to be educated to appreciate work in industry as part of their 'civic' education (towards 'collective values'), and as a panacea for criminality and poverty. And yet, among them, the toil of dependent employment is widely associated with industry. The industrial population mainly lives in the periphery. Like most *popolino*, locals are of course familiar with small-scale production but they do not usually have an industrial background or direct experience of manual work in industry.[23] They feel foreign to proletarian values, lifestyles and aspirations. Above all, although they are quite aware of the rights enjoyed by industrial workers, they associate industrial employment with rigid practices and unrewarding toil on the assembly line, in an unhealthy and dehumanizing environment, under strict supervision and often under stress. It also means that they have no control over profits and little say in the organization of labour and that they cannot manipulate the quality, quantity and scheduling of their work. In a word, for these people who put a strong emphasis on being their own masters and on not being dragged down by their work, industrial employment generally means 'alienation'.

These negative values do not, however, extend to all formal employment. Over the past few decades important cultural changes have occurred among the *popolino* in connection with their improved access to public-sector employment and the increasing permeability of the system. Such public-sector jobs do not mean exploitation or proletarianization. They are seen as undemanding employment which guarantees a stable income (however low) and at the same time allows a fair degree of flexibility in work practices and abundant free time – to be invested mainly in entrepreneurial initiatives. It is precisely the relative flexibility associated with public-sector employment that makes it appealing to the large number of local people who invest their time, contacts and energy in pursuing it, often with success. This kind of organized labour therefore provides an answer (often problematic) to people's craving for steady employment that does not force them into a completely formalized working life but instead accords with their life-style, sense of independence and entrepreneurialism.

Thus, when *popolino* informants say that they do not like '*a fatic*', they mean they do not like toiling. When they say that they are *faticatur'* (sing. *faticator'*), they mean that they are hard workers who make the most of their time and resources and perhaps extract both satisfaction and good monetary rewards. This use of *fatic'* in both senses generates no confusion, for not only are the two corresponding concepts clearly differentiated in local culture but the actors are always able to say without difficulty which meaning they attach to the word. To put it simply, their culture of satisfaction and fulfilment does not sanction hard work as such; instead, bringing to mind various ethnographic parallels (Wallman 1984; Harris 1986; Herzfeld 1992: 134), it qualifies *how* and *under what conditions* hard work should be performed.

This rejection of alienation in the strict sense raises doubts about the validity in this situation of the Weberian concept of a nemesis of rationalism (Weber 1949). Instead of inspiring the work ethic which is the object of Weber's (1948) celebrated essay, this culture describes work in terms of degrees of emphasis on independence and freedom of choice as essential elements of the direct association between labour and fulfilment. Most significant, the dichotomy between work and toil translates into the terms of the management of existence as something more than the end of life and an accomplishment in itself. This intimate relationship between production and consumption and immediate and long-term goals (material, moral and spiritual) makes it understandable that the local *popolino* generally work more and have tighter schedules than in any formal (or, in some cases, informal) work setting I can think of. It is in these terms of rationality that such work accounts for an important aspect of the idea of *sapè fà* (cleverness) – expressing one's entrepreneurship fully, with a clear commitment to a culture of generosity which would be too simplistically explained as a form of solidarity or as calculating management of exchange and personal image.

The nature of entrepreneurial action

Lino, Michele, a qualified social-services employee now in his forties, and Ciro, Michele's father-in-law, exemplify central aspects of *sapè fà* – as opposed to being *'n addurmut'* (a sleeper) – which inform the *popolino* definition of success and failure. They have constructed relatively successful styles of entrepreneurship which are in many ways similar despite their different attitudes towards the favour system and the relationship between work, self-interest and fulfilment.

Michele's position results from a long and laborious process in which finding a secure job and obtaining an invalidity pension are two key stages. About twenty years ago he was, he says, 'still a desperate good-hearted man liked by most but poor, without a secure income and without *maniglie*'. One of many children, he began to work in his early teens as a delivery boy for local shops because he was 'not so good at school' and his family 'needed the money'. Later he became a miserably paid unskilled worker in a local workshop where he slowly gained skill and, because he was accommodating and respectful towards his bosses, regular, though still informal and precarious, employment. This, he hoped, was only a temporary predicament, his main goal continuing to be a secure formal job.

In contrast, Lino, who also became informally employed very early, did not really need to work at the time. Not only, as he discovered later, was part of his pay secretly provided by his father (a seasonal manual worker) but he received pocket money regularly from his mother, who, since she married, had established the profitable stall business which Lino and his siblings later inherited.[24] Lino was restless and insubordinate to his employers, finding these relationships 'humiliating', and to his teachers, whom he considered old-fashioned and tyrannical. When his father died, Lino, who was thirteen, gave up school to help at the stall. He also invested his meagre savings in selling garments door-to-door and in other unlicensed trades. Another important difference is that whereas Michele never became involved in collective action in his pursuit of employment and of other goals, Lino campaigned for a public-sector job with others.

In this pursuit Lino was motivated more by a specific crisis than by the desire to be formally employed. It was when he and his brother, Luigi, were forced out of their street trades by the combined effects of an outbreak of cholera and the economic depression of the early 1970s that he became the informal leader of a small group of local traders who joined thousands of old and new 'unemployed' demanding steady jobs. Some of these protesters drew an income from other activities, as did Lino, who was managing an unlicensed transport business. Others were still in business but had placed their businesses in their wives' or other relatives' names.[25] These unemployed (real and bogus) found leadership in the left, parliamentary and extraparliamentary, in a situation in which the city had not yet experienced leftist government.[26] Many writers on Naples and many former Communists believe that this leadership created a new consciousness wherein jobs were rights rather than favours. I have argued that this is only partially true (1993). The attitude of Lino and his mates towards clientelism was certainly affected by their experience of Socialist ideas and organized action, but it would be wrong to argue that they became engaged in a class struggle or developed class consciousness. Moreover, they say that they already knew they had the right to a steady job; the problem was primarily how to satisfy this claim. Following the example of many, Lino's group resolved this dilemma by bridging the gap between collective protest (and achievement) and individual goal pursuit. While continuing to protest with the others, they constructed independent routes to minor but steady public-sector jobs. In particular, Lino, Luigi and a friend used a bureaucrat and a social-service employee who were supporting the campaign of a politician of the centre-left. They reciprocated with their votes, but Lino declined to comply with the politician's demands for services and campaigning.

Lino's negative experience of politicians had begun much earlier in connection with a powerful lawyer and Christian Democrat MP, Esposito, whom his mother had met through a local shopkeeper, signora Pina (described in a later section). In exchange for a sum of money, Esposito had helped to resolve the bureaucratic problems associated with the adolescent Lino's marriage to Luisa, who was pregnant. Later, when Lino was arrested in connection with the petty cigarette-smuggling he had just started in cooperation with a friend, his mother had managed, through Esposito, to get the charges dropped.[27] For Lino the money and electoral support Esposito demanded were an acceptable price to pay. He had lost all the money (his and Luisa's wedding gifts) he had invested, but he was grateful for having escaped jail and, in fact, a criminal record. Soon, however, Esposito began to exploit expectable gratitude: acting in a way that recalls old-fashioned patronage, he claimed services and regularly sent his office boy to fetch goods from the stall gratis. Lino bitterly resented both Esposito's arrogance and his mother's submission, and when she died he severed the links with him.

Having learned from experience, Lino now not only restricted his relationship with this new politician to a single exchange but also decided to be more true to his own ideas and avoid depending on politicians in his goal pursuits. He, like many locals, establishes relations with potential *maniglie*, to whom he may give gifts as part of undefined and delayed exchanges which may or may not occur. But he also says, 'Nun voglio stà suggett' 'a nisciun" (I don't want to be subject to anyone). Twenty or thirty years earlier the politician might perhaps have found a more sympathetic audience. However, as locals of Lino's generation were becoming increasingly committed to new values, they were also becoming increasingly aware that resources alternative to politicians could be found, albeit with some difficulty. The *popolino* refer explicitly to values of self-respect and practicality when they say, 'Chi pecora s' fa 'o lupo s'o magn" (If you behave like a sheep, you'll become a wolf's meal). They despise sheep and say that it is better to have as little as possible to do with politics.

Lino's experience of politicians and the favour system has strongly affected his career without really restricting him. On the contrary, he exemplifies the way in which the balance between success and failure is established, among the local *popolino*, by degrees of ability to refer to alternative values and to construct and use resources other than allegiance to political 'benefactors'. This is a result of symbolic and moral negotiations and pragmatic choices which require a rethinking of power relations and the relationship between agency and structure in Naples. Complex operations of thought allow Lino and other locals to behave in an apparently contradictory way without becoming involved in politics or crime and without having to compromise their identity as honest and independent individuals.

Over the years, Lino has improved his position. The disadvantaged young man has become a deputy supervisor and has expanded his stall business, now registered in the name of his son. With the help of their daughters, Lino and Luisa have also opened a shop selling goods entirely different from those sold in the stall, and they have become multiple-property owners.[28] In the situation of mass diffusion of favours, Lino uses his contacts among professionals, trade-unionists, bureaucrats, and ordinary people to solve various problems and obtain benefits, some of which are supposed to be universally available by right and some of which formally do not exist. Lino reciprocates with favours and free or discounted merchandise or, less frequently, with money or electoral support.

Quite unlike Lino, Michele managed to gain a formal steady job when, he says, he was really losing hope. Almost too old to marry and still able to offer no security, he took the view that the worst of times was also the time for one more push of the wheel. Compromising with his pride, he approached Pasquale, a childhood friend, for an introduction to the Christian Democrat councillor for whom he had canvassed in the quarter, and when new social-service jobs were advertised over which the politician had control Pasquale reminded him of Michele. The good news came directly from the politician who, in Michele's own words, accepted 'a present, just '*nu fior*' [a flower, to stress the non-material value of the gift] but didn't exploit the situation; he knew I was penniless.' Later, the councillor directed Michele to the 'right people', who shortly afterwards helped him obtain the training he needed for the job. Pasquale married into Michele's family. Thus Michele escaped subjection to a master regarding employment. In accordance with the values that motivated the self-employed entrepreneur Lino to continue – and later expand – his business, Michele quickly and gratefully gave up 'toiling in the workshop'. Perhaps more important, he began to understand key processes of *sottogoverno* – in administration, bureaucracy and politics. Nowadays it is in his improved network that Michele finds solutions of a kind to normal crises, and to more serious problems.

Michele did not become wholly dependent on Pasquale or the councillor. His universe includes a large number of contacts (kin and non-kin) of both sexes, who are widely diversified in their social positions, power and residence (throughout Naples and, in some cases, outside it). Michele gained formal employment by investing in his local network, but it was starting from his work environment outside the quarter that he established what he calls 'relations of friendship' with various contacts through whom he achieves goals unattainable in the past. For example, using the system to his advantage, he has obtained a disablement pension to which he may well not be entitled.[29] Michele's key contact in this goal pursuit has been Avitabile, a well-connected professional and bureaucrat whom he met through a trade-unionist. Avitabile having asked nothing in return for the favour, Michele made him a present and continues to be grateful and to use him occasionally for similar favours on his relatives' or friends' behalf. For instance, through Avitabile's connections he got his brother-in-law, Giuseppe, classified, and then employed, as an invalid.[30]

In spite of having constructed alternative resources, Michele, unlike Lino, has continued to vote for and ask favours of his political benefactor. This, in a sense, reminds us of Ciro. Ciro, who comes from a nearby neighbourhood but has lived in the quarter since he married Giovanna, a local woman, was middle-aged when repeated failure in gaining formal employment and, he says, 'the unpleasant memory of toiling in many precarious jobs' (including manual labour in small workshops) motivated him to work hard at establishing useful contacts in the hospital where he was undergoing long-term treatment. He became a friend and supporter of an important doctor and Christian Democrat activist through whom he entered active politics. First, in contrast to most local canvassers, he joined the party. Then he campaigned successfully for a powerful candidate by mobilizing relatives and friends in his original neighbourhood, in the quarter and in the network he had constructed over the years as a prominent member of a religious association.[31]

The working partnership between the Christian Democrats and the Church, particularly the parish priests and their lay collaborators, that is well known in Italy (Allum 1973, Kertzer 1980) was notably efficient at the time, and, although it lost some strength over the 1970s and early 1980s following Vatican II and the Communist Party's alliance with Catholics (Pardo 1993), it has been recently rejuvenated by overt papal support for the Christian Democrats, who have now scattered in various new centre parties.[32] Of course, as research elsewhere in urban Italy suggests (Prato 1995), this has been complicated by the formation of Catholic groups outside the party. Nevertheless, in the quarter the attitude has long been dominant that the Christian Democrats are the people 'any good Catholic should vote for'. In little more than a year, Ciro's canvassing had produced a professional qualification and then a public-sector job for him, and two years later he obtained a similar job for his wife and one for his son. With time, he expanded his network, establishing useful connections with middle-ranking bureaucrats, professionals, clerics and with what he describes as *pezzi grossi* (sing. *pezzo grosso*, big shots; or Neapolitan *piezz' ruoss'*) – party candidates whom he has supported since his benefactor retired from active politics.

The Ciro I met bore no trace of the hardship and desperation of his recent past. He has capitalized on his time, information and contacts establishing a reputation as a reliable broker who grants favours for cash. Through him, people gain jobs and job transfers, avoid statutory military service, deal with legal problems, and obtain benefits such as council or state grants, pensions and speedy hospital care. Apart from a small percentage, Ciro says, the relatively large sums of money go to his contacts and expenses.[33] Occasionally, however, he helps the poorest among his favour-seekers by 'persuading the contact to charge less'. This carefully controlled form of generosity extends to the small-scale moneylending business which he and Giovanna started around the time she gained formal employment. The two have thus constructed a relatively comfortable position, investing their money in property ownership and their identity in an acceptable though basically instrumental image. Ciro's self-representation broadly coincides with local people's description of him as a useful though not particularly generous or good-hearted person whom they respect 'because he isn't too usurious and doesn't pretend to be charitable'.

It would be naïve to expect moral sanction of Ciro's informal activities in the quarter or to believe that here respect can be easily imposed rather than earned. Ciro provides services (favours and loans) which people want and for which, should other strategies fail, they are willing to pay. He is only one of the *ammanigliat'* [*i*] (sing. *ammanigliat'* [*o*], well-connected) people who have made a profitable business of inefficiency in the public sector. Whether caused by overregulation, inadequacy or corruption, inefficiency has produced competition throughout a social system in which a connection between services and profit is simply supposed not to exist. This approach of Ciro's, indicative as it may be of one aspect of the *popolino*'s entrepreneurship, cannot, however, be assumed to be representative of their morality and action.

Combining different domains of livelihood: entrepreneurial action between poverty and prosperity

Combining different domains of livelihood is an aspect of personal entrepreneurship crucial to all levels of local life, from relative poverty and deprivation to relative prosperity. Rafele and Peppe, two neighbours of Michele, and two other informants, Carlo and Domenico, exemplify significant positions on the continuum between these poles with particular reference to important values in the relationship between production and consumption.

It is thanks to Michele's generosity, I was told, that Rafele has a pension and a job. Years back, Rafele's lungs had been seriously damaged by handling poisonous glue in a small workshop.[34] As his health deteriorated, the only job he could find was in a neighbour's shop, as a factotum, for a regular but miserable wage and without insurance or the other benefits of formal employment. After Michele had helped Rafele to obtain an invalidity certificate and then an invalidity pension, the shopkeeper helped him to find a second job. The *sanzar'* (unlicensed housing broker) 'o Russo had decided to sell the goodwill of his small businesses (he also obtained documents on other people's behalf) and retire, and Rafele bought the goodwill with part of his pension arrears and, despite competition, managed to increase his custom even outside the quarter. When I met him in 1985, he was helped by his twelve-year-old nephew, who later took over the business gratis. Rafele said, 'I've my invalidity pension and would have felt dishonest taking the boy's money.' Relatively rewarding goal pursuits and brokership improve actors' positions in future transactions, contribute to the development of their resource systems and increase the occasions on which they may become temporary favour-bestowers. Moreover, there is a feedback between this causal relationship and actors' self-esteem.

On a level quite different from the episode involving Rafele, generous Michele has helped his friend Peppe to obtain an invalidity certificate and hospitalization for his wife without having to wait the usual several months. Peppe, who is formally unemployed, runs a profitable business. Some years back, following his wife's advice, he gave up his manual job in a small workshop producing clothing to sell clothing to petty traders throughout the Centre-South. His wife has worked in one of these workshops since she was a teenager, rising from the rank of (unpaid) apprentice to that of skilled worker and, now, manager. In unspoken reciprocation for Michele's favours, Peppe allows him to operate a clothing trade of his own without capital by charging him at cost and only for the clothing he sells. Similar deals with others allow Michele to sell merchandise as varied as shoes, handbags and perfume. While his wife sells mainly within her local network, Michele's customers are his workmates, his superiors, the service users, and their relatives and friends. Sometimes he also establishes favour relations with people who buy from him or their relatives, taking advantage of the fact that, as he says, 'in a workplace like mine you meet lots of people'.

It would be reductive to say that the practical results of people's commitment to doing what is morally demanding provide a safety net allowing even poor and downtrodden people like Rafele a sense of security. There is, however, sufficient evidence to suggest that the relationship between values, norms and action in exchange and entrepreneurship affects their lives in such a way that we have to think very carefully before defining them as resourceless and marginal. It plays an equally important role at the opposite end of local livelihood, generating conduct that is normative and rational – clearly motivated by expected returns which are neither short-term nor necessarily tangible.

Thus, within the framework provided by a relatively high level of competition, the combination of various monetarily rewarding work activities that characterizes the entrepreneurship of people like Michele and, in a different way, Lino, does not usually generate identity conflict. It is interpreted positively by the local community. To their mates and to themselves, these people are not greedy; they are 'clever' because, having managed to obtain a secure job, they 'don't sleep on it, as they could easily do'. Some who are formally employed extract an extra income from the private, sometimes illicit use of the resources of organized labour and from extra activities like those performed by Michele in the workplace. Some, like Lino, Luigi and Antonio, quickly perform their jobs and, while formally still at work, run stalls, shops or other businesses registered in the names of figureheads. Some perform 'black labour' for shops, workshops, garages, etc. Others manage their own informal enterprises.

Carlo, a public-services employee, trades informally in radios, television sets and household electrical appliances which he stores at home and sells, evading taxes, within his and his wife Assunta's network. Carlo's nuclear family[35] is participating fully in the new unlicensed business he has set up with the cooperation of a neighbour woman and her daughter-in-law, and Franco, a nephew of his who works as a freelance van driver. On Saturdays Assunta, her two daughters and the neighbours produce home-made gnocchi, which Franco and Carlo's son deliver to shops throughout Naples and the province using the van of one of the firms for which Franco works. Alongside shellfish, mixed nuts and cakes, fresh pasta, particularly gnocchi, is traditionally a must for the Neapolitan Sunday (and generally festive) lunch. Although Neapolitans continue to take pride in their culinary skills, in recent years market demand for fresh pasta and other such ingredients has increased. Many *popolino* have joined the bourgeois in the habit of buying home-made food instead of spending time making it themselves. The products marketed by enterprises such as Carlo's are made appealing by their quality and relatively low price. The unlicensed nature of their production and distribution keeps costs low and facilitates shopkeepers' tax evasion. Carlo, who manages organization and finance, has quickly expanded the custom he originally constructed through a friend who runs a food shop in the periphery. In response to market demand, he is now considering giving up his other activities and borrowing the money required to develop the business further by diversifying the types of pasta and involving other relatives and friends.

Domenico, having recently obtained a modest but steady job in a large firm, has given up the unprofitable informal work (as a repairman) which he started when still a teenager. Instead, now in his fifties he is selling pirated cassettes and videos and sports equipment within his and his family's local network, at work and, occasionally, in a stall. Stallholders willingly make room for his small temporary stall because, they say, it costs them nothing to help but, quite clearly, they are also engaging in an unspecified exchange for potential access to his contacts in the trade unions and the bureaucracy. Initially, Domenico used the formal guarantee of his steady income to buy merchandise by instalments. Now, having systematically reinvested the profits in the business, he has managed to repay his debts and to save money. As does Carlo, he plans to use his savings and borrowed money to expand his enterprise and involve members of his household and possibly relatives.

These traders, even when they tend to specialize, can quickly switch to other kinds of merchandise should their personal circumstances or changes in the market or simply convenience direct them to do so. Moreover, in the normal management of their businesses they rarely pass up a bargain, and when such occasional merchandise is too different from that regularly sold they set up temporary extra stalls, entrusting them to their wives, children or temporary associates. Finally, as I have said, those who are not traders or skilled tradesmen and cannot or do not want to perform distinctly criminal activities (such as drug dealing, extortion or theft) most often participate in 'quasi-legal' ones such as selling smuggled cigarettes or tickets for the clandestine lotteries.

These activities have never been described to me as morally wrong; rather, they are presented as profitable and legitimate sources of extra income. They belong to the complex interplay of moral themes, expectations and motivations that underlies both these people's distance from industrial values and their combination of different resource domains in

their entrepreneurship. Moreover, as we shall see, this interplay leaves isolated the few who will not work because they find easy money appealing
even if it implies criminal action. The effect is the progressive, and observable, marginalization – cultural, moral and social – of this minority.

The cultural construction of personal position

A discriminative role is played in these economics of work and entrepreneurship by the cultural construction of choice and action. Lino says that
his formal income gives him peace of mind and respectability but covers
only basic expenses. It is, instead, his trades which, besides giving him
satisfaction, produce the money necessary to improve his household's livelihood and to acquire what is not immediately needed. Thus, while investing in his formal career, Lino has opened the shop and, he says, is working
on 'improving [his] manners'. Like most *popolino*, he does not, however,
directly – or strictly – associate wealth with virtue.

Perceptions of work, I have said, change with circumstances and individuals, and they have moral and practical significance at a level much
deeper than that of individuals' awareness of the connection in modern
society – often oblique and disproportionate – between effort and reward.
In particular, the emphasis put on appearing to work at a leisurely pace
and deriving satisfaction from one's labour depends on the meanings of
'surplus' or 'need' that can be attached to one's own and one's fellows'
hard work. The explanatory value of these meanings extends in a complex
way to the expectable results of such work. Sometimes described as sacrifice, hard work that justifies self- (*and* group-) description as *faticator*' is
usually seen, in the framework of cleverness, as a way of improving one's
life which, apart from serving tangible purposes, produces returns in terms
of self-esteem and satisfaction.[36] Case-material may help us to reflect on
this apparent contradiction in terms.

Michele and his wife, Nunzia, regard themselves as co-producers of
their household's economic welfare. Their household can count not only
on Michele's formal income and the tax-free money he earns from his
informal activities but also on the unemployed Nunzia's work activities,
particularly trading and the informal work she does at home for a small
workshop in a nearby quarter. Through her mother, Giovanna, Nunzia
gets as much work as she can manage. This job is a result of Giovanna's
relationship with the owner of the workshop, whom she has met through a
neighbour. Giovanna and her grown-up children (two of whom are
unmarried and live, characteristically, with her) are paid piece-rates for
packing at home the goods produced in the workshop. This activity has

altered the organization of Nunzia's and Giovanna's households, their internal relationships, and their members' schedules. Nunzia says, 'My older children have to do more housework, shopping, etc., and have to look after their brothers and sisters.' Her older son has now asked her if he may do some packing work after school as a way of earning pocket money. In spite of the objective difficulties for the household's organization brought about by their multiple activities, Nunzia and Michele do not describe their work as toil imposed upon them by need. They stress, instead, the positive aspects of surplus and fun in their identity as *faticatur*'. The extra cash is partly saved or invested in new enterprises and partly spent on clothes, holidays, eating out, celebrations, presents and other goods or activities that enhance their self-esteem, networks and image.

Thus, the positive meaning of surplus is injected into the representation of work, consumption, social position and, ultimately, personhood. Nunzia typically says, 'I don't really have to work. Michele has a secure job, and we aren't desperate for money. I do this extra work to improve our position [they are saving to buy a larger flat] and escape from routine.' Luisa gave a similar description of the work she did in the early years of her marriage, when she resumed the 'black labour' she had done in her family home for a small workshop. The money she made went into the accumulation of the capital to buy their home.[37] These themes of surplus or need do not depend, then, on the presence of a formal income; they are equally relevant when an enterprise or informal job can be regarded as a secure source of income. Whether or not these people are formally employed, to them their hard work is not toil; it is, instead, evidence of cleverness which contributes to their households' betterment. Equally, they say, their children's work is not exploitation but, rather, a good way for them to earn pocket money, learn by experience, and stay off the street and away from drugs. Moreover, it is widely believed that a wife may contribute to her household's welfare not only through her paid work but also by acting as a connection between the private and the public domain and by bringing together different networks and resource spheres.

At the opposite end of the scale of values in this culture of work there are those who cannot cope or cope only with difficulty and who work hard without producing satisfaction or surplus. Paolo, a stallholder of Lino's age, was originally pointed out to me as an example of poverty and failure. In the past few years he and his wife, Enrica, have established a fashionable and remunerative shop, but when I met them they were just managing to survive despite Paolo's double work,[38] Enrica's knitting jumpers for sale, and their older son's working in his free time in the stall and on Sundays as a bar assistant. Paolo, I was told, was 'unfortunate, but also *fess*' [stupid]. He knows the importance of contacts, but he does nothing to acquire and use them. Instead, he and his wife and children toil for crumbs. He hasn't even managed to get the petty recommendation you need for a [trading] licence.' Thus, until recently, Paolo has had little reason to feel fulfilled. In line with values that mark the opposition between work and toil, whatever Paolo's and Enrica's perception of their work activities, to their peers theirs was 'a sort of life nobody likes leading'. This local judgement was not mitigated by the fact that Paolo had relatively more free time than his busier mates, formally employed or not. Paolo proudly said that he spent his free time outdoors with his family, but to many this only stressed his inadequacy. Michele typically said,

He can do that because he isn't tired and has nothing to think about, no special responsibility. But what does he go out with his family for? At the most he can afford to go to Mergellina [a promenade by the sea], in the midst of traffic jams and without even having the money to buy an ice-cream, and he can't have proper holidays. He doesn't have the money, you know, and he can't borrow at interest because he can't give any security.

The changes in the couple's position are reflected in the changes in the symbolism of their self-representation and modes of consumption. The relationship established by the *popolino* between personal appearance (and behaviour) and the ability to manage livelihood beyond immediate need is directly relevant to actors' competitive approach and perception of others. Surplus must therefore be translated into recognizable symbols. If Antonio's management of his appearance is an overstatement even by local standards, that of Paolo and Enrica provides a more ordinary example. Their invariably poor clothing, shabby aspect and lack of 'true leisure' once emphasized their failure in a way as visually powerful as the gradual expansion of their business, display of jewellery, frequent *scampagnate* (eating out) and plans to see their children married with 'appropriate pomp' now emphasize their improvement. These symbolic statements – according to some observers 'baroque excesses' – are predictably much more low key when people believe that they may be the object of envy and evil eye. At the same time, the *popolino* are explicitly contemptuous of what they regard as transgressions, especially by the bourgeoisie, of the positive relationship mentioned above. Because they believe the bourgeoisie to be economically and socially better-off, they regard their sober appearance and behaviour as inconsistent – evidence of their *purucchiamm'* (penny-pinching) and inability to enjoy life.

Segregated women or competitive entrepreneurs? Redefined priorities

In spite of objective differences, most local households find important common ground in the strong interaction between the moral, symbolic, social and economic activities of husband and wife. Most *popolino* women in their thirties and forties quickly dismiss the question of how they regard themselves with the response that they are housewives who are interested in the welfare of their families and in 'keeping up to date'. Bringing to mind issues debated in other European ethnographies (e.g. Herzfeld 1987; Loizos and Papataxiarchis 1991a; also Wallman 1984), prolonged conversations and case material show them expressing their identity in a variety of important spheres, well beyond the limits of domestically oriented action and of economic significance. The career of Luigi's wife, Anna, illustrates a widespread process among local women (and men) whereby changes in mentality, values, self-image and behaviour are associated with new attitudes towards work, work conditions, entrepreneurship and competition. Her case also highlights the significance of other factors. She has established her identity as an independent-minded woman, clearly drawing on the fact that here the biological dimension remains important mainly in ritual life[39] but no real superiority is attributed to men over women (or vice versa) in everyday life. In her pursuit of betterment, Anna 'cultivates herself', stressing her and Luigi's interest in 'good magazines' and 'cultural television programmes', and she says that she wants her children to be equally independent and better educated. Like many *popolino* of her age, she left school after the *licenza media* (approximately O level), when she was only fourteen years old. This does not, however, seem to have restricted her or her children in their motivations, expectations and careers.

Whereas the children of Michele and Nunzia place greater emphasis in their pursuit of 'good positions' on the help they can get from their father's contacts than on achieving qualifications, Anna's and Luigi's daughter and their older son, more in tune with the contemporary trend, are studying hard to become a qualified clerk and a technician. Paolo and Enrica's daughter is doggedly pursuing a similar goal while lending a hand in the shop. Lino and Luisa's older daughter, Barbara, who is engaged to a local man, is attending university while working as a trainee accountant. She strongly identifies with the women-achievers in the professional and political arenas whom she learns about both from the media and from direct experience. Lino implicitly underlines important changes in gender relations and the culture of social position when he says, 'Having a member of the family at university is something to be proud of. Moreover, a professional whom I trust fully is now managing the finances in the family's businesses. And, you know, she is also assisting a relative and a friend in their businesses.' Having won her argument with her parents, Barbara's younger sister is studying with the aim of starting her own business. In accordance with new patterns of socialization, she met her like-minded fiancé (from a similar quarter) at a disco. This is not unusual nowadays, for, although socialization in the quarter is not restricted by true segregation of the sexes, it is subject to what the young call 'the rules of gossip'. They can interact more freely in extralocal situations, where the risk of gossip (for them and their families, they stress) is minimal. Long-lasting friendships among young people, mainly of the same sex but often of different social positions, have sprung from encounters at school, fashionable bars and discos, holiday resorts and church-sponsored events.

Local women also increasingly share with men the moral and emotional responsibility for the household. And, although it is women who continue to be educated to domestic tasks, especially among the younger generation, as elsewhere in South Italy (CENSIS 1988) they tend to share with their husbands not only the responsibility for its economic welfare but also child-rearing and housework (cleaning, shopping, cooking, etc.). These young women's 'emancipated' and unsubmissive attitude is positively reflected in that of their male contemporaries. Both in one-to-one interviews and in the conversations we had in the presence of their significantly[40] argumentative fiancées, young men proudly stressed their egalitarian views. Some couples also referred explicitly both to the advantages of modern family planning and to the equality of sexes as a constitutional right,[41] and the men said that they were open-minded, and expected their future wives' emancipation, career choices and, in some cases, education, to lead to a working role even more active and rewarding than that of older women like Anna.

This situation is explained only secondarily by the fact that in recent years the link between women's honour and prenuptial virginity has lost most of its symbolic and social value. Prenuptial intercourse is, of course, not a new thing among the *popolino*. What is relatively new is that, in contrast to the symbolically disordering extramarital sex, it is much more tolerated than it was, say, twenty or thirty years ago. Although unambiguous censure – much weaker than in the past – does occur in the rare cases in which prenuptial sex brings about pregnancy (contraception and medical information are widely available and used), an abortion may well be seen as a viable alternative to an early or forced marriage. Thus, in line with important changes in the explanation of sex, nowadays loss of virginity outside marriage does not invariably carry symbolic expressions of guilt and is very seldom the motive for bitter disputes and 'reparatory marriages'. In defiance of 'old-fashioned' views and important Catholic principles, such behaviour no longer inevitably precludes honour, respect or future marriages.

In other words, the *popolino* have crucially revised their priorities. The parents of these young people are trying, above all, to give them the best options in terms of socio-economic competition and mobility. The value of virginity remains as important for women as that of marriage (for both sexes), which is crucial to a person's symbolic normalization, but neither value is any longer the indispensable condition for women's self-esteem and good reputation. This has greatly helped to open up opportunities both in women's own careers and in the collective competitive prospects of their households before and after marriage, thus further undermining the equation – some call it absolute – between (men's) honour and (their households') economic welfare. In addition, the greater degree of freedom and, according to my informants, emancipation, which corresponds to these new priorities in values, norms and modes of action, finds expression well beyond the categories of work and employment. The culture of personal well-being and betterment which widely affects local life and its normative aspects has inevitably engendered a redefinition and updating of certain sex-related tasks and norms of proper behaviour and of the associated inequality. Of course, roles remain gender-structured in the minds and conduct of the *popolino*, but in this flexible situation the concept of proper behaviour is normally negotiated in such a way that it would be difficult to argue that it plays a particularly restrictive role and that a gender-oriented monopoly of normative control really exists.[42]

Although these changes are particularly obvious among the young, significant background for them is found in the lives of many *popolino* of their parents' generation. Anna's case material reveals important aspects of the female side of this issue; in particular, her work history shows that her attitude can be traced to her youth. After leaving school, following her mother's advice she became an apprentice in a local workshop, but because she found working under a *padron'* exploitative and oppressive she was always quarrelling with her bosses and changing jobs. Anna and relatives and friends who have known her since she was a child attribute her insubordinate and restless nature to the radical views she had picked up at school, from the media and from her older sister.[43] Determined to avoid industrial employment, the young Anna rejected the help of a relative who, at her mother's request, had found her a steady job on the assembly line in a factory. This attitude contrasts in many ways with that of women who live in the industrial districts of the periphery, for whom such work is often an unpleasant but crucial and reliable source of income and an important asset in their lives before and after marriage (e.g., Pacifico 1982). Anna's account of this decision reflects the distinction between toil and meritorious work, providing a further example of the difficulty of opposing social norms to rational conduct.

The moral value and rationality of Anna's choices began to be vindicated and her general attitude more clearly explained when, shortly before she married Luigi (who was a neighbour), she obtained permission from her parents to help him in managing his business. This, Anna says, cost her a fierce struggle in the family and, initially, ostracism by some locals, but it was in this way that she finally managed to work independently as a self-employed trader and to be able 'to decide what to do and how and when to do it'. Not only is the Anna I have met popular and respected in the quarter but, as in the case, say, of Peppe's wife, over the years her managerial ability has become more sophisticated and, as Luigi himself proudly says, she has emerged as the dynamic entrepreneurial soul of the family business. As she puts it, 'Luigi's got the experience, but I'm the one who looks after the finances, expansion of the business and public relations.' Recently, Anna has played the determinant role in engineering a major change in their enterprise by successfully competing with other bidders for a lucrative and much sought-after shop. Having heard from her sister-in-law about the shopkeeper's intention to retire, Anna started to raise capital very early. At the same time, she pre-empted other possible bids by using her *savoir faire* and her contacts in the shopkeeper's household, improving her acquaintance through her sister-in-law. Thus, she managed to put her case in the best possible way – she wanted to improve her household's position, she argued, adding that she would take good care of the shop and its custom – and eventually bid successfully for the shop.

The story of Gina, a relative of Michele now in her forties, is remarkably different. Up-to-date on fashion, songs, films and television programmes, she is poorly educated, falling well below contemporary local standards. Although she is no less argumentative than, say, Anna, and is clearly concerned with not appearing ignorant and destitute,[44] she shows little interest in education, formal or informal, and generally seems quite restricted in her action and choices. Her work history shows relatively little variety; since the age of twelve she has worked for small unlicensed workshops, either at home or on the premises. She provided a vivid illustration of her attitude by referring to her present job for a local workshop as exploitative but convenient because she could work at home. Not only is her entrepreneurship confined to selling smuggled cigarettes, soft drinks, toys and other little things in her *basso* but also she mismanages the resources available to her; and this includes the network to which she is potentially connected through Michele who finds it difficult to help her because, he says, she is not motivated to improve herself.

This attitude is reflected in those of Gina's husband, who works in a small workshop, and their children. Their sixteen-year-old daughter, who only managed to finish elementary school, is at home 'learning to be a housewife'. Their sons, both in their early teens, spend most of their time playing in the alley, vandalizing property and, despite being underage, gambling on the machines in a club nearby. With Gina and her husband's approval, they say that they will soon stop wasting their time attending school, where they feel frustrated and ill treated. However, given the low level of entrepreneurship expressed by their parents, the boys have little hope of becoming involved in a business like that in which Carlo's children or even Rafele's nephew are employed. Gina hopes that they will escape drugs and criminality through honest employment in the workshop where their father works. Such work, like that of the young Michele or Ciro and of Paolo's son in the old days, will probably bear meanings opposite to those of fun and surplus that characterize the home labour of Nunzia's children and the cooperation in the family business of Luisa's.

Gina and her husband express a mentality and values which are shared only by a minority of their *popolino* contemporaries, despite common origins, residence and age. Of course, the declining normative status of such values should not make us forget that, with some significant exceptions, they were more common in earlier generations. Above all, Gina's outlook contrasts sharply not only with that of Anna, but also with that of many other women of her age (or older) who represent themselves and behave less radically.

As we proceed, the cases of other local people of various social positions will help us to cast in a broader framework the explanation that I have proposed of the similarities and contrasts between Anna (and Luisa, Nunzia and Peppe's wife) and Gina and between Paolo, Lino, Michele and Ciro as they are reflected in their personal choices and in the general approaches of their households. I do not dispute that certain cultural aspects found among the *popolino* might be invoked to construct arguments about honour, virtue and shame, as has indeed been done from various perspectives in the literature on South Europe. I strongly suggest, however, that this would amount to an otiose theoretical superimposition, for these three concepts do not affect in any special way the morality and rationality of these people's ordinary lives, or of their 'civic spirit'. An informed view of the relationship between the objective situation and actors' self-representations needs to take fully into account the socio-economic and moral importance of values such as independence, insubordination and competition *across* gender divisions.

In a number of cases the people themselves may well overemphasize the power of either sex in household and extrahousehold relations, but observation suggests that the *popolino* family is certainly not a unitary group under male authority characterized by women's indirect but strong influence. The claims of matriarchy and, alternatively, of women's suppression in some writing on the *popolino* are equally unsubstantiated in the contemporary situation. I recognize both the power of women (*popolino* and bourgeois) as central figures in network construction and as mediators and the significance of the benefits they and their families derive from their composite entrepreneurship. Given that it is mainly (though increasingly not exclusively) mothers and older daughters who look after children, I also do not deny that there may well be some ethnographic truth to the saying 'The hand that rocks the cradle rules the world.' But it would be very difficult to accept the stereotype that, at least since Anne Parsons's study (1962), has been attached to *popolino* women (particularly to the husband's mother) as the omnipotent driving forces of male behaviour. It would be equally difficult to argue that local women are segregated, overcontrolled members of the local community – housewives oppressed and economically marginalized by motherhood (Belmonte 1989 [1979]: 87–94), housework and 'black labour' done at home (Cetro 1984) and doomed to socio-economic marginality by the normative implications of a backward morality. These difficulties become particularly obvious when changes in the conceptions and symbols of gender are contextualized in the complex relations between such important social domains as household, kinship and neighbourhood (Chapter 4). For now we can suggest that the main explanation for backwardness and poverty – and for relative success, emancipation and motivation for betterment – lies in actors' differential ability to manage material and non-material resources entrepreneurially. It does not lie in their gender, or in the simple fact that they are *popolino* and live in this run-down quarter of the centre. This means that our analysis must focus on values and beliefs in their complex relation to action.

Moral and spiritual themes in the normative explanation of 'deserving good', 'failure' and 'success'

The grassroots significance of the saying, 'Ajutat' ca Dio t'ajut" is clearly expressed in actors' combining resources of different kinds in their goal pursuits. Graphically expositive of the error of considering the *popolino* fatalists, their mobilization of financial resources, time, information and contacts is part of their broader symbolic and moral investment in the affective and spiritual aspects of their lives and in the supramundane domain of their universes. Within this framework of strong continuous interaction, individuals' ability to make such investment injects crucial strength (moral and psychological) into the explanation, and the performance and results, of action and choice.

Success often elicits competition. It also provokes envy and encourages conflict and ostracism, in this culture raising issues of the evil eye, misfortune and the related strategies of protection and defence. Sometimes people avoid showing their success. More generally, they make identity investments in recognizable forms of generosity and the associated meanings of goodness and worthiness. These investments also produce results which encourage entrepreneurship as an important, though not always deliberately planned, secondary effect. Reiterating an earlier point, it would be more naïve than straightforward to argue that these choices are either gratuitous actions or disguises for predatory motives. We have studied how actors' commitment to behaviour that makes them feel worthy translates into various forms of generosity and unpaid work on other people's behalf. In keeping with the eschatological value of work and entrepreneurship in their lives, such behaviour intervenes in the connection that, according to Communist orthodoxy, exists between personal initiative and incapacity for selfless (and long-term-oriented) action, allowing ordinary people like Michele to conform more closely and clearly to local ideas of satisfaction, goodness and success than, say, professional favourbestowers like Ciro. The power of people like Michele to say 'I make myself loved' is directly related to, and benefits from, local recognition that they have constructed their positions without ruthlessness. An important corollary is that they can say that their resource options potentially include almost everyone they know in the quarter and outside it.

Michele's representation of his local universe as a warm, supporting fabric of strong links is met by the description his relatives, friends and neighbours continue to provide of him as clever and good-hearted. When discussing him, people said that his favour-seekers needed only to make 'small presents' to his contacts and provided examples of the help he offered of his own accord, as in the case of Rafele. Equally, I was told that, although Michele draws an extra income from providing his professional services privately, he never charges anyone who cannot pay. He behaves similarly with people who could become useful, but he links such behaviour to his good-heartedness and wish to be helpful rather than to the (relatively more instrumental) 'One never knows' strategy earlier mentioned. It is clear that such generosity produces results in terms of satisfaction and contacts for the generous individual and material and non-material benefits for others. It is equally clear that Michele can be generous because, and insofar as, he has constructed good non-material resources in terms of contacts and information as well as identity, and that the moral and practical dividends of such generosity help him to be a better entrepreneur. Therefore, as in his case, both generous individuals and their significant others can say that an improvement in their positions is likely to serve more than their own self-interest.

People like Michele recognize that they are regarded as useful persons in the neighbourhood, and they reject the cynical explanation for what they describe as people's shows of affection. For example, turning on its head his own representation of his investments in others, Michele says, 'People don't need to cajole me. Everybody knows that I help when possible. People feel grateful, not just obligated.' To accept that the opposite could be true would obviously imply too strong a challenge and probably an identity crisis. It would also introduce a 'polluting' *incognita* into the relationship established in this culture between personal motivations, their value and the moral and spiritual significance of the corresponding behaviour. This is so obviously problematic that even the more coldly (and instrumentally) managed entrepreneurship of people like Ciro includes negotiated forms of generosity.

This morality of generous behaviour is better understood by taking into account the strong link between actors' culture of well-being and their religious beliefs. 'We all must account to God,' they say, adding, 'If you do good God will protect you, and so will your own dead.' They also say that they want to be remembered after death. Like a good life, a good death and the corresponding condition in the hereafter depend on the care, support and memory of the living.[45] The belief is indeed widely shared that a sinful, heartless or particularly unfulfilled life condemns one to oblivion and to prolonged suffering in life and after death (Kilpatrick

1921). The role the living are believed to play in the condition of the dead thus acquires a profound explanatory role in people's actions.

The connection between the symbolism of the supramundane and actors' practical ethics is precise and important in the definition of ultimate ends across the whole spectrum of social and economic variation in the quarter. Under stress, Michele, like other *popolino*, makes spiritual investments in his relationship with the souls in purgatory[46] and with the saints of whom he is a devotee. He keeps a family shrine and expresses gratitude for the general improvement in his life by spending money and time in supporting a local religious association and in renewing a street shrine dedicated to St Anthony, for which he has obtained the formal blessing of the local priest.[47] Similarly, Lino's behaviour has been significantly affected throughout his career by this belief in the mutual influence between the living and the dead. He tries to 'be honest' in order to comply with the moral expectations he believes his dead relatives (especially his parents) have of him, and he tries not to displease the spirits whose presence he feels about him. In accordance with local morality, he also maintains that his good nature and substantial honesty allow him to hope for the protection of the sacred part of his supramundane universe.

Local people tend to establish individual relations with saints. They may supplement individual requests with collective action, but in many cases the collective aspect is altogether absent. Paolo and his family pay periodic visits to the sanctuary of the Madonna of the Arch[48] 'to pray and bring her a candle, a flower', but they do so in private, doubting the sincerity of what they call 'collective displays of faith'. An important aspect of this issue is illustrated by the behaviour of Lino, who seldom goes to church but remains a devotee of the Madonna of Montevergine and generously supports the local annual celebrations. Moreover, recognizing the power of the Church, he encourages his children to socialize in the parish. In the past, however, he was a regular churchgoer, and after he was released from jail he visited the Sanctuary of Montevergine with Luisa and his mother to fulfil a promise the latter had made to the madonna during the crisis. They walked the last few kilometres to the church, taking candles, flowers and some money. More money was given to the local priest to say a mass for the soul of Lino's father, who Lino was sure was protecting him.

This, in a sense, is analogous to the behaviour of Rafele, who, since the recent improvement of his fortunes, has begun to look after a small street shrine in his alley. Rafele does not believe that he obtained the pension *because* of supramundane intervention any more than Lino believed that the madonna actually released him from jail or manipulated the conditions of his dramatic predicament. Equally, Michele is well aware of who he should thank for his job, as is indicated by his vows of gratitude and, perhaps above all, by his commitment to expanding his network. There is no significant evidence that these people believe that the problem is magically solved or taken away by the supramundane powers that they approach. Nor do they show a resigned attitude – before the will of God – to the opposition between merit (and hope) and experience. However, their belief in supramundane influence over earthly matters – as a general value – motivates them to show gratitude to the entities they consider closer to them (including the near dead) for having fulfilled their pleas, causing them to meet and obtain the help of the right persons in their problem-solving and goal pursuits.

It is in this framework of belief and hard work that my *popolino* informants stress moral and spiritual values which allow them to circumvent, or negotiate, through symbolic and psychological control, both existential crises and the strictly material and instrumental aspect of their lives. Nevertheless, in line with the maxim quoted at the beginning of this section, it is usually clear to all those involved that other resources need to be mobilized. Recently, on the occasion of an accident suffered by Luisa, Lino used his contacts to obtain a speedy hospitalization and good treatment for her. At the same time, he privately 'addressed a hopeful prayer to the Volto Santo'. He has not visited the sanctuary, nor has he made a habit of stopping to pray before the local street shrine dedicated to this image of Jesus as many of his elders would probably do. But he does contribute financially to the local annual celebration, caring little, he says, 'that the organizers will probably pocket some of the money. Luisa is better, and I promised the Volto Santo an offering. I'm just keeping my promise. It's the thought that counts.' As in the case of Rafele, this coincidence of such an offering with a specific crisis makes Lino's devotion seem more transactional than usual. Such superficial understanding would, however, get in the way of grasping what these people are doing.

Steven Lukes, in arguing that norms do not usefully contrast with self-interest or outcome-oriented motivation and that the meaning of 'outcome' should be very broad, asks us to note that, 'with enough ingenuity, any kind of action, however expressive or traditionalist, can be fitted into the means–ends schema' (1991b: 148). This argument has strong connotations in contemporary anthropology (see, e.g., Davis 1992). I suggest that this context of value and belief helps us to understand the rationality of various forms of generosity and of the money, time and work devoted to the dead and to religious celebrations.

Ciro's actions provide an example of the extent to which ordinary people can behave instrumentally and still be able to explain their relative success also in terms of the benevolence of the sacred supramundane. His money-lending does not have a particularly strong mercenary aspect, but the sinfulness attached to usury (discussed in detail in Chapter 5) and to the instrumentality of his action do make his position problematic, symbolically and morally. That Ciro has been speedily successful only complicates things further; since it cannot be explained by criminal involvement, it is explained by the benevolence of the spirits. Indeed, Ciro himself says that he once saw the Monacello in the building where he lived years ago,[49] describing the experience and the emotions as positive: 'It must have been a benevolent spirit, because since then my life has improved considerably,' he says, in apparent contradiction with his belief in the role of the Volto Santo.

We know that, regardless of a person's success, the pursuit of betterment is directly associated with greed only when it is overtly rapacious. Contrary to this case of Ciro, the study of people like Michele suggests that, when there is no obvious reason to feel particularly guilty, gratitude and devotion are simply associated with well-being. Because such well-being is part of the broader idea of fulfilment, it allows the necessary construction of what Parry and Bloch call an 'ideological space within which individual acquisition is a legitimate and even laudable goal' (1989: 26). Generosity and devotion thus provide recognizable reason to hope for the benevolence of the saint and the associated sense of worthiness. Sometimes this complex relationship between the living and the dead and the symbolic orders to which they belong may be so heavily stressed as to tempt the observer into dismissing it as evidence of irrational and chaotic behaviour motivated by a precapitalist mentality. To a careful analysis it is, instead, recognizable as an important aspect of a moral framework which, far from producing casual results, allows people to derive a sense of security that plays a fundamental positive role in their careers.

The supplicant's hope of supramundane intervention is justified by his good-heartedness and the related 'good conscience' and 'deserving good', not merely by his offerings and promises to the saint; ultimately, supramundane benevolence is explained by having a relatively good life, not simply by the solution of one particular problem. Of course, although these interactions are essentially unspecified and not necessarily instrumentally motivated, they do involve risks, proportional to the psychological and spiritual investments. However, this aspect is rarely conceptualized or emphasized, because admitting its importance would challenge actors' rationale for moral behaviour and, perhaps, success.

An important phase in Paolo's career helps to illustrate the principle of negotiations about moral values and personal relationships with the supramundane and the practical significance of these negotiations. At the time of the original fieldwork, Paolo depended heavily on others, and everyone seemed to get the better of him. As we became acquainted, he often complained about this and about his misfortune, saying at the same time that he owed his small unlicensed enterprise to the good-heartedness of signora Pina. Signora Pina helped Paolo and Enrica, they say, because she was moved by their 'neediness', particularly after they were finally warned by the police about the unlicensed stall they ran in a high street nearby. They found themselves out of work and, above all, with no way of earning a living, since they lacked the entrepreneurial approach of people like Lino, or even Rafele. They reckoned that their only – inadmissible – option was to become involved in criminality. As Paolo puts it, he 'was made to understand' that he could become employed in the drug business but, he stresses, that was 'too dirty'. Having spent their meagre savings, he and Enrica ran into debt with relatives and, perhaps most important, began to lose hope and health. Their desperation was widely known in the neighbourhood, but it was only when Enrica persuaded Paolo that it was worth talking to signora Pina that they found help.

Local people say, 'C'avimm' ajuta' ll'un' cu ll'at'' (We must help each other). Stressing values of human solidarity and generosity, signora Pina persuaded some local stallholders (who were obliged to her for favours linked to council permits, fines and accountancy) to make space for the 'desperate' Paolo to set up a small stall. Only when Paolo became better off did these people ask him first to pay a fee and then to move. He was thus forced to sublet a new space for the stall, paying four times the council rate.[50] That signora Pina did not overtly ask for or expect reciprocation from those stallholders only compounded the normative aspect of the transaction. This middle-aged widow is locally known for her commitment to disinterested benefaction. She was described to me as 'a good woman who's on good terms with everybody' but also as a good Catholic who probably feels guilty for having been unfaithful to her late husband and then, having become a widow while still young, for continuing an illegitimate sexual relationship. In her case, the 'disordering' condition of widowhood (Pardo 1989: 108–9 and 114) underlines sexual behaviour that is strongly transgressive because it is purposefully unreproductive and must, hopelessly, remain so. That she maintains a humble attitude is seen as providing no mitigation for her sin.

Among the *popolino* sexuality is linked to sin in many ways. It is not, I repeat, that this leads to widespread chastity. However, in this case, because extraconjugal sex occurs in obvious defiance of the basic rules of sexual behaviour and because its 'dryness' cannot be explained in the local terms of family planning, it does much more than cause guilt. It is so symbolically disordering that it is believed to lead to a precarious position after death. Such unmitigated sexuality is regarded as a staining violation of the Christian explanation of sex and marriage, according to which sexuality is transformed – even sublimated – into sacrament.[51] This is, to local people, a legitimate value expressed, confusingly, by the very Church with whose ministers signora Pina and other bourgeois 'sinners' are on such good terms and whose political electioneering they staunchly support. Such confusion does not, however, seriously jeopardize the symbolic and moral order of local life. Instead, by justifying the negotiated character of the *popolino*'s relationship with Catholicism, it – more or less directly – expands the domain of morally legitimate or acceptable behaviour, promoting further flexibility and scope for negotiation in thought and action. Such transgressive behaviour is nevertheless socially problematic, for, quite apart from what people actually do, it is too obviously inconsistent with the established and workable rationale of normative behaviour and the corresponding ontological constructions. Therefore, it must be domesticated both in the recognizable and ordering authority of expiation before God (Bolle 1967) and in society. As in other similar cases, for local people God's punishment of this sinful woman is attested, sadly, by the suffering created by her premature widowhood and her daughter's ill health.

Signora Pina never explicitly discussed sin and its nature, particularly regarding her illegitimate relationship. Quite unlike my *popolino* informants, she accepts the suffering caused by the premature widowhood and ill health that cripples her household as ineluctable in the context of the Christian rationale of *memoria passionis*. The relation of her religious beliefs to her practical life does not, however, inform an attitude of passivity or self-containment. On the contrary, her actions in the very different cases of Lino and Luisa's premature marriage and of Paolo and Enrica's work situation provide only two of the many examples of the positive effects of her negotiation of such a relation in practical life. Signora Pina's helpful behaviour is a direct answer, *in society*, to the Christian theodicy that explains human suffering as a test of faith and as a means to the punishment of the soul and to its subsequent redemption (Bolle 1967; Meyer 1967; O'Neil 1912). It testifies to her social and ontological redemption and, perhaps, her spiritual, transcendental atonement (Adams Brown

1920). Not only do these practical meanings of redemption encourage hope in a mitigation of the consequences of her sins – particularly, the *natura vitiata* (LaCocque 1987) of her daughter's painful condition – but also they allow her to feel more worthy even of a not-too-painful afterlife in which she may enjoy the good memory of the many whose *pietas* and sympathy she has earned.

The supramundane (sacred and non-sacred) and the related operations of thought are important resources at both a moral and a spiritual (and, then, a practical) level and at an explanatory level. For instance, when persistent adversity, misfortune or 'strange' negative events cannot be explained in terms of envy, evil eye or sin, they are explained, especially among the *popolino*, by the malevolence of spirits such as the Monacello or, more problematically, by a combination of these explanations with the practical effects of moral choices. When Paolo and Enrica made the decision to return to Naples from the North, where they had lived for some years, they gave up relatively good material conditions. They had a 'decent rented flat' and were fully employed, Paolo in a large garage and Enrica in a small workshop. They felt oppressed, however, by such dependent work and by social relations which they described as 'too cold, impersonal and regimented', and they missed the quarter. Back in Naples, they made unsuccessful attempts to start their own small workshop for the production of leather goods. However, taking a view almost opposite to that of his mates, Paolo described himself as honest rather than incompetent. He associated his failure to start the workshop with influence of evil spirits. Enrica remains mildly sceptical, but for Paolo the coincidence of the violent deaths of all of his partners with repeated mishaps (breakage of equipment, inexplicable cancellation of new commissions, delays in deliveries, etc.) was not 'just' a casual series of events. He never explicitly described the evil spirits as *causes* of his failure. Instead, he established an explicitly causal link between these mishaps and the subsequent poor prospects of the business and various other problems caused by lack of access to bank loans and insufficient organization and administration. He gave up the business, however, when he realized that, should one more person die, the number of deaths would match the number of crosses they had found painted on the walls when they first entered the place.

Equally, Paolo now concedes that, *taken separately*, his children's poor health could be due to inadequate diet, poor environment, and lack of specialist care and his financial precariousness and job situation could be explained at least in part by his weak entrepreneurship, lack of contacts and defeatism.[52] At the same time, he says that minor accidents (falls, cuts, minor losses of money, etc.) could be explained by the misfortune brought down upon him by *uocchie sicche* (dry eyes; see Pardo 1992: 262) in the form of envy of his family life.[53] It is the *coincidence* of these accidents with *recurrent* and *increasingly negative* events that he explains by the presence of ill-disposed spirits in his life. In this belief, before settling in the flat where I interviewed them Paolo and Enrica had moved twice because Paolo 'felt uneasy'. The fact that he was less explicit regarding the flat where he now lived may be explained by the beliefs alluded to above, that spirits are unpredictable and that humans, having made of these spirits the almost exclusive embodiment of the uncontrollability of the supramundane, can only seek to avoid displeasing them by keeping silent about their presence.

The rationale for Paolo's belief that such spirits were not irreparably unfavourable has only recently become clear. Now that their finances have improved, Paolo and his family have moved to a larger and better apartment, but against Enrica's counsel he has left their old flat partially furnished and has struggled financially and legally (against eviction) to hold onto it. Through symbolic reversal, Paolo now attaches stróng positive meaning to the flat, saying that he feels affectionate towards his previous home because it was while living there that his life began to improve. Quite in accord with important aspects of the *popolino*'s culture of the house and their moral explanation of success, he says that he feels 'good' and 'accepted' in his new home, but he also sees in his personal history sufficient reason to try to retain the full value, *material* and *non-material*, of his previous home. Among the *popolino* the positive identity of a house has a name, Bella 'Mbriana.[54] This is a kind of abstract personal entity quite unrelated to the spirits of the dead that is believed to influence one's good fortune. By keeping the place, Paolo hopes to keep the goodness/Bella 'Mbriana that he associates with it, but he also provides a practical explanation: 'You never know, there's shortage of housing, the flat is well located, and one day one of the children might need it.'[55]

There is an aspect of Paolo's moral attitude in the old days of misfortune that requires further attention. The *popolino*, we know, normally approach both mundane and supramundane contacts when dealing with serious problems such as physical or mental health, dangerous circumstances, unusually prolonged unemployment and drug addiction (on this last issue, see esp. Chapter 3). Stress on one or the other of these resources depends on personal experience and management of value and belief. For example, as Paolo was desperately short of mundane contacts, in dealing with his daughter's prolonged illness he could count only on the free but slow, formal ways of the health service and on his strong faith in the Madonna of the Arch. Apart from visiting the sanctuary regularly, he had his car blessed there and kept her image on the windscreen. Before the child was hospitalized, he and Enrica took her to the sanctuary in lonely pilgrimage, faithfully pleading for protection and help. When she recovered, they took her 'to that beautiful madonna again, to thank and show her the healed child'. This madonna is conspicuously present in Paolo's and Enrica's family shrine and Paolo keeps her image in his wallet.

Thus, in his misfortune, Paolo referred to very different domains of the *popolino*'s idea of the supramundane – the liminal spirits, the sacred Madonna of the Arch, and the Bella 'Mbriana. Because, like Lino, Ciro and many others, he does not contrast the beliefs and powers attached to these various entities, he can say that misfortune was brought down upon him by people's envy, that the spirits haunted his family's life but did not seriously dislike him, and that he trusted that eventually the madonna would help relieve him of his desperation. And, while he now says that he is grateful to the madonna, he also clearly believes that the Bella 'Mbriana played a benevolent role in his family's improvement. His self-perception and behaviour are consistent with such belief.

By reason of concreteness and personal well-being, it is, then, customary for religious doctrine and representation of the afterlife to be negotiated so that supramundane beings of all sorts become important elements of the explanation of success and failure, fortune and misfortune. This kind of negotiation of facts belonging to tangible reality and those belonging to moral and spiritual life allows for events that coincide in space and time to be not necessarily conjoined in thought *and vice versa*. Nevertheless, such coincidence corroborates belief in the reciprocal influence between the mundane and the supramundane. The practical, spiritual and psychological value of this aspect of the *popolino*'s culture invites reflection on the fact that what may appear as an illusory or wilful manipulation of 'reality' poses the crucial question of what is meant by being rational.

This issue is vividly illustrated by Lina, a self-made trader in her fifties whose behaviour strongly draws on the link established by the *popolino* between good health, financial well-being and happiness on the one hand, and various kinds of supramundane protection on the other. Lina, who was pointed out to me as a particularly successful example of personal ability, describes herself as a 'good entrepreneur'. She does not mind showing off her wealth and contacts among the clergy, criminals, doctors, lawyers, policemen, bureaucrats, prostitutes and 'abnormal' persons such as transvestites, homosexuals and the mentally or physically handicapped.

People say that Lina has the Monacello *'mmiez' 'e cosc'* (between her legs), alluding to the use she may have made of her attractiveness to further her career but also meaning that she holds onto the spirit and enjoys his total benevolence. This is also a case of symbolic transfer of male attributes associated with strength to a successful female entrepreneur whose 'virility' is generated, or perhaps only stressed, by the powers of the Monacello. From her response to the related jokes it is clear that she too believes in this profitable relationship.

It might be argued that failure is explained in terms of supramundane influence (and of disadvantage) by the individual himself, as in the case of Paolo, whereas the same explanatory themes are reversed when success is thus explained by one's envious fellows. This may be true with regard to spirits (and to certain aspects of competition), but too many locals, including Lina and Ciro, have given an important role to the protection of the sacred supramundane (and to personal ability) in explaining their and their family's well-being for this hypothesis to have broader value.[56]

Although Lina, like signora Pina, is a devotee of the Madonna of the Arch, there are important differences between these two women. Signora Pina, like other local bourgeois people, practises her faith in a reserved and church-oriented way and avoids indulging in manifestations of popular belief that are tolerated with difficulty by the Church such as keeping a private shrine and looking after a skull/soul in purgatory. Instead Lina displays her devotion publicly. She keeps in her shop a large, perpetually illuminated shrine dedicated to the madonna (a smaller one including the images of her dead is found in her bedroom) and performs the cult of souls in purgatory. Typically, however, she also donates generously to the local church, which probably plays a role in her good (people say 'useful') connections with clerics. Moreover, Lina is generous in a way which is only apparently more straightforward than signora Pina's. When discussing both Lina and Ciro, local people link the meanings of sin directly to what they describe as their instrumental-minded, relatively unscrupulous entrepreneurship. Lina, however, makes spiritual choices that are uncontemplated by Ciro. She practises disinterested beneficence with the evident intention of emphasizing her good relations with the sacred (though in many ways unofficial) supramundane and perhaps also of justifying hope of her redemption. At the same time, her rationality and behaviour incorporate religious belief in a way that goes beyond the symbolic and moral implications of this domain of local culture. Lina regularly helps poor and abnormal persons either directly (by finding them jobs) or through charity.

This kind of behaviour obviously agrees with the Catholic idea of the link between benefaction and atonement, with the rationale according to which the *popolino* make moral use of supramundane resources and with the processes by which devotion and faith and the related operations of thought affect entrepreneurial action. But it also belongs to a wider symbolic and spiritual strategy by which Lina keeps an entrepreneurial eye on much less orthodox routes to spiritual well-being. 'Abnormal' persons, we shall see, facilitate relations with the non-sacred supramundane. The fact that these 'unorthodox' relations are said to play a positive role in Lina's life exemplifies, in this combination of dichotomous sides of the supramundane, an aspect of the negotiation of thought at a level of complexity confronted by more ordinary entrepreneurs only in a limited way and only following personal betterment.

The motivation of people like Michele, signora Pina, and even Ciro to construct and maintain a successful approach that is morally consistent (and not just a manipulative prettification of their entrepreneurial capitalism) should not mislead us into thinking that they are, for this, less rational or entrepreneurial. Whether or not these people are aware of their tendency to overstress their probity in certain circumstances, they are obviously aware of the relation between their generosity, their sense of self-worth and the good opinion of others. A heartless person risks social ostracism and God's punishment. This belief provides the basis not for the crippling implications of shame but for an anxiety of guilt and punishment that strengthens people's concern with deserving good[57] – bringing about observable results.[58] Such concern plays an important role in terms of individual and group identity, helps reproduce and multiply jobs, facilitates access to formal and informal benefits and encourages not only the construction or expansion of capital but also the reproduction of generosity in the form of actions which are described as meritorious.[59]

Degrees of ability, ruthlessness and honesty

That Paolo obtained help only when it became absolutely necessary is no indication of his local standing as a person. It is, rather, that by confining himself to toiling to earn his living he lacked the local prerequisites for fulfilment and good reputation. Moreover, given his limited resources in money and contacts, he had little to offer in the exchange system, and this inevitably limited the practical value of his good-heartedness and willingness to provide moral support. Paolo's case became more intriguing when he reluctantly mentioned some underworld contacts. On one occasion he had happened to defend a local criminal from a street attack, earning his outspoken obligation. I asked Paolo why he did not use that resource to improve his position or at least to put an end to the arrogance of some locals. Having harshly said that he wanted nothing to do with criminals, Paolo stressed that he and Enrica 'come from humble but straight families and want to live honestly'. It is widely believed in the quarter that criminals are not so omnipotent as they seek to appear and that 'things can often be obtained otherwise'; asking their help is an implicit admission of failure. In support of an earlier point, this aspect of imperfect competition suggests that, whatever the situation in the past, there is good reason to doubt that the *popolino* easily fall under the 'protection', hence domination, of criminals and become obligated to or employed by them. On a broader level, given the blurring of boundaries that I have described, Paolo and Enrica's semi-legal activities are not seen as making them dishonest. However, the successful performance of such activities requires an ability to use the right contacts and enough money to make one's way out of difficulties with the police and the tax collector. Paolo and Enrica called their choice of avoiding corruption a moral one: 'Asking favours means accepting that you can't get things you've a right to. You must be good at compromise and flattery, and you must accept corruption as a way of life.' With Enrica's manifest approval, Paolo goes on to say, 'My problem is that I'm not good at that.' The relatively rigid idea – by local standards – of honesty and proper behaviour on which they base their self-esteem is insufficient explanation for their past failures. Equally, their fear of becoming involved in corruption and not being able to cope is a poor excuse because others cope relatively well without being dishonest. Significantly, Paolo and Enrica avoided publicly expressing their attitude, for it implied a rejection of the legitimacy of using favour-bestowers which was difficult to sustain. Indeed, their recent action shows that their interpretation of honesty does not exclude them in principle from the favour system. By the time I returned to the field in 1988, they had managed to finance an expansion of their stall business by borrowing from relatives and, with great difficulty, from a local moneylender. Having repaid the debt, they were about to borrow again to expand further. They also hoped to legalize their business by establishing the right contacts to ease Paolo's way through the exam for the licence, which he had failed twice. They believed that they needed money because they could not reciprocate with favours and because, since there was so much competition for local places, they would have to buy a lease from the man from whom they were subletting.

Instead, soon after, Paolo and Enrica made the best of a crisis caused by one of the periodic council campaigns against unlicensed street trades in central Naples. Having had to close the stall, they sold out and used the money and a loan from Enrica's mother to open a small shop nearby. Enrica's brother-in-law, who worked as an assistant in a similar shop, provided the necessary experience and trading network in exchange for partnership in the business. They were forced to close several times until Paolo managed to obtain a licence, with the help, he says, 'of a policeman who used to persecute me but later took pity on me. He's a good man, after all. He knew I wasn't well-off and charged less for the favour. I give him and his friends good discounts.' Thus, Paolo and Enrica eventually indulged in what to an outsider is bribery but, taking into account the broader situation, could be better described as a way of capitalizing on their time, experience and money without too seriously violating their values. Given the direct role that moral values, like useful contacts, play in these people's cultural construction of successful or unsuccessful entrepreneurship, there is reason to doubt that Paolo's and Enrica's self-representation will really make them less successful than, say, Luigi and Anna or Lino and Luisa, who also say that they are and want to remain honest, linking their honesty to spiritual values.

It appears that, as in the complementary case of their more successful peers, Paolo and Enrica's way of life, strategies and failures (or misfortunes) stemmed from the combination of their unnegotiated identity choice (to be 'better people') and their moral rejection of the entrepreneurial tactics of mobilization of contacts and symbolic and monetary resources. Therefore, beyond the simple explanation that Paolo and Enrica were blindly superstitious and incapable of making positive choices, it seems that, unlike the 'deviant' but skilful and successful Lina (or signora Pina), they behaved as 'conscientious objectors' in local competition, apparently not realizing that their view of the relation between moral principles and practical action would crucially disadvantage them. It is difficult to say whether Paolo was criticized and described as *fess'* for his obvious failure alone, or also because he dared not explain it by making public his principles. Whatever the case, now that he has achieved some success his past situation is reinterpreted by his mates as evidence of the turns of fortune in the life of a man. At the same time, not only does Paolo continue to feel honest but his supramundane universe seems to have acquired a particularly positive identity in his symbolic and moral system and a correspondingly positive role in his action.

To summarize, we can reasonably suggest that the moral attitudes of people as different as Paolo and, say, Lino influence their perception of their universes, their places in them, and the inherent relation among symbols, choices and actions. Even people who show similar attitudes, for instance, to favour relations – such as Michele, Lino and Luigi – are significantly different in the stress they put on this aspect of their management of existence and on the related psychologically protective concepts.

The well-connected Michele has managed to become a successful entrepreneur without making brokerage a permanent job and source of income. Nor does he use beneficence as a necessary strategy for expiating his 'sins' as signora Pina and, in a sense, Lina do. We have seen how elaborately, and without ever mentioning corruption, Michele draws on his contacts to give moral power to his entrepreneurship, avoiding inconsistency with his idea of honesty and good conscience. Michele is midway in these cultural negotiations. At one end of the spectrum there are people like Lino, who feel morally consistent but do not bother to present all their transactions normatively or to prettify corruption – which, nevertheless, they seek to avoid. At the other end there are people like the Paolo of earlier times, who base their lives upon a relatively more rigid view of honesty, morality and disinterested affection. Later I shall examine in more detail local attitudes towards honesty, corruption and the favour system, and more generally the morality of entrepreneurial action, in relation to the young and local bourgeois people as well. The evidence examined so far nonetheless provides fair warning against simplistic short-cuts. It is not just a question of set standards and a few deviations from such standards. It is, instead, important to recognize that the *popolino*'s idea of an honest and respectable person and of admissible behaviour is made particularly complex by the symbolic negotiability of the strong continuous interaction I have described.

It is through the negotiated adaptation of the notions of ability, affection and good-heartedness that Lino has managed to maintain a good reputation as a man who has made himself respected without unnecessary ruthlessness or corruption. But, in contrast to signora Pina, who in expiation of her sins extends her generosity to many, he restricts his good-heartedness, affection and trust to what he describes as a deserving few. In accordance with the local culture of entrepreneurship, Lino does not need to justify his semi-legal dealings to consider himself and be regarded as an honest person. He does, however, use these themes as selected resources to explain certain facts, such as his remaining honest while having relations with criminals and, in the past, corrupt politicians or his spending considerable time with me without material gain. That despite such restrictions Lino is locally popular and described as successful raises the crucial issue that he enjoys this position because he has mastered the moral and normative aspects that make relationships between people good. Like Luigi, whose friends have the duplicate keys to his car and who willingly gives of his time and moral support, Lino is generous in the small exchanges of everyday life. Many describe him as good-natured and sympathetic with people in trouble. Above all, he acts in such a way as to be described as both generous and clever.

In spite of all his efforts, Michele is nowhere near such a position. He is described as generous, but he lacks the personal resources in which Lino is wealthy. This has several drawbacks. Perhaps because of his anxiety to be regarded as generous and selfless, Michele tends to neglect or conceal the more coldly transactional aspects of his entrepreneurship. This choice seems to weaken his image as a clever man and perhaps his credibility. These aspects of entrepreneurship are, in fact, highly valued in the quarter as it is recognized that they need only be not too predatory to be morally domesticable. Nevertheless, Michele's attitude is neither irrational nor inexplicable. Given his normative consistency in the past, now that he is successful, he is particularly concerned with avoiding transgression of the unspoken rules of proper behaviour. He is observably aware that such transgression involves the risk of losing the advantages of belonging to the order of local life (and to the intimately related system of exchanges) and, especially, the sense of security that comes from such belonging.

Agency in a multifaceted economy and moral framework

This Naples material raises central issues in the contemporary debate on the management of livelihood and, more broadly, of existence in the West. The Neapolitans of the old centre may be commonly regarded as a poor and superstitious underclass with a criminal mentality, but the empirical study of their culture and action across generations, gender divisions and social organization suggests a very different view. The observable widespread blurring of boundaries between legality and illegality does not correspond to a widespread involvement in criminality, violence and antisocial behaviour. Linking informal work with illegality not only would be simplistic and misleading but would require ignoring the complex relationship between norms, values and goal pursuits that allows the domestication, in terms of ability and honesty, of behaviour that to an outsider may well appear semi-legal or illicit. On another level, we have begun to see that the economic structure of this quarter includes far more than small-scale production, cottage industry, etc., and that more than just cash for consumption is derived from work activities and exchanges. Here work is a shifting fact of everyday life and life-cycle entrepreneurship that fits no particular 'mode of production'. To put it simply, if the marketistic model of entrepreneurship restricts our understanding to the tangible activities of individuals, the mainstream sociology of work and employment takes us no farther than grappling with part of the material benefits for which people work and of the way in which they do so. Important questions as to their expectations, motivations and culture of work, exchange and betterment of life remain largely unanswered.

The study of the political, cultural and socio-economic framework in which people operate is, I believe, a necessary condition for understanding not only this specific relationship between production, investment and consumption but also actors' management of existence in the broad sense. Case material on the entrepreneurialism that structures apparently contrasting attitudes (e.g., Lino's and Paolo's) has highlighted the significance of various activities that intervene in the relationships between work and employment, formal and informal. In the attempt to negotiate control over their lives, these people express not fatalism but, challengingly, an attitude to these categories far more flexible than some observers may be inclined to concede. The resulting situation is sufficiently complex to encourage us to look well beyond the economic and financial relevance of work activities which, whatever their 'use-value' (Firth 1979), give satisfaction and are therefore worth creating in themselves.

We have examined various cases of interdependence between the formal and the informal sector, but it has also clearly emerged that such interdependence is not a condition of 'coping with life'. Within the limits posed by risk and uncertainty in choice and action, actors' positions are causally related to their culture of work and of satisfactory entrepreneurship and personal fulfilment. Most significantly, case material shows how it is possible to escape deprivation by concentrating almost exclusively on the domain of the informal. I do not wish to suggest that the formal arena – and particularly organized labour – has no influence in cases like, say, Paolo's, for, after all, signora Pina is formally employed, and Paolo himself has finally gained a formal position. I do suggest, however, that it does not appear to play a fundamental or discriminative role. This multifaceted economic framework is deeply influenced by the action of formally employed *and* formally unemployed 'hard workers' who prove to be more or less successful but always busy entrepreneurs. Their careers, defying the opposition between employment and work, may benefit from but may also remain basically independent of their positions in relation to formal employment, production and consumption. Indeed, this culture of work and accumulation and investment of capital is articulated in a complex and diversified way which accounts for but also goes well beyond industrialism.

Above all, the line between success and failure appears to be drawn by individuals' ability to combine resources of different kinds in a highly negotiated and flexible way. These resources include entrepreneurial ability, varying amounts of money and time, the qualified use of contacts, symbolic negotiations and moral and spiritual values. We have discovered that feeling fulfilled and secure in inner and social life depends on the strength and quality of the relationship between morality, belief (religious or otherwise) and practical action. Quite beyond a materialist interpretation of rational choice and conduct, this perspective accounts for the variety of actors' motives and the changes in the way in which they combine their skills, expertise and knowledge in their performances. Examination of the younger generation will help us to address this relationship at a further level of sophistication and to begin to look more closely at the complex role of individual action, morality and thought in the structure.

3

Entrepreneurial morality and ethics among the young: changing social and cultural relations

In this urban setting, norms and values are not given, inscrutable social facts made unchallengeable by tradition or by formal definition. They are part of a process of 'active selection' (Lukes 1991b, 1991a: ch. 18) and redefinition through which the *popolino* construct their careers. Within the (relatively flexible) boundaries of right and wrong, good and evil, the combination of interest and disinterest and its representation are negotiated in response to much more than practical goal pursuits, or abstract notions of the collective good. Case material on the entrepreneurial morality and ethics of local people who at the time of the original fieldwork were in their twenties, in comparison with their immediate elders and with teenagers will help us to address the nature and scope of change in this complex relationship between social norms, personal identity and the rational pursuit of interests.

Contrasting norms and values with outcome-oriented motivations, I have said, would misleadingly simplify our task. This point is illustrated by the way in which the strong continuous interaction between different resources is affected by young people's construction of their motivations, expectations and culture of fulfilment in terms of their view of their place in society. Negotiated change in these crucial domains of life, I shall argue, brings about a morally and practically significant redefinition not only of culture and social relations but of the agency/structure relationship.

Local young people collectively show an improvement on their immediate elders' ability to carry entrepreneurialism beyond established patterns without necessarily coming into conflict with the recognized social and moral order. Often, among them, the *popolino*'s culture of honesty and morality interacts with very general left-wing sympathies and plays a more tangible role than in the previous generations. Far from being simply a response to material conditions, these values combine with improved education and identification with certain bourgeois aspirations to influence actors' attitudes to life and, in particular, the construction of their significant universes (mundane and supramundane).

The ethical role of self-worth and the supramundane in a problematic setting

Most of the young locals whom I have met take a sophisticated view of the local idea of cleverness. Among them, as among Lino's contemporaries, the emphasis is on a blend of inner strength, determination and quickness of mind that rejects ruthlessness, but they appear to link these values to moral and ethical principles more common among the local bourgeoisie. Giovanni and his girlfriend, Lucia (now his wife), and Enzo are representative cases.

In describing his view of cleverness, Giovanni gave the example of his mother's father, who died years ago but with whom he retains symbolic and identity links. This grandfather had established a local reputation for his entrepreneurship, agreeable attitude and wisdom. Giovanni imagines him in purgatory because, 'He was too shrewd to be sent straight to heaven and not wicked enough to be in hell.' This kind of statement reflects a view of the ecclesiastical representation of heaven and hell as unlikely – they are, respectively, boring and hypocritical[1] and appropriate only for really evil cases. It indicates the relevance of a culture of management of existence, also among the young, wherein religious belief is negotiated in a way that transmutes the social and psychological finitude of death into a supramundane condition conceivable (and negotiable) for self and significant others. According to the *popolino*'s interpretation of the Catholic theology of the afterlife, under normal conditions purgatory allows, for a period of time, the survival of spiritual individuality. Then, as the years pass and the work of mourning is accomplished (Pardo 1989: 111–13), the soul is believed to reach a state of deserved serenity. It is to this state that the *popolino* refer when, in wishing someone well, they say, "E sta' int' 'e schier' 'e ll'angel" (You'll be among the angels). At either theological extreme there is too little scope for mediation and negotiation for the *popolino* to feel sympathetic. On the contrary, while the near souls are, transiently, in the theologically ambiguous condition of purgatory, they are believed to have the power to intercede with the supramundane sacred hierarchy on behalf of the living, who offer them relief in the form of memory and prayers. According to my informants, souls in purgatory – known and unknown (see Chapter 2: n.46) – need such relief because they are in a situation of precariousness and uncertainty in many ways similar to that of the living, described as an 'earthly purgatory'. Significantly, people do recognize the suffering in purgatory after death as a prerequisite for the achievement of grace, but they also regard their earthly precariousness as negotiable through hard work. The orientation of their goals is observably consistent with such a view.

Giovanni believes in purgatory, but unlike his mother he no longer goes to the catacombs where the cult of the 'forgotten souls' is performed because, he says, it is 'una cosa d'altri tempi' (old-fashioned).[2] This attitude is stronger among local teenagers who also show an interest in church-related (particularly leisure) activities that is alien both to the generation of Giovanni and to that of Lino. In the same line, while his mother occasionally offers a mass to her father's soul and often visits the family niche where his bones rest, Giovanni's relationship with this important near soul is restricted to private appeals for protection and help through intermediation. He expressed a familiar theme among the *popolino* when, referring to his search for a steady job, he said that his grandfather would help him if he could. 'Maybe', he added, 'he expects me to help myself. Anyway, he knows what I need.'

Giovanni's attitude to earning a living and, more generally, managing existence is symbolically consistent with his moral representation of and identification with the notion of resolution of existential precariousness (*his* earthly purgatory) through entrepreneurial work. This is reflected in his behaviour and aspirations. While describing himself as somewhat unlucky and handicapped by his origins, Giovanni has struggled his way to a good local reputation. Steering clear of ruthlessness, he has successfully invested money and other resources in deferred (but also direct) exchanges and in materially rewarding activities in the legal and semi-legal arenas. Now steadily (and formally) employed, he has been a reluctant 'black labourer', working as a shop and workshop assistant, delivery boy, bill-poster for political parties, etc. In his late teens he became briefly involved in unlicensed door-to-door selling and in smuggling cigarettes and watches, but, given his concern with maintaining an honest appearance and a 'clean sheet', he gave up these activities when he realized that he could not long avoid 'becoming compromised with the law'. Instead, he started a 'legitimate' business in which he profitably evaded taxes. His family operates similarly. At the time I did fieldwork, the household's income included profits from his mother's unlicensed trade, rent from a local flat and his father's pension; Giovanni's brothers, who still lived with their parents, contributed with part of their earnings from formal and informal jobs and trading activities.

The contemporaries of Giovanni show an interest in legitimation that, though observably greater than their immediate elders' (i.e., the generation of Lino), is nowhere near that expressed by many teenagers. For example, in their pursuit of emancipation, the children of Lino, Luigi and Michele express little sympathy for entrepreneurial activities based on the blurring of boundaries between legality and illegality. At the same time, although Giovanni and his contemporaries have similar objectives, they tend to place their action in the framework of negotiated legitimacy already examined, dealing in this grey area skilfully though less overtly than their immediate elders. More generally, their culture of management of existence denies conflict between such dealing and the desire for formal legitimation, and they distinguish sharply activities which are unmistakably evil and criminal from activities which are relatively 'honest' and 'human'.

Giovanni's relationship with the law and the police is symptomatic. He describes don Peppino, a policeman contact for many locals, as one of the *maniglie* who helped him to avoid paying or to negotiate the fines for tax-evasion in his business. Direct bribery, often in kind, was also an option. 'Whenever I put my "presents" in a police car', Giovanni says, 'I saw cartons of food, wine, T-shirts, etc.'[3] Echoing the remarks of others (*popolino* and bourgeois), he describes these policemen as dishonest busybodies whose behaviour is somewhat understandable because they are paid miserably.

Thus, when I met him Giovanni operated in the semi-legal arena truly believing that he was honest, and, like many of his mates who also were formally unemployed, he considered it right to register as unemployed and receive the limited social security. He was aware of the Camorristi's interest in people like him: 'It'd take them time to trust me', he said, 'because my family are not criminals, but they'd appreciate that I'm not a *tossico* (pl. *tossici*, junkie) and have a better education than most.' Meaningfully, he added:

My family's living here would guarantee my reliability. However, I'm not interested in such easy moneymaking. I couldn't hurt or abuse anyone, or steal anything. You don't have to become a criminal to earn a decent living. It's a matter of pride, you know; it's the rubbish of the quarter who become Camorristi. Moreover, I'm too concerned with my family's respect, which I'd lose.

Again, he expressed his concern with retaining the benevolence of his significant dead.

At the opposite pole, the behaviour of a local ordinary family into which a Camorra-connected young man has married suggests that a degree of acquiescence may sometimes be forced upon people by circumstances without necessarily becoming the approval and support that here are so central to individuals' choices and sense of well-being. Indeed, the low moral and practical value of Camorra membership in the entrepreneurial eye of most locals, particularly the young, contributes substantially to the observable, probably irreversible, decline in such membership. Moreover, although local criminals appear to continue to recruit easily in a few well-identified and specifically criminal strongholds, even here criminal values are losing their appeal and family ties or origins cannot be assumed to determine involvement in crime. Instead, I have recorded cases of young people born and brought up in the *abbient'* ('environment', underworld)[4] who have escaped it, opting for the unappealing alternative, in their dilemma, of forgoing the financial advantages of a criminal life and breaking links with their friends and relatives, sometimes even their parents.

Tony, an ex-convict whose friendship played a key role in encouraging some local villains to agree to extended private interviews, exemplifies a complication of this issue.[5] He describes himself as someone who is trying to get out of the underworld ('ascì 'a int' all'abbient''). He says that, born into an honest household, he committed a serious crime ('of honour', he and other informants specified) because he had no choice. 'I lost the respect of my family, however,' he adds, 'and haven't seen them since, while my in-laws, who have to struggle to make a living, are less rigid, more under-standing.' Significantly, given the criminals' recognized rapaciousness, 'becoming honest' gives access to the strong sense of identity that ordinary people derive from the interaction between the practical and moral and spiritual aspects of their lives. This is why the 'easy choice' of becoming a criminal is not an option for most ordinary young people, while, from the other side of the fence, the decision to go straight (*cammenà dritt'*) is increasingly regarded as something which 'isn't easy and requires guts but can be done'. I am not predicting that this will become a widespread pattern in the Naples underworld. It is true that magistrates, heroes for many locals, have exposed important aspects of corruption and crime. But, given histor-ical examples, it is impossible to say whether the improvement that many Neapolitans are clearly beginning to enjoy will be allowed to become an established fact. It is difficult to judge whether what remains of the stranglehold of crime and corruption will be tolerated in everyday life by ordinary people or whether, instead, a process will take place similar to that by which the *popolino*, like other Southerners (Prato 1993), have silently but effectively challenged despotic and predatory relations of power.

Local attitudes to criminality appear to draw strength from the uncompromising condemnation of drug dealing and addiction. Drugs are seen as the main explanation for the widespread petty crime that makes everyday life so hazardous, conveying, at the same time, a ruthlessness that has no equivalent or inspiration in local culture. Drugs are antisocial; they defy established forms of social control and frustrate entrepreneurialism and investment of money. As Lino puts it, 'Drugs force you to spend money instead of encouraging you to devise ways of making it. *Tossici* are the scum of society. It's a shame, because most of those who now beg for money, steal, or go about mugging people used to be promising kids.' Moreover, it may be encouraging that, while drug dealing and addiction are relatively widespread among Giovanni's contemporaries, many younger locals – especially teenagers – express an intolerance of drugs and the associated culture as strong as that of their parents.

Addicts are despised quite regardless of emotional or social ties – the harshest comments often being reserved for closest relatives. But addicts who show a will to fight *'a scign'* (the monkey, as heroin addiction is called) and to re-enter ordinary life usually enjoy the support and help not only of their immediate kin but also of their extended family and neighbours. Such a will is recognized as significant evidence of the culture that rejects passive submission to adversity and suffering in terms of the Christian rationale of a test of faith and a means to redemption, preferring, instead, positive action intended to 'help God to help you'. Accordingly, local people's strategies regarding drug addiction are as complex, resourceful and multifaceted as those employed in most other fields of existence.

A good example is provided by Concetta, the widow of a respected local *rammaro* who lives on her savings, a small pension and money from her married children. The way in which she coped with her younger son's drug addiction was in fundamental accord with the rationale of interaction between different resource domains. By the time Concetta obtained Enzo's promise that he would try to fight *'a scign'*, she had experienced all the anguish and monetary ruin that usually mark a household's experience of drug addiction. Desperate, she was determined to act quickly. Enzo had tried before, experiencing the misery and, he said, the shame of failure. This time, however, he seemed truly determined, swearing to his commitment by the Madonna of the Arch and by the soul of his father. From our conversations it emerged that Enzo was motivated not only by consciousness of degradation and by guilt for the pain he was causing his family but also by a haunting sense of lost opportunities and inadequacy. As a relatively successful student, he had been the hope and pride of his poorly educated mother and siblings; having become an addict, he had dropped out of school and had been abandoned by his university-student fiancée. Above all, he was aware of the harrowing prospect of falling into a hopelessness that is normally inconceivable in the entrepreneurial culture to which he belongs.

Having obtained a promise of monetary help from her other children and from her sister, Concetta called upon resources that she regarded as extremely problematic; she asked Giuseppina, a former prostitute who now deals in smuggled cigarettes and clandestine lotteries, to mobilize her contacts in the underworld to help persuade Enzo's creditor drug dealers to accept payment in instalments. Giuseppina's contacts also helped her persuade the dealers not to supply Enzo with heroin now that he was so resolutely fighting addiction. The villains agreed to help out of respect, they said, for 'donna Concetta as a mother' whom they had known since childhood. However, the strategy of this 'poor mother', as she was described, 'facing a crisis that can strike anybody's home' included other resources as well. She mobilized her and her relatives' and friends' contacts among doctors, who provided assistance with unusual assiduity, and a paramedic neighbour made himself available free of charge. Concetta's other sons, sons-in-law and a neighbour readjusted their households' schedules to keep watch over Enzo, who throughout this critical phase was allowed to go out only with a male companion who could control him, also physically.

Enzo's recovery was rewarded with full readmission into ordinary life. Now he was no longer the object of the distrust and ostracism to which the bearers of the drug culture are subjected. He still had to cope, however, with a shattered life and an uncertain future; he found it impossible to return to school. Having to abandon hope of a professional future did not, however, mean losing heart completely – after a brief experience abroad as a waiter in a family friend's restaurant, he gave up for good the idea of emigrating, arguing, as many young Southerners are now doing, that he would rather fight for his right to live where he felt he belonged.[6] Thus he started working in his brother's shop, later became engaged to a girl from a nearby quarter, and after his marriage was made a partner in his father-in-law's stall business.

The resolution of this crisis was marked by symbolic statements of a moral and spiritual kind as powerful as those which had characterized the crucial phases of addiction and recovery. Concetta, who is not a regular churchgoer, is thankful that the madonna has given her and her son the strength to accomplish their aim. Having received this grace, they walked to the Sanctuary of the Madonna of the Arch in fulfilment of a promise made by Concetta years earlier and then faithfully reinforced through periodic solitary pilgrimages. Concetta and Enzo behaved no differently from other locals in similar circumstances. They donated money, votive candles, a syringe in silver and gold and a naïve-style painting reproducing the main stages of the crisis. Later, Enzo returned to the sanctuary with his new fiancée, who promised her wedding dress to the madonna as a sign of gratitude, devotion and hope of her future protection. As for Concetta, apart from her public acknowledgement of the madonna's listening to her faithful pledges, she continued to give money and support for the local yearly celebrations as she had since she learned of Enzo's addiction. On a more 'private' level, a silver bas-relief of the madonna testifies, by the durability and value of the metal of which it is made, to her profound and permanent devotion. Above all, perhaps, it symbolizes her capacity for belief in the madonna's continuing protection of her family.

In a similar line, Giovanni wears a gold necklace with a medal engraved with the image of the Madonna (of Montevergine); a protective sticker of the Volto Santo adorns the windscreen of his car,[7] but he rarely expresses his faith formally in church. As a child he visited Montevergine annually with his mother, but he has stopped doing this because he feels embarrassed. Recently he has visited the Sanctuary of the Volto Santo to ask protection for his father, who has had a heart attack. He has done this in a sober, solitary fashion, emphasizing the private, but not necessarily 'inner' character of the religiosity of many young. We have examined the importance Giovanni attributes both to being clever and to feeling worthy. The spiritual and identity value of supramundane themes in his life is synthesized by his sense of closeness to the 'innocent soul' of his dead baby brother and by his feeling 'closer to the sacred' when he meets Maria, a middle-aged assiduous performer of the cult of souls in purgatory and a 'mystical person' who is also a family friend. Giovanni explained that, because of her virginal and hieratic attitude, Maria's physical inability to procreate (she has an undeveloped uterus) is seen in the quarter as evidence of God's wish to preserve her purity from the pollution of giving birth. Normally, such inability would put Maria outside 'normality' in a quite different way. Because unintentional, it would be seen as evidence of incompleteness and of past sins rather than sinful behaviour, but it would still be interpreted as a sign of an uneasy relationship with the sacred supramundane and perhaps of God's punishment and rejection. Instead, she is treated almost like a saint. Belief in her quasi-holiness gives her the power to assure others of their own worthiness. Giovanni says, 'If you aren't at peace with your own conscience and with God, you can't feel such a sense of tranquillity and emotion when you're near such people as Maria.'

Other aspects of Giovanni's spiritual universe bring to mind the issues of rationality and belief discussed earlier. He says that belief in entities such as the Bella 'Mbriana are the product of ignorance and superstition, but he also says that, if he is wrong, his good spiritual life and his and his family's prosperity would confirm his mother's belief that their household enjoys the favour of the Bella 'Mbriana. Similarly, along with his father, he only half-believes in spirits but he acknowledges that his mother and siblings may be right in their belief that the family enjoys their benevolence because events unexplainable by common sense that occasionally happen in the house are generally positive. Money has been found which nobody can account for, members of the family have often won in the lottery and all enjoy good health or have recovered quickly from illness. The role of modern medicine in these recoveries is acknowledged (and made more efficient and comfortable through suitable contacts), but silver votive objects, representing the parts of the body affected by illness have also been taken in solitary pilgrimage to the Madonna of Montevergine.

The negotiations of theoretically conflicting aspects of the *popolino*'s belief system practised by people of Giovanni's generation are made more complicated and sophisticated by an element of scepticism which is much weaker among their parents and even among the contemporaries of Anna, Enrica and Lino. However, it is by taking into account that these negotiations play an important role in the interaction between moral and spiritual resources and material resources that we can understand the ethical position of people like Giovanni as an expression of a new syncretic relationship between norms, values and rational conduct. Young people's attitude towards semi-legality and criminality raises important questions in this respect. Cases like those of Giovanni and Lucia (and of Enzo and his wife) help to cast doubt on arguments of the *popolino*'s weak morality and indolent disposition to crime and drugs as easy ways to escape the responsibilities of life. Even within their generation this continuum is negotiated in practice, stretching the limits of the permissible so as to include most of the semi-legal activities which are locally considered normal aspects of entrepreneurship. There are, however, important differences which need to be stressed. Not only do they, like their elders, uphold a cultural framework by which they avoid true and wilful crime but also they seem much more motivated to emphasize formal, legal legitimation.

Entrepreneurship, education and contacts: the rationality of identity
Although Giovanni's self-description basically agrees with the local culture of cleverness, he has had to struggle to combine contrasting

aspects of his identity and vision of the future and domesticate them into a locally acceptable form. Like most other locals, he enjoys feeling part of a network of relatives and friends upon whom he can count. When he says that socializing with 'better people' outside the quarter has been crucial in his emancipation, he is culturally in tune with a maxim repeated by many *popolino* in describing their view of personhood and the betterment of their lives: 'Fattell' cu chi è meglio 'e te, e fanc' 'e spes" (Associate with your betters and go to expense). He traces his view of personal betterment to the influence of his petty bourgeois father's ideas, his experience as a student and activist in leftist organizations, and his relationship with Lucia, who represents an important part of his identity and of his future. Following an increasingly common pattern, Lucia (like Ciro and Giovanni's father) is from another quarter of the centre. More unusual for their age-set, she is a university graduate. The daughter of a public-sector clerk and skilled craftsman who runs his own small workshop and of an illiterate 'black-labourer' housewife, Lucia has performed various work activities throughout her adult life. This only partly explains why, after six years at university, she was only halfway through her four-year course when we met. Younger people such as Lucia and Lino's daughters, who are also studying while working, show a determination to succeed that reminds us more of the bourgeoisie, but until recently the Italian university system allowed such delays, producing thousands of so-called phantom-students.[8]

Giovanni had given up secondary school to start working for cash. It was not that he needed money; he was receiving more pocket money from his parents and his siblings than most of his schoolmates. Nor did he reject authority as did Lino and Anna. His motivations lay elsewhere. I have said that attitudes towards education are changing quickly among the *popolino*. Lino's pride in his children's success at school and his approval of his younger son's choice to become involved full-time in the family business instead are quite representative of the contemporary situation, in which young people's choice to be students up to university level enjoys a normative status as positive as that of their peers who leave school to enter what they call 'real life'. They do not have to engage in problematic negotiations over identity and value. Certainly they do not have to cope with a situation in which, even in Giovanni's day, those who continued to be students in their late teens were subjected to mockery and contempt as idlers – in a sense, as poor entrepreneurs. Because his siblings had left school in their early teens and his mother was illiterate, Giovanni felt out of place, in his late teens, as the only member of a household in which everyone was earning money. He felt 'humiliated to work under a *padrone*', but he knew that this was only temporary. Typically, his mother regarded such work as inappropriate and undesirable for an educated young man. Having 'understood' his choice, however, she helped him to become self-employed by mobilizing her financial resources, experience and contacts.

By the mid-1980s, Giovanni had developed profitable entrepreneurial skills. Although, like Paolo, he said that he would prefer a less manipulative kind of life, it was obvious that such a life would probably not make him happy. He did, in fact, say that he felt superior to many of his mates because of his better education and social relations. But, voicing a common theme in the quarter, he also said that he felt watched and judged by his grandfather, in comparison with whose entrepreneurship his own seemed to him mediocre. As his financial and social position improved, he began to come to terms with the dilemma brought about by his midway position in relation to changes in local values and modes of action. For example, having coped with the identity problem of living up to his share of his and his immediate elders' idea of being clever, he decided that the choice he had made years before to leave school and work for cash could now be safely reversed. Under pressure mainly from Lucia, he included the pursuit of a secondary school diploma in his strategy for self-improvement. Having obtained the necessary information from Lucia's father's contacts in the educational system, Giovanni used his brother's trade-union network to buy the benevolence of a member of the examination board for one million lire (about £400). A teacher who was obligated to a trade-unionist friend of his brother gave him specialist tuition on the most important subjects, charging only half the usual fee. Lucia and some of her university friends – who, Giovanni says, felt sympathetic with what he was trying to achieve – helped him with the remaining work without charge. At the same time, behaving basically like Concetta, Michele and other older people, Giovanni offered prayers and the promise of an *ex voto* to the Volto Santo.

In pursuing the diploma Giovanni had clear hopes of embourgeoisement. This new choice, emphasizing the combination of education with entrepreneurial ability, appeared to have strong normative status. Giovanni was criticized by some of his mates because he participated only occasionally and half-heartedly in the activities in which they spent their free time and money – gambling, endlessly chatting on street-corners, going to expensive discos, etc. But he was also the object of their admiration, for he carefully managed potentially contrasting values (including distinctly bourgeois ones) without violating local webs of solidarity. Over the years he has continued to do so, exemplifying the negotiated conjunction of tradition and innovation that can increasingly be observed in the quarter and outside. In the process, he has become increasingly competitive with his father's relatives, all professionals who treat his family contemptuously.

The mixture of cooking-up marks and studying for the examination exemplified by Giovanni's strategy[9] is explained in part by the widespread belief that while qualifications are useful and prestigious it saves time to buy them and in part by the fact that Giovanni was interested not only in *looking well educated* but also in making sure he would *obtain a diploma*. This attitude contrasts, in a sense, with that of Enzo, who appeared to be truly interested in studying and resented not being able to do so.[10] Giovanni is, however, like many other locals in pursuing qualifications through contacts but regarding information and knowledge as important assets in economic and social competition and, more generally, in the construction of a better future. The complexity of this attitude is well expressed by Lino, who says, 'I don't want to remain ignorant and be overwhelmed by anyone who speaks better than I.'

When asked, many contemporaries of Lino express a commonsensical low regard for formal education. But, we know, they have invested hope and money in their children's education, at the same time establishing contacts that may be useful to their future. Some have chosen expensive private schools in the belief that they provide better education and better options. Most significantly, this is the case of Tony, whose children have attended a private kindergarten and elementary school located, he says, in a 'good area, where they've made friends with the children living nearby who also go there'.[11] Tony typically believes that 'although there are lots of unemployed graduates hanging around, a *titolo di studio* [qualification] gives an advantage'. He looks forward to enjoying 'the pride and satisfaction of having the kids educated and living quietly in a better area, out of the fray I've experienced in my life'. But he also says that he has let school be a choice rather than an obligation for his children. Given that this (widespread) approach may produce a variety of results, it remains to be seen what effect this will have on their choices.

Politics and choice in the redefined culture of honesty and fulfilment

These identity and normative themes among the young are reflected in their relationships with the system with particular reference to favour relations. Regarding the political arena, many young people whom I have met embody a variant of the action of, say, Lino and Michele, a step beyond that of Ciro and Pasquale. Giovanni, Lucia and Enzo, for example, are even more disenchanted than Lino is with politicians. They do, however, make an exception for the Communists, from whom they have picked up the political aspects of their idea of honesty and to whose ideas they were introduced by their teachers, by the activists who did political work in central Naples in the 1970s and, less frequently, by their families (Enzo, following his grandparents' example, has 'always voted Communist'). Like many other Neapolitans (*popolino* and bourgeois), they describe the Communists as more honest than many other politicians but also as too rigid in their views. Of a Communist in his network Giovanni said, 'He doesn't do favours because he says he's against clientelism. But I need favours. Moreover, the Communists I know are too intellectual and set apart from ordinary people.' This view, shared by many, has affected his choices.

One day in the spring Giovanni invited me to drink to his future relationship with a Social Democrat councillor whom he had just met through a relative and who promised to be a useful *maniglia*. Soon, encouraged by this new powerful acquaintance, he persuaded other formally unemployed friends to join him in forming a cooperative. Knowing that the politician was interested in their votes and in the dividends he could derive from controlling tens of unemployed youths, Giovanni thought that he would probably keep his promise to help them obtain small contracts (subsidized by the town council or the regional assembly) for road work, gardening, etc., and, hopefully, steady employment.[12] Only in a very restricted sense, however, was this man like the small political bosses described by Allum (1973: 14–15), who controlled dependent people. When I returned to the field, two years later, I found that Giovanni and most of his mates had acted in accord with the flexible and diversified power relations that are observable in the contemporary situation. They had developed alternative strategies in their pursuit of secure jobs. At the same time, because the Social Democrat had helped some of them, they had voted for him at the local elections despite their sympathy for other parties. Most of them, however, like Lino as a young man, had refused to campaign for him, finding it humiliating to work for a party whose ideas they did not share.

It is quite beyond the notion of 'patronage', I suggest, that the *popolino*'s attitude to party politics illuminates important aspects of power and political organization. Central in this attitude is the clear distinction they draw between the politician as a person and the party to which he belongs. Their emphasis on the personal aspect allows them to deal with politicians as favour-bestowers without having to recognize that they are indulging in political corruption. The choices of Giovanni and his friends suggest that his generation has brought ahead a process of change in values and behaviour whose relevance to power relations began to emerge in the early 1970s in Lino's generation. Not only are their resources in the favour system not limited to politicians and trade-unionists or to professional favour-bestowers like Ciro but, because they show little interest in becoming professional brokers, for them (as for Lino today) voting for a candidate is reciprocating his favours in a specific way. The theoretical 'inconsistencies' (Firth 1985; Overing 1985) that mark the associated classification ('person', 'politician', 'political ideas', 'party') do not create practical problems for these young entrepreneurs. Addressing quite directly central issues of exchange (Parry 1986), the rationale by which these inconsistencies are reconciled with personal identity, philosophy of life and action is part of the actors' ability to negotiate their choices in a way that allows them to extract better results and feel more fulfilled than the majority of their immediate elders. For example, because nowadays Michele is not dependent on one particular party or politician, he explains his political canvassing as a form of gratitude and as a personal favour he does for deserving candidates. In contrast, Lino, we know, tends to restrict his dealings with politicians to direct and occasional exchanges.

Given Giovanni's stronger aversion to politics and corruption, his stress on the politician as a person allows him to mobilize values vaguely similar to those mobilized by Michele and to extract benefits from various politicians without having to invest any more than Lino and at the same time to avoid the *overt* cynicism of Lino's behaviour. Giovanni can thus conceptualize his cynicism in a way which does not contrast too sharply with his 'Communist ideals'. On the one hand, his action differs from the more limited interpretation of vague normative concepts exemplified by Paolo. On the other hand, his political sympathies are obviously very far from generating an attitude like that of Ciro, who, having started his practice in 'the old days, when people were not so cynical towards politics', explains his campaigning in terms of his belief in the party's ideas and describes his asking favours of his party comrades as 'natural'. Giovanni and his like-minded mates seem to be ideally reluctant but, in fact, successful entrepreneurs equipped with local knowledge of the favour system and of the options for negotiation or defiance of its exploitative bias.

Benefaction and capitalization of gains and losses in the formation of new enterprises

Towards the end of my stay, Giovanni began to improve his position through cooperation with Andrea, a middle-rank clerk in his fifties[13] to whom he had been introduced by a relative who knew him well. Giovanni synthesized local views of Andrea's entrepreneurial style by describing him as an admirable hard worker and a clever and intelligent *maniglia*. Apart from working in the social services, Andrea has for many years operated a small business based in a local office but spanning the city. This activity has helped him to expand his network among lawyers, accountants and other professionals, making him a man for whom favour-bestowing is a profession.[14] As do Ciro and Pasquale, he charges a fee for his services and occasionally shops gratis at his favour-seekers' stalls and shops. He differs from those two, however, in being respected because, though making no secret of his sympathies for moderate parties, he is successful without dirtying his hands in politics. This is important, because the independence of his favour-bestowing of political contacts and of traditional patterns of clientelism meets the value requirements that have emerged from the case-studies of Lino and Anna and, more strongly, from the study of young locals. Andrea's relationship with Giovanni is enlightening.

In spite of his initial enthusiasm about the Social Democrat, Giovanni gave evidence of his distrust of politicians by adopting an independent strategy. Having learned that Andrea had sacked his assistant, Giovanni applied for the job. Andrea was, it turned out, experiencing a serious crisis; one of his contacts had mishandled a delicate question involving a powerful (and allegedly criminal) local family, and he was under pressure from *pezzi grossi* contacts because of the sacked assistant's criminal contacts and recent involvement in illegal dealings at the expense of the factory where he was formally employed. These problems and his wife's mental illness had brought his activity to a standstill. Since Andrea does not believe in spirits and is admittedly only lukewarmly religious, in coping with this crisis he invested mainly in his mundane universe, keeping a watchful eye on issues of identity and local reputation. Soon after Giovanni's application, he decided to reorganize his activities. Closing the office, which had long since ceased to be a necessary physical point of reference for his favour-bestowing, was one aspect of this strategy. When this reorganization – and part of the reason for it – became known in the quarter, Giovanni and his mother pressured their relative into persuading Andrea to turn the office over to Giovanni. Andrea's willingness to comply with this request is explained, beyond straightforward good-heartedness, by an interplay of various issues addressed earlier in our analysis of generosity.

Andrea saw Giovanni's interest as an opportunity to convert a total loss into a partial gain. After all, he would avoid having to dispense with the office altogether at relatively low risk and with good potential. He would have to invest time in training Giovanni. He knew that now, given the crisis, these assets – his time, that is, and the office – were relatively devalued. He could nevertheless be generous, improving his moral situation and earning the obligation of a potentially successful man of locally uncommon resources (Giovanni) and of his relative. His inability to continue the business did not in fact diminish either the normative or the financial value of the favour he was granting.

Andrea did not miscalculate. Giovanni overtly expressed his gratitude for a business which required ability, was recognizably above average and, especially, had been entrusted to him by 'a man of the calibre of Andrea'. Andrea's behaviour suggested that he knew all this and carefully managed this knowledge and the relative power to use it. He said he was sure that Giovanni was the right person for the job because he had ambition, skills and, above all, education. This is why he had preferred him to a (less well qualified, he said) relative who also wanted the job. Soon it became clear that Giovanni was extracting sufficient benefits (money, as well as self-esteem, prestige and contacts) from the business to nurture an enduring sense of gratitude on which Andrea could count in redefining his own entrepreneurship. Andrea was experienced enough to know that obligation which can be explained as gratitude and is not devalued by tyranny is the best possible encouragement of the favour-receiver's reliability.

Moral values were central to this transaction. Until this crisis, Andrea had been known as a clever, business-minded mediator. Now he was also a good-hearted man who could count upon the affection as well as the esteem of people who were locally respected and popular. However, neither Giovanni's gratitude nor Andrea's expectation of gratitude was simply an emotion. Giovanni did not change his attitude when it became obvious that Andrea actually needed him or when he no longer needed Andrea. This suggests not only that Andrea's moral expectations were justified but also that they were a valuable rational (and normative) investment for the future. Thus, Andrea converted a potentially disruptive series of events into a fundamental improvement, through negotiated redefinition, of the symbolism and morality of his entrepreneurship and social position. It is significant that he redefined his identity not only in relation to his contemporaries but, perhaps above all, also in relation to the 'new values' embodied by the young.

Andrea's strategy is not uncommon. It raises the issue that the *popolino*'s entrepreneurial culture motivates them not to abandon resources (material and non-material) that they can no longer use. As in the case of their attitudes towards the house, their main goals are often satisfaction, fulfilment and the pursuit of security, but tangible returns (direct and indirect) also play a role. For example, we have seen that Paolo has struggled to keep his previous home as both an important locus of identity and a resource option for his children. Even the instrumentally minded Ciro tries to behave along these lines. Long before I met him, Ciro had retired from the administration of the local religious association which he had used as a platform for his brokership and political canvassing. By the time he retired, this activity had become mainly time-consuming for he, like Andrea, was well known and could easily dispense with this physical point of reference for his activities. Nevertheless, he had postponed his retirement to promote his image as a 'man of modern ideas' who encouraged the young to enter the association's hierarchy and as a responsible member who was concerned with ensuring the best possible future for the association. Again, though aging and ill, and despite Giovanna's encouragement, he hesitated to hand over his moneylending and favour-bestowing businesses to his son and son-in-law. As we have seen, many *popolino* have ceased to depend inevitably on the politically powerful, and it is mainly among the local petty bourgeoisie that the Church retains importance as an intermediary with the establishment and the sacred supramundane. However, although Ciro's contacts among clerics and especially his old-fashioned brokerage have lost popularity among the *popolino*, the basically instrumental nature of his entrepreneurship still forbade him to relinquish his power for fear that this might jeopardize his local standing and the interests of his contacts. He failed to negotiate a successful way out of this dilemma, finding himself in a problematic position unknown to more flexible favour-bestowers both professional (Andrea) and non-professional (Michele).

Although on a number of occasions the *popolino* may favour immediate rewards, even in the more instrumental cases this is absolutely not a determinant aspect of their culture. For instance, Andrea could have imposed some form of reciprocation upon Giovanni and his relative, but he chose not do so, knowing that this would transform the dependable positive results of a deferred, unspecified exchange into the crumbs of a single transaction. Practical inconvenience apart, it would also have been regarded as too ruthless by the local community, involving moral risks which he was too expert to take. However, to ensure good future returns[15] he did more than simply turn the business over and sit on the reasonable hope of non-tangible benefits. He not only trained Giovanni and advised him on fund-raising but also helped him find the appropriate premises – 'all this gratis', remarked Giovanni, 'whereas usually you have to spend millions for the goodwill alone'.

Giovanni used the bank loan he obtained in the name of his formally employed brother[16] and the money borrowed from his family to start the business, pay the low rent and redecorate the office, which he did cheaply with the help of a neighbour builder. Giovanni also economized by borrowing some of the furniture and equipment from friends and buying the rest cheaply through his mother's network. It is only in apparent contradiction with such economizing that he publicly inaugurated his new business by giving an expensive party (largely funded by his mother) on the premises. Relatives, friends, neighbours and local notables attended the party bringing well-wishing presents. The positive meanings of such support (as opposed to the ever-present danger of envy and evil eye among one's group) were duly legitimated and strengthened by the formal religious authority of the local priest's blessing. The office was tidy, well organized and strategically well placed, and Giovanni and Lucia adorned it with posters, fresh and plastic flowers and a discreetly placed image of the Volto Santo.

Important changes in the relationship between norms, values and action began to emerge in the study of Lino, Michele, Anna and Paolo. The process by which Giovanni's and Andrea's styles of entrepreneurship have been successfully combined has highlighted the undramatic but substantial metamorphosis of activities and meanings in the new approach to such relationship, especially among the young.

Constructing the future
The changes embodied by Giovanni, Lucia and, in a more limited way, Enzo highlight not only an improvement on the entrepreneurial style of Lino's generation but a new syncretism of *popolino* and bourgeois values, motivations and expectations. Giovanni, for instance, behaved like many *popolino* when he registered the office business in Lucia's name, thus leaving open other options for himself. He continued his door-to-door selling and occasional work as an electrician for private firms, working only part-time in the office. It was, therefore, Lucia who actually ran the business, while continuing university and doing some home tailoring with her mother for a fashion firm. Later, however, as Giovanni gained formal employment and Lucia, having graduated, became a teacher, they gave up these informal activities as a 'necessary step' in their personal betterment, in the sense of embourgeoisement. Similarly, in describing Lucia's work

activities (past and present) and her studies as evidence of their emancipated views and open-mindedness, they exemplify an attitude to personhood that is becoming common among younger locals, whose parents
emphasize in words and deeds their 'modern views' on gender relations in
the household and in society. Such arguments may not always be sophisticated, but their complexity contributes to these people's rejection of what
they call 'backward' mentality and behaviour. This attitude is part of the
process by which many *popolino* households have become enterprises
whose competitive identity is upheld by *all* members on increasingly *equal*
terms.

While working in the office, Giovanni continued to manage the cooperative, guaranteeing its cohesion. Having lost interest in the expected
immediate rewards, he hoped for the politician's gratitude and help in his
and Lucia's pursuit of non-manual formal employment. Nevertheless, he
continued not to restrict his options to his relationship with this or other
politicians. He invested his time, contacts and work in the pursuit of a
better life, drawing on a redefinition of his *popolino* background, entrepreneurial spirit and local identity as well as on distinctly non-*popolino* and
non-local resources. Almost a year after he and Lucia started their business, Giovanni became a factotum for a contact of Andrea, a professional
to whose studio he travelled daily at his own expense. Instead of regarding
himself as being exploited and dragged down, however, he emphasized
that he was expanding his network, at the same time improving his Italian
and his manners and learning how to deal with 'more refined people'.
Giovanni also believed that this man could help him to find a steady job,
and eventually his choices and investments were rewarded when he
obtained one of the state jobs for which he had applied. He and Lucia formally turned the business over to Giovanni's younger brother and to a
friend, who until then had sold goods door-to-door and done odd jobs in
the quarter, and his fiancée, who was a poorly paid tailoring assistant.
'They couldn't marry on those bases,' Giovanni and Lucia said; 'We're
happy we have been able to help.' He and Lucia retained an interest in the
business, which has recently been expanded and relocated.

Such behaviour has produced more than an improvement in the couple's
image as persons who are both clever and generous and who can therefore
feel worthy. It has also produced new job opportunities. Apart from the
important sense of localness, it is these issues of quality of existence that
motivate relatively successful people to make their success locally acceptable instead of severing 'relations with persons who are not useful economically'.[17] The case of Giovanni and Lucia, who have established

residence neolocally, suggests that such relations are normally kept and carefully cultivated even when the successful entrepreneur moves to another quarter.[18]

In conclusion, compared with their elders, young people appear to be advantaged by a new approach – at once selective and syncretic – to belief and morality and a redefinition of the concepts of ability and self-respect encapsulated in the *popolino*'s idea of *sapè fà*. Their management of the relationship between values, norms and self-interest plays an important role in the construction of ethical concerns which influence their choices and their use of local and non-local resources but do not appear to restrict them in their careers. We have studied how it is possible for people like Giovanni to construct successful careers and even pursue embourgeoisement – in terms of education, employment, manners and social relations – without rejecting the *popolino*'s culture completely and without having to overstress the normative aspect of their action as some of their elders do. The negative value they attribute to drugs and criminality interacts with the interest of people like Andrea in better-educated locals, opening up access to information and to opportunities in business and cooperation with professionals that remain largely inaccessible to less well-educated local people such as Lino (or in some cases are becoming accessible to them indirectly, through their children). At a higher level of abstraction, I shall argue, the redefined rationale by which many local young people manage to construct what they see as a better future, quite unexplainable as 'false consciousness', underlies attitudes to power that exemplify important changes in social relations and organization.

4

Acceptance vs. discernment: the morals of family, kinship and neighbourhood as resource options

Except in the moral and affective core areas of family and close friendship, relations of kinship and neighbourhood in the quarter are symbolically, normatively and practically flexible and become resource options in terms of the same entrepreneurial rationale that informs the relationship between action, morality and thought in other important domains. I shall argue that it is this rationale – not the given or, alternatively, the extremely vague nature of normative rules – that generates a graded series of positions between the poles of acceptance (acquiescence in crime, indiscriminate familism and gender oppression) and discernment (the calculation of risks and the management of value and position) and, to a certain extent, between the poles of sentiment (female, emotional, volatile) and structure (male, stable, solid).[1] It is according to this gradation of positions that family, kinship and neighbourhood relations become part of broader universes of resources.

Good, problematic and useful neighbours

Neighbourhood relations are diverse, following the main lines of the entrepreneurial action that contributes to the pursuit of fulfilment and a sense of worthiness. It is basically in terms of the strong interaction between morality and action that neighbours are included in or excluded from an individual's universe of resources. The exchanges analysed in Chapters 2 and 3 have shown that not only is a relationship between good neighbours (here often childhood friends) morally rewarding, it may also produce contacts that are instrumental in gaining formal employment, thus making neighbourhood relations part of political and economic ones. The cooperation between households discussed in the following section provides a typical example of the inverse process. Considering the basic aspects of entrepreneurship encapsulated in this culture of neighbourhood relations, I would suggest that there are important similarities, for instance, between the actions of Lino and his fellow protesters, those of Giovanni and his mates in the cooperative, and the working relations Giovanni has established with brokers and professionals through Andrea. It is equally important that various benefits can be obtained through locals such as Ciro. Of course, neighbourhood relations also strongly affect the informal sector, as is suggested, for example, by the transactions between Michele and Rafele (and 'o Russo) and by signora Pina's action on Paolo's behalf. And they are important in the formation of new enterprises, as in the case of the business started by Giovanni with the help of Andrea via a relative, the informal trading constructed by Michele and his wife Nunzia through a formally unemployed friend, the business set up by Carlo in cooperation with his kin and neighbours, and the strategy by which Anna obtained a much sought-after local shop.

It is now clear that my earlier analysis of the conceptions of gender relations must be understood from a perspective that takes into account variations in the significance of gender in different situations and contexts, including problematic ones. Case material has helped to illustrate how the redefinition of the socio-economic, conceptual and symbolic aspects of gender bridges the opposition between sentiment and structure in the order of neighbourhood relations. The economic value of the choices and entrepreneurship of Anna, Lina, Giovanna and signora Pina has indicated the role played, in terms of structure, by local women in their forties and fifties. Comparison of their situation with Gina's on the one hand and with that of Lucia and younger women on the other has highlighted the increasing strength and normative status of this process, which now draws also on women's position in relation to socialization, emancipation and the pursuit of embourgeoisement. A later section expands on the (equally crucial) issues raised by this redefinition of gender relations in the domains of household and kinship and between these domains and broader networks in the quarter and outside it.

Local villains are usually negative figures in my informants' conceptions of social and moral order; 'real criminals' are problematic, and in many cases bad neighbours, who create moral disorder and ruthlessness and whom – I was told – it is best to avoid. Stressing the point which I have made earlier on the importance of understanding actors' categorizations of the field of illegality beyond the simple dichotomy between conformity to and deviance from formal normative rules, real criminals are described as embodiments of an evil that cannot be atoned for: they will be punished, not forgiven, by God. Well beyond vague disapproval, this condemnation is directly linked to their violation of two important aspects that justify the expectation of supramundane protection, moral reputation and sense of self-worth. Criminals' blatant disregard for the morality of fulfilment that underlies the local culture of respect places them unambiguously outside the field of legitimacy in which local ordinary people construct their personal and local identities. The crucial, and discriminating, opposition is between respect springing from an individual's accomplishment of the recognized values of success and fear. This opposition is encapsulated in the general tendency to judge villains' behaviour 'on its own merits'.[2]

In a sense ambiguously, my informants' negative judgement of today's criminals also draws on comparison with villains of the past, whose collective representation granted them a more normative image. According to local memory these old-style villains were *uommen' 'e rispett'* (men of respect) who would not harass ordinary people going about their own business and who 'did justice with words and hands', intervening on behalf of the weak.[3] It is common belief that nowadays the Camorrista imposes his will through fear, not respect. To support this view, Lino described a recent experience. In a mixture of anger, sarcasm and contempt shared by his mates who were present, he reported how, in the course of a day, he had had his moped stolen, recovered through Gaetano, a local young criminal to whose band the thieves were said to be connected, and then stolen again, this time for good. Lino omitted to report this second offence to the police, who are notoriously inefficient in these matters. Nor did he return to Gaetano, who obviously lacked authority or, worse, Lino suggested, the will to put the locally legitimated idea of justice before predatory criminal self-interest.[4] Thus, Gaetano's action ended up stressing precisely the gulf that criminals appear to resent between the criminal culture – and the related sense of priorities – and that of the great majority of local people.

In the light of ordinary people's construction of self-esteem, it is not surprising that even those – such as, for example, Lino – who say that they have friends in all walks of life, including the underworld, discerningly state that 'there is no honour or prestige in being a Camorrista'. At the same time, I have recorded the mixed feelings of many *popolino* about the effective, if occasional role of the criminals in local policing. With the approval of his mates, an informant typically said, 'they've good reason to try to be helpful. They couldn't operate if we didn't mind our own business', adding that especially if one has family one does not want to have bad relations with 'chella ggent'' (derogatively, *those* people). 'Even police-men don't live easily if they don't acquiesce,' he stressed,[5] 'and if you denounce them and they're jailed before they can reach you, their pals'll take revenge on their behalf.'

As a further precaution, when discussing these problematic neighbours in public both the *popolino* and the petty bourgeois avoid the words Camorrista or criminal, instead using expressions such as 'those of the *abbient*'' and 'those in the street'. Sometimes local villains are transferred to symbolically manageable domains by being described as 'childhood friends', 'the children of relatives or friends', or 'relatives who have taken the wrong way'. Often subtlety prevails. For example, older *popolino* condemn criminals while exchanging greetings with them ('for the sake of peace') and giving them low-profile help in serious matters such as illness or infirmity. They say that they are motivated by 'humanity', apparently without realizing – as members of the younger generation clearly do – that although helping criminals may not mean condoning their actions or becoming their accomplices it does mean risking acquiescence in criminal-ity.

Ordinary people's attitude to criminals is, thus, marked by a streetwise defiance and fearful acquiescence that may seem confusing. The case of Concetta, like that of Lino, shows that the *popolino* do mobilize criminals (directly or indirectly) when criminals can provide services unmatched by their more ordinary contacts. But, because they normally enjoy an unequivocally legitimate place in the moral community, in doing so they have no reason to worry about the risk of moral pollution. The local culture of honesty and proper behaviour suggests caution in interpreting people's acquiescent pragmatism as evidence of an anti-state or anti-police attitude. Instead, there is reason to believe that a role is played by the scant hope of effective police action which would rid them of criminals without jeopardizing their informal (and semi-legal) dealings. Luigi, for example, stresses that he avoids asking favours of people whom he dislikes, and that like most others he has constructed his position independent of criminals. In spite of this, however, and in spite of the incompatibility of his sense of identity with criminal values and Anna's strong disapproval, he also says that people with connections in the *abbient*' may sometimes be helpful. On various occasions he has coped with criminals' disruptive behaviour through the brokership of his best friend, Genny, a dealer in falsely labelled clothing and leather accessories who has such connections. He in turn relies on Luigi's network to cope with bureaucratic and legal prob-lems. However arbitrary the individually erected barriers between criminal and non-criminal dealings may be, Luigi's ethical flexibility in this field cannot be objectively described as a form of acceptance. A crisis caused by arrogant criminal favour-seekers and resolved through other criminals may help to clarify this point.

Some time ago a local criminal acting on behalf of a notorious Camorrista asked Luigi 'the favour' of selling him his local flat for a 'fair price'. Luigi protested that he and his family had temporarily moved because the flat needed repairs but it was their home and they were fond of it. This response was met with threats which, typically, challenged basic values of local socio-economic relations. Having ruled out approaching his police contacts as useless, Luigi immediately mobilized Genny, who took him to Amalia, the wife of a recently murdered boss and a top dealer in the clandestine lotteries. In sympathy with 'the injustice Luigi was suffering', Amalia arranged a meeting with the bidder, demonstrating that she was well aware of the power she derived from her position. Luigi described how, as part of her competent mediation (Gulliver 1977) in the dispute, she made a successful appeal to the bidder's good-heartedness and to his 'having a family too' stressing that her friend Luigi needed the flat for his family. Similarly, when another Camorra-backed bidder tried to take over Luigi and Anna's shop, Genny, who had done business with the man in the past, persuaded him to go elsewhere, and the man now claims to be at 'don' Luigi's disposal.

An incident experienced by Lino and Luisa exemplifies from a different angle the way in which the presence of criminals in local life distorts social relations. The episode shows that serious – but, in a sense, ordinary – circumstances may interfere with an individual's attempt to stay on good terms with criminals while generally avoiding dealing with them. When the ongoing quarrel between Luisa and a Camorra-connected new neighbour over the maintenance of a common area reached a critical point, the woman summoned local villains through a relative. Luisa, believing she had right on her side and confident of the support of other neighbours who also resented the woman's arrogance and dangerous relations, refused to apologize. The confrontation escalated further and, since male criminals rarely attack women physically, the villains threatened to shoot Lino in the leg. Lino acted quickly. With Luisa's approval, he asked a childhood friend, now a notorious criminal, to intervene on his behalf. The quarrel was eventually settled, as the couple's contacts via friendship in the underworld proved sufficiently useful to counterbalance those enjoyed by their opponents via kinship. The remaining grudges were kept carefully private in the interest of all those concerned, including other residents who now enjoy the relative tranquillity of the new situation in which this problematic household is making a point of being accepted.

Lino was asked for no reciprocation. In cases like this one friendship may facilitate the management of underworld-connected crises because it allows the actors to avoid problematic reciprocation and obligation. The position of ordinary people who control this kind of resource may allow them to mobilize criminals as (problematic) friends rather than protectors, but this position is not without its limitations. Lino's claims of friendship with some local villains *as persons* do not make him less disenchanted about crime or less determined to use these people only in extreme cases. Not only is he well aware of their social and moral marginality as criminals but also he knows that he is one of the few exceptions to a situation in which the criminals bestow their 'friendship' within the very narrow limits imposed by their business interests. In line with a classical theme in the study of friendship and trust (Simmel 1964:307–29; Silver 1989), it is, then, Lino's greater knowledge of them that allows him greater control of uncertainty about their behaviour. The risks he takes in (carefully) dealing with them are correspondingly, and proportionally, assessed; because *they* respect him, he stresses 'drawing on experience', they are very unlikely to claim reciprocation or compromising favours.

Lacking the kind of knowledge enjoyed by Lino and the resources either to operate as potential favour-bestowers themselves (as does Michele) or to gain indirect access through brokers (as do Luigi and Concetta), other ordinary locals lack sufficient rational ground to deal with these neighbours, extract benefits and avoid compromising involvement. They therefore tend to limit their use of criminals mainly to coping with crises caused directly by the criminals themselves or by their presence in the neighbourhood.[6] And, in doing so, they must be satisfied that they have no choice. The theme 'You must always be careful with *those* people' not only has full practical value but, as is clear from the case of Andrea, may well become a matter of 'professional' life or death.[7]

Of course, it is also true that, although there is much less to criminals' social and cultural significance than meets the eye, in real life people simply cannot afford to be too censorious of neighbours who are at once dangerous, relatively powerful, and potentially useful. Successful entrepreneurs such as Michele share with most locals the view that the criminals' attempts to impose themselves as unsubstitutable resources are pointless but they occasionally compromise, taking risks which are justified, in their view, by the hope that resolving one such crisis will reduce the likelihood of future ones. However, this simply does not happen when, in the majority of cases, actors' investments in criminals are not endorsed by values such as friendship. On another level, networks of the kind constructed by, say, Luigi may well allow relatively safe handling of illicit liaisons in coping with certain crises and at the same time be relatively unproblematic for the favour-seeker because they do not involve direct obligation to the criminals.[8] Arrangements of this kind are uncommon, however, also because they are dangerous and relatively unrewarding for the brokers. As for the criminals, they know that true feelings of obligation to them are out of the question.

Obligation to criminals is a complicated issue. In social exchange, personal obligation is generally a strong motivation for reciprocation (direct or deferred), but it does not operate mechanistically. We have seen that in this culture obligation is governed by negotiated decisions which are in line with the complex relationship between morality, social norms and personal entrepreneurship. We may reasonably say that criminals' benefaction and the obligation linked to it do not structure action or social organization. When criminals are involved, reciprocation is subject to discernment, tending to occur under duress if at all. Defying it may be dangerous, but such defiance is not believed to amount to a transgression of the values normally attached to obligation. There is, of course, individual variation in this arena. For example, any dealing of Paolo and Enrica with the underworld would inevitably involve them in criminality. Indeed, to preserve their relative independence and avoid acquiescence in deed (though probably not in value), Paolo and Enrica had to take drastic measures. This choice meant giving up the security and tranquillity that they might have enjoyed in exchange for Paolo's doing a 'favour' for a boss. They knew that, in their case, the boss's 'reciprocation' could soon become a source of obligation that would cost them dearly. Criminals tend to establish dependence, people say, not to become dependent, and they only 'sell' their protection for loyalty, support and services. This is precisely what most locals are unwilling to give them.

The choices of young people like the children of Lino, Luigi and Michele represent a simplification of these processes in the form of an unqualified and sustained exclusion of criminals from their resource systems. They argue that of course *chella ggent'* are violent, dangerous and protected by their fellows, but their power is limited and can be made to have less and less influence on local life. These young also embody one possible solution of the dilemma found among their immediate elders, such as Giovanni, who 'realistically' – he says – negotiates his idea of honesty to explain his past semi-legal dealings but is as extreme as Michele in his contempt (he says 'repugnance') for criminals. Moreover, while valuing entrepreneurial skills, Giovanni has developed an attitude towards some of his mates' cunning and frauds that agrees with his pursuit of embourgeoisement and the more formal ethics of proper behaviour associated with it. Giovanni knows from experience that his greater control over education and information allows him to cope without the help of local villains or even of people like Genny and Giuseppina. He also knows, however, that having a better education does not straightforwardly facilitate these choices. Contrary to the experience of most younger people, in his case education originally generated a frustrating mixture of moral and practical difficulty and identification among some of his friends and neighbours. Only with time did it begin to interact constructively with more traditional (and widely shared) resources such as the esteem and respect of his family.

The *popolino*'s informed discernment regarding their criminal neighbours as resource options underlines the error of seeing them as inclined or subjugated to crime. In general agreement with the point made by Gambetta (1988) with reference to the Mafia, actors' choices give us no reason to assume that they are responding positively to criminals' ability to create a market for their protective services and are willing to purchase them. More importantly, people's discernment highlights an underlying complexity in the apparently obvious conclusion that the continuously negotiated balance between moral and practical risks and gains and losses which defines relations of friendship and neighbourhood depends on the positions of the persons involved. Because in this situation of imperfect competition actors' positions are significantly affected by their entrepreneurship and ability to manage the interaction between different resources and domains of morality and action, this balance is not determined a priori by the power of criminal patrons over powerless clients any more than it is determined a priori by political clientelism; or by individuals' formal location in society.

Household and extrahousehold relations as negotiable domains of meaning and action

Regardless of gender and age, the local *popolino* and petty bourgeois have a common attitude regarding household and extrahousehold relations as resource domains. They are strongly concerned with the ideal of being safe, happy and quiet in their homes. It has been claimed that among the *popolino* family ties are informed by an instrumental interpretation of primary relations,[9] but the material available to us suggests that it is in the much broader and more complex terms of strong continuous interaction as defined earlier that these relations are resource systems. Among my informants, having good and reliable neighbourhood, kinship and, above all, family ties is one of the basic requirements for security, because close relatives and friends play a crucial role in their way of life and of death and in their conception of the afterlife. In this case, too, people's actual practices are widely identifiable as part of negotiated positions between the poles of acceptance and discernment in relation to identity and goal pursuit.

The concept and scope of kinship and the associated morals vary with actors' experience of the value of *parentela* (kinship relations) and the possible alternatives. My informants' genealogical maps invariably include all the technically ascribed positions in this system of bilateral kinship. This does not necessarily imply set meanings. Their 'kin/non-kin' universes show that, when it comes to giving moral and affective weight to relations, the balance between *parenti* (sing. *parente*, kin) and *amici* (sing. *amico*, friends) is not strictly ruled by incorporation. Depending on circumstances, friends may in fact be given priority over kin. On the other hand, the nuclear family – the main household model – invariably has the status of a core element of a broader and variously significant framework of relations. Under certain circumstances, affines, friends and neighbours may be symbolically included in and ritually bonded to this core through godparenthood (which may or may not facilitate alliances) and shifting alliances and through participation in family celebrations. Morally, parents and, to a certain extent, siblings never move out.[10]

The nuclear family is the locus of cohesion, satisfaction, trust and projection into the future. It is an important demonstration of its members' success that meets some fundamental requirements of the Christian theology of marriage. In the context of the redefinition of the symbolism of proper behaviour in relation to sex, this view of marriage remains an important aspect of social relations, for it provides the rationale – and the crucial objective grounds – for the individual's existential 'normalization' (Sattler 1967:266) and placement in a moral context that allows hope of God's grace. Unsurprisingly, then, although divorce and non-marital cohabitation are tolerated (especially among the generation of Luigi and Anna and younger) they are in fact rare. More generally, contrast and rivalry are certainly not unknown in local households but they do not normally carry sufficient weight to jeopardize this culture of the family as a crucial moral entity in terms of personal identity, career and relations with the wider society.

Paolo's nuclear family, for instance, provides him with a psychologically safe haven where he can escape and perhaps domesticate the sense of his troubles and shortcomings. He would have otherwise been unable first to reinterpret his failures in a way that is acceptable to his identity and then to construct a successful business. While in Paolo's case these operations of thought based on family identity have only a limited effect on his personal entrepreneurship, they are directly important to that of persons as different as Giovanni and Michele.

Complex aspects of discernment (and the consequent pluralism) are highlighted by the comparative analysis of my informants' universes. Their concepts of kinship, kinship relations and kinship solidarity are sufficiently flexible[11] as to include kin in the category of closeness according to criteria which often transcend the presumable strength of individuals' formal (even ascribed) positions in the kinship system – stressing the point that relations among kin are not necessarily kin relations. Indeed, to say that most local people have a large proportion of their kin residing locally and that they value family relationships is not to say that the moral weight of kinship relations should be taken for granted. The kinship segment is not always the largest and most significant part of their mundane universe, and association with kin may well not have priority.

Processual analysis of the relationship between Ciro and Michele (and, in a sense, that between Michele and Pasquale) sheds light on the way in which the fabric and strength of kinship links and of their relation with the non-kin network can be influenced by personal position and career rather than the other way round. In discussing the councillor who helped him, Michele said, 'I've voted and canvassed for him. Now he's no longer in politics, but I always call him on his name-day . . . Once he even tried to reconcile Pasquale and me.' Michele was referring here to an incident provoked by his father-in-law, Ciro, who without consulting Pasquale or even Michele had asked the councillor to help him out of unemployment. This had provoked a quarrel with Pasquale, who regarded Michele as responsible for Ciro's behaviour. Ciro's attempt had failed because, Michele says, Pasquale had asked the politician not to help him. The councillor's behaviour was largely predictable. That of his two favour-seekers and supporters highlights powerful normative aspects of *parentela*. Aware of the importance of kinship relations, the councillor did what most ordinary people would have done, summoning Michele and Pasquale to his studio and insisting on a reconciliation because 'such things shouldn't happen between prospective in-laws'. The politician, of course, had much to lose, but he was also in a position to contain the damage or even turn the situation to his advantage. He capitalized, in particular, on the fact that a broker's local position also depends on the relative reliability of contacts higher up. In the first place, he reported Ciro's behaviour to Pasquale, thus reducing the risk of losing Pasquale's electoral support for an unknown factor.[12] Michele was popular among his friends, relatives and potential favour-seekers, but his personal resources obviously fell short of the experience and ability he shows nowadays in such matters. Presumably, he had also not yet developed the canvassing power and knowledge of *sottogoverno* which I observed during the fieldwork. Since favour relations still had elements of old-fashioned patronage, however, the politician had to preserve his image of loyalty and reliability with a safe supporter. He manoeuvred to keep his support intact by referring to moral and normative themes directly and commonly connected to the local culture of social relations in the kinship system and in larger networks. Otherwise his image would have suffered from a public quarrel (even if over a partially private affair) between two persons locally regarded as pathways to him.

As for Pasquale, up to a certain point he behaved as a professional broker is expected to. 'He had reason to feel offended,' Michele said; 'Ciro is my father-in-law, but he shouldn't have done such a thing.' This is important, for, although the kind of favour-bestowing performed by Pasquale was much less common than in the past, it would lose most of its residual symbolic and practical strength if its basic criteria could be so easily evaded. In respect to the network domain involving the politician, relations of (acquired) kinship – existing and potential – provided insufficient cover for Ciro's transgression[13] and for Michele's responsibility, and they did not give Pasquale sufficient motivation to be sympathetic. Certainly, they were not so valuable as to prevent or mitigate his indignation. However, part of these relations gave sufficient strength to the politician's argument and normative performance and, perhaps because of their still undefined character, in fact complicated the whole transaction enormously, with unpredicted (because in large part unpredictable) results.

It was in regard to the moral and normative value of these relations of kinship as such and their interplay with his broader universe that Pasquale's entrepreneurship proved inadequate. He got one side of the situation right, for it was precisely because Michele was a direct connection of his that, in this culture, Ciro's behaviour was overtly offensive and potentially crippled his power. He entirely failed, however, to limit his indignation appropriately. Michele said, 'I told Pasquale that, as I didn't know what Ciro was up to, I wasn't responsible for his behaviour. He should've accepted my apologies.' Referring to their kinship link as further reason for

Pasquale to be understanding, he added, 'He didn't because he's '*nu spuorc*' [a dishonest].' Insufficient flexibility made Pasquale miscalculate the full significance of his advantageous position. In particular, he failed to capitalize on the moral assets produced by the fine balance among Michele's obligation, his continuing interest in the politician, and his position as an in-law. Pasquale miscalculated the risks accordingly, thus irreparably jeopardizing the power that he derived from the deferred, unspecified nature of their exchanges. He lost both as an in-law and as a broker.

Michele, we know, had paid virtually nothing for the favour and therefore remained obligated. Had Pasquale been a more dynamic broker he would have forgiven Michele, and he would probably have done so in a ritual and public *chiariment'* (clarification) symbolically ratified by drinks or a meal. This would have been not only a morally rewarding event, constructively forestalling a crisis, but also a boost to Pasquale's prestige and power among Michele's family and network and in the quarter in general. Instead, Pasquale espoused a moral and ethical interpretation of the relations involved which was becoming increasingly obsolete not only from the independent-minded perspective of people like Lino but even from that of 'traditional' brokers like Ciro.

Thus Pasquale unwittingly gave Michele good reasons to withdraw his respect and, implicitly, feel free from obligation and, in a sense, from kinship loyalty without transgressing the basic moral rules. Pasquale is now 'retired', but Michele feels morally justified in continuing to resent his behaviour. And yet, whether Michele realizes it or not, his transformation from a downtrodden supplicant to a relatively successful and independent favour-bestower has been affected by the practical and symbolic implications of that crisis, brought about by a mismanagement of the normative rules (and the changes in those rules) according to which kinship links are included in or excluded from broader universes. This was, indeed, the time when he began to make choices and pool varied resources in his performance of increasingly sophisticated forms of exchange. This was also the time when he began increasing his investments in his family, neighbourhood and other powerful contacts.

Michele's tactics underline the complexity of the issue of flexible kinship relations, particularly among the *popolino*. Kinship links may motivate choices; they have moral and practical relevance in actors' resource systems, and in problem-solving people think of their kin and their kin's contacts first. But kinship is not always the first area of choice, and well-connected people do not always become resource options for their relatives.[14] This culture of social relations (and exchange) was instrumental in Michele's option not to feel betrayed by Ciro's behaviour. He could, instead, 'understand' Ciro through an opportune adaptation of the morality of 'having a family to support' (*tengo famiglia*) according to which so much – bad and good – is done or not done in Italy. 'Ciro was trying to resolve a very critical situation for his family,' says Michele. 'He didn't behave well, but he had been unemployed for a long time.' By the same logic, Michele even helped Ciro financially. Having chosen not to sanction Ciro's serious violation of the unspoken rules of the favour system, he acted in accordance with local criteria of judgement and proper behaviour. He represented Ciro's self-interest as virtuous because imposed by family responsibility and his forgiveness of him as respectful behaviour. He, who would later perform favour-bestowing on very different bases, managed to do so without jeopardizing his image as a rule-abiding broker by mobilizing, in a negotiated form, the same culture of good relations among *parenti* to which the politician had resorted to reconcile him and Pasquale. This strategy produced good moral returns, improving his image among his kin, to whom he is a respectful, understanding and forgiving man. It also produced deferred material advantages such as, for instance, Nunzia's informal job.

Therefore, so far as kinship relations are concerned, variations in the definition of closeness seem to depend on the actor's personal history and management of the complex relationship between values (such as respect, affection and generosity) and norms (particularly regarding the implications of social exchange) and the pursuit of interests. Kinship relations, like other social relations in this urban setting, do not depend on criteria of 'familism', 'localism' and 'clientelism'. The resource spheres of kinship and friendship are defined entrepreneurially (though, of course, not because of this 'amorally'); their boundaries shift and their links are strengthened or severed accordingly. It is once again a matter of negotiated choices. And, once again, the local *popolino* show discernment in viewing kinship ties as not necessarily translating into better options. For example, it is particularly significant that, as pointed out earlier, Ciro has long hesitated to hand over his obsolete and declining brokership to his son and Andrea, in substantially similar circumstances, has chosen to turn part of his business over to a non-relative (Giovanni). It is, of course, equally significant that Giovanni and Lucia turned their office over to both Giovanni's brother and one of Giovanni's needy friends.

However, moral and practical strategies can be activated by people as different as Ciro and Giovanni in order to maintain the balance between acceptance and discernment in this field of *parentela*. For example, Ciro maintains his business-mindedness in dealing with his son, as with other kin, particularly regarding moneylending. Moreover, when he does not charge them for the favours he grants them, he willingly accepts expensive presents. He thus allows his kin, including the virtuous Michele, to feel morally justified in maintaining some distance from him. Aware of this, he is occasionally generous and organizes expensive consensus-constructing family meals.[15] Giovanni revises his tactics of personal betterment according to circumstances, while helping to improve his siblings' and friends' positions with subsequent benefits for his own position in his family and in the neighbourhood. Equally, family identity may justify moral choices (such as those of Giovanni, Paolo and Michele regarding the underworld) or help to modify them, as Luigi does under Anna's pressure. This, we have seen, may be complicated by family origins, as, for example, in the case of people who enter or seek to escape the underworld.

Kinship and gender in the dynamics of exchange

As local people prefer to stay in the quarter, joint households are sometimes a necessary arrangement;[16] particularly in the form of coresidence of nuclear families linked by kinship ties. Lino and Luisa, who lived with Lino's mother for several years after their early marriage, share their experience with many of their generation. Nowadays, despite the fact that most couples are older at marriage,[17] objective restrictions (especially the shortage of housing) may well be met with an initial period of coresidence, usually with the husband's or the wife's parents. On the other hand, sons and daughters often support their parents morally, financially and socially until death.[18] Apart from emotional motivations, relations of reciprocity are dictated by the inadequacy of the welfare system, particularly regarding housing and services for the very young, the old and the sick.

What people say does not, of course, always agree with what they do. This is particularly evident from the perspective of gender relations. For instance, quite unsurprisingly for a bilateral kinship system, children share inheritance equally, mainly objects and money but also, in the current increasingly better economic conditions, immovable property. However, despite an obvious interest in presenting a harmonious picture and despite civil law (Art. 462), they do not always do so equanimously. In the present situation, given the absence of any culturally explicit inequality in principle between men and women, the role of women in economic competition and the not strictly kinship- and neighbourhood-bound character of their personhood combine to produce disputes which involve sisters and sisters-in-law as well as brothers and brothers-in-law.

By the same criterion, it is a matter of pride for the bride and groom to contribute equally (with the support of their parents and sometimes of their older siblings) to paying for the wedding – which can be very expensive in Italy – and the setting up of the new household. Although they do so according to their financial resources, they tend to follow a customary but negotiable division of spheres of competence. According to the broad guidelines of the 'chi ten' pav'' (the one who can, pays) principle, the bride and her parents usually buy the linen and take care of the furnishing of the kitchen and the bedroom, thus largely exceeding the scope of the traditional *corredo* (trousseau).[19] The groom (sometimes with his parents' help) does the rest. When he buys the house (not strictly a 'male' task), its furnishing becomes almost entirely the bride's concern. A large proportion of money-borrowing is explained by the compulsion to perform these marital duties. Of course, this places the above-mentioned economic principle of marriage at the core of the complex framework of negotiated norms, values and interests that characterizes this setting. This is particularly intriguing because, although Italian law identifies only the goods acquired after marriage as automatically common property,[20] my informants (and their families) customarily regard property acquired before marriage as the object of the couple's common responsibility rather than of their separate rights.[21]

Sometimes financial support is given to siblings after marriage as well, as in the case of Lino and Luigi, who give a monthly allowance to their widowed sister.[22] More often, relationships within the household and with other kin (siblings, in-laws, etc.) and their households are marked by favour exchanges (e.g., the cases of Michele and Pasquale and of Michele and Gina's husband) and financial cooperation (e.g., the cases of Carlo, Domenico, Rafele, and Giovanna and Nunzia and of Giovanni and his brother). Moral support is usually ensured together with support in terms of time, information and other non-material prestations.

In line with a point made by Davis (1977:176), these strong links between children and parents (before and after the household breaks up), between siblings, and with in-laws appear to be facilitated by geographical proximity, affecting, in turn, the moral and socio-economic composition of the neighbourhood. Newly-weds, I have said, tend to stay in the quarter, and their parents help them do so. Alternatively, they stay as close as possible and keep constantly in touch. When one of the partners is from another quarter, the couple's housing resources and work activities influence residence, which may indifferently be uxorilocal (e.g., Tony, Ciro and Giovanni's father), virilocal (e.g., Enzo) or neolocal (e.g., Giovanni and

Lucia). All my informants, *popolino* and bourgeois, almost completely regardless of age and residence, see their parents (and parents-in-law) and siblings regularly (weekly and, most often, daily), spend with them equal shares of traditional holidays (Christmas, Easter), participate in socializing celebrations such as name-days, birthdays, baptisms, christenings, marriages and funerals, and exchange invitations for Sunday lunch with them and with other close kin.

I have argued that the contemporary *popolino* household – an increasingly egalitarian institution with regard to power – has the appearance of an enterprise whose relation with the wider society (including in many cases kin) is typically competitive. This competitive identity is enhanced by women's role in the extradomestic spheres, economic and other.[23] Of course there are divisions of labour and areas of conflict. But, given the redefinition of the symbolism and conceptions of gender relations, they do not appear to entail the risk of disruptive clashes, for they no longer necessarily correspond to an opposition *tout court* between sentiment and structure. This opposition is, indeed, blurred in this situation of entrepreneurship, and some double standards may well remain, but they are not paralleled by strong double standards about sexual behaviour. Even if we consider that nowadays there is more awareness of constitutional rights, this does not appear to be simply a case of a direct equation of women's increased significance in the household and the wider society with their relatively greater economic contribution and sexual freedom. Observation and actors' accounts suggest that this is instead a case of a complex relation among moral, symbolic, emotional and practical factors which affects women – as well as men – as autonomous human beings. The fact that keeping the construction of personhood independent of the biological dimension is clearly not a straightforward task, I would stress, should not blind us to the fact that in this situation the biological is made to play its role without generating segregation but instead contributing positively to the moral and practical order of life.[24]

The relative balance in the relationships between husband and wife and between brothers and sisters is certainly more obvious among the petty bourgeoisie and among the *popolino* of the generation of Giovanni and Lucia and younger. However, the situation among people of Luigi and Anna's age highlights an important part of the background situation and important changes in the relationships between parents and their children. It is, in fact, true that in their case, also, obliging a mother or a wife continues to be likely to facilitate relations with her son or husband. Not only, however, are the relationships between the young siblings and the engaged couples whom I have met more egalitarian (they say more modern) and in tune with the observable redefinition of the categories of sentiment and structure, but also they are in tune with the progressive weakening of the link between women's personhood and the categories of marriage and kinship. At the same time, the relationships of women like Luisa and Anna with their sons – and, in the cases of Luisa and Nunzia, with their daughters' fiancés – appear to be based on a kind of discernment (on both sides) that, without jeopardizing traditional links of solidarity and reciprocal support (like those between Giovanni and Enzo and their mothers), generates in many local households a relatively more pluralistic and openly debated attitude than in the past.

The female side of local life provides enlightening examples of the role of relevant kin in actors' discriminating and (within limits) shifting sense of kinship and in their construction of career and self-image. Throughout her life, a woman usually develops a certain amount of control over a wide network. Mothers, sisters, wives, fiancées, even daughters and sisters-in-law are important protagonists of ordinary life. Although this neighbourhood does not have the claustrophobic characteristics of its rural counterparts (Davis 1977: 78–9), in it women are experienced repositories of information and managers of certain areas of gossip[25] and of both discursive and confrontational language. They are mediators *par excellence* in the household, the kin group and the neighbourhood. They start or mediate quarrels and crises, are often key figures in business competition and in cooperation among relatives and sometimes friends or neighbours (e.g, the cases of Carlo and Domenico and of Giovanni), and may have power as links via marriage to locally powerful persons (Ciro, Giovanna, and Michele, in the case of Nunzia). In short, they may upset crucial social relations just as they may be instrumental in strengthening them.

Of course, although these relations are governed by rational processes made up of normative and moral pressure and interest, they involve an important emotional element. Cases like that of Concetta (with particular reference to the villains' normative explanation of their response to her pledges) indicate how the emotional power of women may become an asset (though, it is worth stressing, not an omnipotent one). Such cases also provide an example, from a more orthodox perspective, of the practical value of good-heartedness and generosity.

Middle-aged women and, to a large extent, men play an important role. Because of their age, they usually control wider resources; they also bear less problematic meanings because, though still sexually distinct, they stress their parenthood and their erotic neutrality through symbolic action, body language and speech. The combination of these aspects gives them an aura of maturity (and reliability) and special symbolic power in the processes of intermediation, network management and favours because it pre-empts (in large part) conflict should the favour-bestowers or the brokers they approach be of the opposite sex. The relationship between Ciro's wife, Giovanna and Imma, a middle-aged neighbour, provides a good example of women's position in the system of favours and, more generally, in the management of resources in the quarter and outside it. Imma's husband, Eduardo, is a skilled worker and a high-ranking member of a local religious association. Imma is formally unemployed, but she is well connected in the informal sector. In her relationship with Giovanna, she therefore plays the predominant role in the exchanges of commissions for 'black labour' (at home). And, spending more time in the quarter, she plays a similar role regarding gossip and small favours in the daily routine. Imma also works as a broker, earning small unspecified commissions on Giovanna and Ciro's moneylending and favour-bestowing. Like most local women in her position, when Imma is free from housework and 'black labour', she joins other women for a chat in her mother's *basso* in the same alley. This puts her in contact with a large number of people, some of whom ask her to introduce them to Ciro or Giovanna for a loan or a favour – sometimes with good results.

The situation is complicated not only by the monetarily significant exchanges between Giovanna and Imma but also by the disinterested actions and exchanges of non-material favours between their two house-holds. Ciro, for example, has helped Imma's brother to obtain a pension and a job without charging money for the favour. On a different level, Giovanna mentioned that she and Ciro had stood by Eduardo and Imma by being – 'in a very different epoch', Giovanna stressed – witnesses at their wedding when others had declined because Imma was pregnant. Through Eduardo, Ciro enjoys a position of pre-eminence in the celebrations organized yearly by the association in the quarter and other special events, such as the filmed, lavishly catered and well-attended public inauguration of a street shrine restored at the association's expense. Recently, Eduardo and Imma's newly married daughter has obtained a council flat through Ciro's connections. This has further strengthened the relations between the two families and between their children.[26]

These activities are in no way peculiar to Ciro's and Giovanna's life-style, nor are they exclusively linked to the power of bestowing favours which people like Ciro derive from their use of the political machine. We know that Ciro's occasional good-heartedness has the moral status of usual behaviour in the case of ordinary well-connected people like Michele. An important difference lies in the fact that, because the reciprocation Michele obtains and expects is mainly non-material, indirect and deferred, this brings no harm to – indeed, strengthens – his and his household's normative position among kin and neighbours, at the same time encouraging his expectations of help and general goodwill from these significant domains of local life in a way that is unknown to people like Ciro. Thus, Michele's accepting small presents as tangible signs of his fellows' esteem and gratitude and as evidence of his popularity agrees with his self-representation.[27] He believes that acting otherwise would raise suspicion about his 'true interest'. These presents settle the matter and make everybody happy. Incidentally, no one describes them as reciprocation for favours, and they are especially welcome at Christmas, or on Michele's or Nunzia's name-day and other important events. I witnessed the amount of presents, flowers and cards that Nunzia received from neighbours and relatives when she gave birth. Above all, back from the hospital, she did not need to buy the necessary help or depend wholly on her relatives. More people than normally volunteer on such occasions offered Nunzia assistance in shopping, taking her child to school, and other routine duties. Nunzia could easily have coped with the help of some of her neighbours and her closest relatives who lived nearby.[28] So many offers did, however, clearly attest to her position in her significant universe. In the occurrence of life-crises individuals assess the strength and value of their kinship and neighbourhood relations. 'It's especially when you're in need,' they say, 'that you size people up.'[29]

Of course, because Michele can grant favours – sometimes important ones – people's kindness is not entirely devoid of calculation, but nowadays the power of a favour-bestower is limited by the existence of alternatives. Clearly, presents and manifestations of solidarity, respect and affection do not stem, in cases like Michele and Nunzia's, from mere calculation or mechanistic respect for rules. They are, rather, investments of energy, time, money and identity (as good-hearted and affectionate people) that are made for the sake of one's self-image and reputation, as well as of foreseeable or even only potential benefits. Relatively limited risks do exist, however, regarding the results local people expect of the investments they make in Michele and his nuclear family. Of course, such risks imply a softening of the specified character of transactions, and compulsion to perform a duty is proportionally weak. Nunzia's kin and neighbours were happy to behave sympathetically because, they said, the couple deserved such treatment. The transactional aspect was as inexplicit as the themes of obligation and duty. On this occasion people's behaviour was, in a sense, overstressed, but it was basically not dissimilar from that characterizing the life-crises of others who have more limited access to *maniglie* or to the power of granting favours. Instead, things are generally more calculated with the households of persons who, like Andrea and Ciro, have made a business of favour-bestowing. They do receive cards and flowers witnessing respect and obligation, but they must usually pay for assistance just as they make people pay for the favours they grant to them. Even their relatives, I have observed, take a more cynical attitude towards them.

The moral reality of social relations
It is difficult to judge whether the European rural settings studied in the past were actually as 'closed' as they have often been described.[30] However, this contemporary urban situation encourages us to take a flexible view of the morality and choices that define the opposition of discernment and acceptance in social relations of kinship, friendship and neighbourhood, and of favours. The analysis of culture, and entrepreneurship and gender, in these important domains of social organization demands further consideration beyond the scope of this book. All that can be said here is that there is sufficient evidence to suggest that the situation generated by the complex interaction between different resources is not particularly predatory; it is not reminiscent of a golden age of community life, nor is it marked by gender oppression as an aspect of the *popolino*'s subalternity as an underclass.

What is most striking is that among local people belief (religious and non-religious) and the normative and moral emphasis placed on action may sharply contrast with the 'closed' appearance that marks certain instances of ordinary life. Of course, it is not unlikely that such appearance may give qualified symbolic legitimacy to actors' motivations and choices. The flexibility of material and non-material actions and the negotiated value attributed to shared rules prevent the coherence of ordinary life from being seriously jeopardized (as is real criminality) by the tension between self-interest and the necessity of redefining it in a morally acceptable way. This activity may not always be conscious, but it is rationally determined. And, relatively regardless of actors' ascribed positions (of gender, kinship, residence, etc.), its results depend on personal experience and ability. It is such results that, in turn, determine the nature of imperfect competition. Change is probably structured in this arena.

In Pirandellian fashion, the ethnography of fundamental social relations among these urban dwellers points to the importance of this complex relationship between appearance and being. Such a relationship draws on deep play between morality and action. At times this may make the observer, the outsider, feel that the definition of reality is less than straightforwardly given and predictable. However, under close scrutiny this never amounts to a real challenge, for, as these people never merely perform,[31] their representation of reality in each particular circumstance is always *true* and, being not merely dictated by custom, its governing rules are entrepreneurially and morally rational. This complex relationship between *performance* and *action*, crucial in actors' and their significant others' perception of the order of their existence, provides no justification for conceptual superimpositions. Of course, I am not claiming that these are unproblematic issues. What I am arguing is that their superficial ambiguity is perhaps enhanced by the fact that too much in Naples is spoken, apparent, obvious – obvious to the point of obscuring reality, which is rarely spelled out or simple and only comes to light with time, ethnographic care and a degree of luck.

5

Transgression, control and exchange: the rationality of the ambiguous and the liminal in life and death

Our study of action, morality and thought has addressed the interaction between different resources without superimposing on the ethnography any separation of the living domain of actors' universes (this world) from the dead one (the other world) or of the material from the non-material. The notion of good-heartedness has proved to be central to the representations of human activities that refer to the supramundane as a locus of identity. Because of its direct relationship to the concepts of deserving good and being at peace with one's own conscience and with God, good-heartedness is intimately involved in the pursuit of fulfilment. At a higher level of complexity, it is through consistency with their standards of good reputation, self-esteem, family security and (relative) financial well-being that actors' management of existence encompasses both the linking of the domains of life and death and the construction of a psychologically, morally and practically manageable human condition.

We now focus on the relation of transgression, control and exchange to order by looking at beings – living (prostitutes, moneylenders, homosexuals and *assistiti*) and dead (especially spirits) – who are regarded as out-of-the-ordinary, ambiguous, often liminal. They complicate the task of management but also make it more comprehensively conceivable. The key ethnographic imperative is that certain individuals' ambiguity in relation to the categories of work, sex, age, normality and abnormality, sacred and non-sacred[1] – ultimately, of good and evil, right and wrong – gives them a taxonomic status with profound implications for local life.[2] A common feature of these individuals is that they are regarded as having special personal qualities and access to special resources among the living and the dead. They respond to unorthodox requirements of the relationship between actors' outcome-oriented action, the moral demands of their identity and social norms.

I have outlined how the commonsensically unexplainable and, within limits, unusual good and wrongdoing are symbolically transformed to facilitate their absorption into normality. Through this process, the liminal acquires powerful though often unstated – even 'secret' – practical importance. Our investigation begins with the social, moral and religious rationale for various conditions of liminality and their relation to transgression and marginality, bearing in mind that the imprecise and complex character of these issues of thought (and of action) is often compounded by the verbal (and perhaps psychological) inhibitions that shape informants' accounts.

Classification in terms of the requirements for grace

My informants' universes include persons who 's'hann' fatt' 'e sord' ma nun haven' ben" (have made money but have no good), are not at peace. They also include persons who are 'scurdat' do Patetern" (forgotten by God),[3] the evidence of which is often some serious physical or psychic imperfection. These persons bear connotations of liminality, but they may also be important resource options. Their condition is complicated by their association with a generally reparable, therefore redeemable, evil that derives from their supposed sin of envy of the normality of others. My flatmates belonged to this category. For the *popolino*, the widow's blindness, the couple's fragile health and the incompleteness and precariousness conferred on them by their inability to procreate and by their lacking a 'proper home' despite their age indicated both their 'strangeness' and God's punishment, perhaps for some heavy past sin.

In the case of the old lady, the perennial bereavement linked to the symbolism of widowhood, her childlessness and her physical disability made up such a strong case of suffering that she was said to be 'for' da grazia 'e Dio' (outside God's grace).[4] She embodied a position of diversity and ambiguity which is the earthly counterpart of that of the spirits that were said to haunt the apartment. In a sense, this case of *macula peccati* (O'Neil 1912)[5] reminds us of the causal relationship established in the quarter between signora Pina's sinful sex and her daughter's crippling illness. The compassion of Lino and his peers for this old woman[6] indicates an awareness of the expiating aspect of suffering (which, incidentally, she rejected) consistent with the Christian theodicy that explains human suffering as a means to the punishment and therefore redemption of the soul. It would be difficult, however, to argue that this theme is prominent among the *popolino*.

These two cases provide a graphic illustration, in local terms, of the controversial theology of sin, guilt and suffering (Bemporad 1987; LaCocque 1987), particularly of their proportional relationship to punishment and reparation (Ricoeur 1987). An important difference between them is that signora Pina is seen to accept the expiatory value of the suffering in terms of the Christian rationale of *memoria passionis* (Bemporad 1987). Moreover, no liminality is attached to her or her daughter, probably because God's punishment in her case is not considered *exceptionally* severe. It is extreme sexual misconduct, sexual ambiguity and meretricious or mercenary work activities that engender liminality. Such transgressions jeopardize the aim of feeling justified at the moment of death (Landsberg 1953: iii), opening the individual, ominously, to special relations *in life* with liminal, unjustified dead. The danger is therefore not only religious and moral but also, more broadly, ontological. On a far more problematic level, child molesters, usurers, predatory favour-bestowers and heartless landlords (Pardo 1992: 260) were offered as examples of strong transgression of this kind. They too obviously fail to meet the moral and social requirements of reparation and then reconciliation with God and society. People say that they *cannot be happy*, regardless of their financial situation.

In practice, however, this culture also recognizes what Robert Hertz calls the (Christian) mystery of man's dual nature as a sinner but a redeemed sinner (1922: 5). In his fascinating work on sin and expiation, Hertz says that because sin pre-exists, it is not the sinner who generates the sin but the sin that makes the individual a sinner (p. 19). In most cases (when wrongdoing is not regarded as extreme and irreparable), the formal intransigency of the symbolism of transgression is subject here to negotiations linked to the sinner's personality and behaviour and to the value attributed to sin and forgiveness. We have studied the mitigation achieved by such ordinary sinners as signora Pina, the not-too-usurious moneylender Ciro, and the much-too-successful Lina. Let us now examine the significance of this fundamental Christian principle in less ordinary situations.

In the cases described to me as serious transgressions of proper behaviour, unhappiness is exemplified by an unusual combination of poor health in the household, uneasy family life, repeated accidents, childlessness, etc., or by a combination of one or more of these troubles with unexplainable calamities. We know that such events will normally be attributed not to God's will but to ill-willed spirits or to envy, evil eye or (rarely) sorcery. However, in the presence of seriously transgressive behaviour they are identified with an undesirable cosmic disorder in which there is no place for God's grace. A singular correspondence between these transgressors' self-perception and the moral attitudes of their significant group gives them practical importance. They are said to enjoy good relationships with the liminal dead (rather than just their benevolence as do lesser sinners like Ciro and Lina) and to have privileged access to the dangerous but useful living.

The *demi-monde* as a special resource

Prostitutes, I was told, are "na cos' 'e miez" (in-between) because of their job. Their intentionally unproductive and mercenary 'sin of the flesh', rarely believed to be motivated by vice, is judged a serious transgression of the Christian rationale of legitimate sex. Their sinful wrongdoing makes them unequivocally ambiguous and liminal. However, because their liminality does not necessarily derive from evil, it is *in principle* redeemable, and it does not in itself lead to their exclusion from ordinary life – rather the opposite.

Giovanni reminds us of a point made by Davis (1977: 92) when he illustrates the structure of meaning around the concept of proper sexual behaviour by saying, 'One has less respect for women who present themselves as good and secretly behave like whores; it's thrown in their faces when they quarrel. Most prostitutes operate outside the quarter, and their dignity must be respected.' The fact that close relations with local prostitutes are considered inappropriate and go unmentioned should not be seen as an indication of their limited significance. Their role in fact extends well beyond the Augustinian theme that, although prostitution is condemnable because it is functional to male lust, it helps to mitigate the polluting power of that lust.[7] Because of their job, I was told, prostitutes are well connected and know a lot about people. Moreover, they give expert advice,[8] and may help people to approach the underworld or deal with drug addiction.

Most that remains unspoken in the exchanges involving prostitutes is, for actors, understood while remaining free of the embarrassing, sometimes dangerous, implications of the spoken. The favour and its granter's discretion are usually understood to belong to the complex process of normalization of these ambiguous women which is facilitated by their relatively self-restrained behaviour in the neighbourhood. Basically, however, it is the management of the very reasons for their diversity and liminality and of the resource domains to which they have access as prostitutes that structures their avoidance of marginalization.

I fortuitously gained direct experience of how risks are reduced on both sides of the exchange. While chatting outside the *basso* of Tina (an unlicensed petty trader like Gina), Rita (a stallholder) pleasantly greeted a passer-by in her late forties about whom Tina made scorching comments. The woman was a semi-retired prostitute who had recently begun selling smuggled cigarettes, thus invading Tina's business territory. Tina was incensed by the prostitute's using her underworld contacts to buy cigarettes at better prices and to establish good relations with acquiescent policemen. However, because for most locals the woman was operating within the rules of 'honest entrepreneurship', to justify her anger Tina chose to attack her as a prostitute: 'Since she wasn't making enough money doing that dirty job, now she's breaking the eggs in honest people's baskets.' Rita's uncompromising reply was, 'You're wrong, and heartless. The poor woman's trying to become honest. You can't blame her if she's cleverer. Anyhow, nobody here is a saint, you know.' Tina of course responded harshly, and the loud voices attracted others, thus provoking further discussion.

This woman, like Giuseppina, has managed to establish that misfortune made her a prostitute – 'she was poor, betrayed and unmarried'. This attenuates her sin (see also *Catechismo della Chiesa Cattolica* 1992: 2355). Above all, hardship being traditionally not unknown here, people's sympathy usually goes to the downtrodden (e.g., Paolo in earlier times). Her second activity is regarded not as evidence of greed but as a legitimate – if 'semi-legal' – way out of prostitution. Beyond the principle that sin and forgiveness are the two extreme moments of an intimate drama (Hertz 1922: 11), this former prostitute's sincerity is underlined by her recognizable motivation for penance and atonement. She devoutly attends the yearly pilgrimage to the Madonna of the Arch, and contributes substantially but discreetly to the maintenance of a local street shrine. Moreover, she may well be prone to bad language, and it may well be true that her knowledge of local secrets deters many from antagonizing her, while giving her power in mediating local disputes. But, again like Giuseppina, she has also constructed an image of discretion and good-heartedness by carefully adhering to the customary rule that those who ask favours of people like her should be overtly involved only in the 'licit' part of the transaction – advice – while the crucial, practical part remains confidential

A prostitute's or former prostitute's help is seldom asked explicitly. Instead, it is usually she who *offers help*, thus showing also that she is relatively free of the envy of the normality of others which is supposed to bias her condition of abnormality.

The tacit character of these women's favour-bestowing has various implications. It may not gain them an obviously important position, but it contributes to their moral reparation. It also facilitates their access to the important non-material benefits associated with the relationship between people's gratitude, obligation and solidarity and to monetary returns in the form of tolerance of competitive entrepreneurship, some aspects of which (especially the advantage given by underworld contacts) would normally be condemned. Rita behaved like other beneficiaries of these non-ordinary women in not mentioning any relationship with the woman but overtly supporting her. This management of secrecy projects what might appear to be clever exploitation of prostitutes (as favour-bestowers) into a complex exchange system that allows these women to escape abnormality and construct a more acceptable entrepreneurship. Under these conditions, social legitimation 'just happens'. The actor simply realizes that, while her sinning (her prostitution) increasingly goes unmentioned, positive stories are slowly and subtly being spread. This is less demanding of the favour-seeker and positively rewards the favour-bestower.

This culture dissociates – on both sides – a prostitute's generosity from monetary payment or interest. Again recalling Hertz's work (1922: 14), this becomes particularly significant when her good-heartedness is supported by her observable expiation, for then she clearly benefits from the contrast between (and complementarity of) the goodness of her true self, sublimated in her vocation to disinterested generosity, and the mercenariness and emotional indifference of the profession into which she is recognized to have been forced. However, as these women sin, or have sinned, too constantly and seriously, the contribution of their generosity to their worthiness is much more unpredictable than in the case of ordinary people and, therefore, like certain aspects of magic, more open to manipulation. They tend to believe that the mitigation of punishment must be their ultimate goal but also that, because redemption is made difficult by the very nature of their sin, their good-heartedness is as significant to their inner lives and hope of a justifiable death as it is to their social and existential normalization.

The disordering potential of the *demi-monde* is apparently seldom conceptualized, and under special circumstances it seems to play an ordering role. In this culture no way has been found (or perhaps even searched for) to incorporate these transactions into legitimate entrepreneurship. However, given certain precautions, these women do facilitate unobvious relationships between the normal and the abnormal (illicit, ambiguous, liminal, etc.) that ideally leave the associated sanctions and the underlying moral framework unchallenged, even strengthened. For locals whose entrepreneurship is sufficiently flexible to include them as manageable resources, prostitutes are the long spoon by which it becomes possible to sup with the devil relatively safely and discreetly. Thus, they are, in a sense, an improvement on brokers such as Genny. We know that these brokers facilitate ordinary people's access to the underworld because their work activities, family origins or patterns of socialization place them on the borderline between licit and illicit in the order of life. And they do so in a situation in which people widely recognize that risk is naturally part of social exchange and that the more calculated risks one takes the greater the expectable results. However, not only are the transactions with them necessarily overt and explicit (though not always specified) but they carry connotations of friendship (in many cases *instead of* reciprocation) which greatly complicate the favour-seeker's commitment to important identity values such as honesty and clean hands. Moreover, although in both cases the favour-seeker remains obligated to the broker rather than to the favour-bestower and the transactions end up with obligated brokers and apparently non-obligated favour-seekers, the risk is greater with brokers like Genny that the broker and the favour-bestowing villain will demand reciprocation. This is perhaps the major single reason that the use of these resources is restricted to particularly difficult circumstances despite their relative availability and superficially uncomplicated character.

Prostitutes, children, usurers: liminality vs. marginality in the morality of resources

The flexibility offered by a degree of secrecy expands ordinary people's options, and it helps the culture of good-heartedness and solidarity to play a positive role in the relationship with practical action. The significance of this latter effect to the social integration of the liminal is apparent in the quarrel between Tina and Rita. Rita called Tina 'heartless'. At the same time, bystanders saw Rita's attitude as a measure of her *own good-heartedness*. This indicates that it would be naïve to regard as strictly instrumental self-interest or hypocrisy the idea that 'one should be kind to an unfortunate prostitute who behaves well'.[9] This idea at once relates to the moral value assigned to one's own goodness and indicates how good-heartedness allows the rational expectation of gratitude on both sides.

The structuration of the liminal, free of moral or religious zeal, is independent of any real segregation of ordinary people from most sinners. There is, in fact, no strict equivalence between liminality and marginality. Marginality is generated by the systematic and serious transgression of the morality of entrepreneurship and, more generally, of a fulfilled life. This distinction between liminality and marginality is clarified by the liminality of children (which is temporary), and that of the *rammari* and moneylenders (which is in some cases dangerously unredeemable and permanent).

Children are not yet men and women, but they will be; their undefined position is only temporary. However, while they are *guagliun'[i]* (boys); *guaglion'[e]* (girls), their roles are limited to certain domains of activity and meaning. Some boys become *muschilli* and, we have seen, regardless of their sex, most children help with housework and from their early teens they may well work for cash, usually part-time, while attending school. They may also be special favour-bestowers, rewarded with pocket-money and, above all, with adults' respect – the most important single element in the construction of a self-respect that includes reliability as well as ability.[10] They can do things that adults cannot or will not do. They may be used to spread or gather information and gossip or slander. They deliver messages or (if boys) fetch men from gambling clubs.[11] They are sent to buy 'shamefully' small quantities of food, and their time is employed on any kind of errand or queue. Thus they provide their occasional employers (usually but not exclusively kin) with symbolic protection from embarrassment and also a way of saving time and stressing that they are busy and respected people. Above all, I was told, in this way children learn about life and the value of money while becoming increasingly self-confident and independent. This experience can be invested in various ways (sometimes illegal), but it generally becomes one of the early bricks in the construction of entrepreneurship.

The existential ambiguity of children encompasses their relations with the supramundane. Generally considered 'innocent souls' (Pardo 1989) exposed to the forces of evil and therefore in need of special protection from the living and the dead, their relations with the sacred supramundane become more definite and direct as they become adolescent – a process in which confirmation (normally in the early teens) is a significant event. Because only adults are truly responsible for relations with the supramundane, as we have seen, children afflicted by physical or psychological problems are regarded as the passive recipients of suffering brought about by their parents' sins. Reflecting this ambivalent symbolism, it is often children who show greater sympathy with the positive spirituality of the house (the Bella 'Mbriana) and greater emotional attachment to their home when the family moves elsewhere, but it is also they who are often the first to feel the presence of spirits.

The symbolism of children and the ambiguity of widowhood and of existential precariousness stressed by poor health, childlessness and lack

of a proper home later in life point to the significance of age in the definition of an ambiguity that does not generate marginality. The case material
on prostitutes would appear to grant a similar status to work, indicating
that, apart from its material value, work contributes crucially to the definition of an individual's existential position not only in the moral and spiritual sense but also in the cosmic and supramundane sense. Similarly, other
special workers, such as moneylenders and *rammari*, are normal people
who become ambiguous and liminal *because of their work activities*.
However, even their symbolism is negotiable and can be converted into a
positive resource.

Borrowing money or deferring payment for merchandise is normal
practice in the quarter. It is equally normal for people to lend small sums
at interest or to sell goods on instalments (and charge low interest) within
their networks. These activities entail no liminality or marginality. When
the petty selling of money or goods at interest becomes a permanent and
principal work activity it, like the work of prostitutes, is often explained in
terms of the morality of 'need'. These entrepreneurs may well be projected
into the problematic domain of ambiguity by the nature of their work, but
because they do not demand extortionate interest rates they are not associated (nor do they associate themselves) with the pure, amoral logic of
profit *à la* Bentham (1787). In line with the religious rationale of man's
dual nature, their existential position is thus distanced from unforgivable
sin and social marginality. Defying contradiction, they continue their
activities, presumably forced upon them by the lack of viable alternatives
for making a living, even when the original motivation ceases to exist.
Since they are already 'compromised', they ask, would it be convenient, or
useful, to give it up?

The important question is why the ambiguity of these special workers,
unlike that of their more usurious colleagues, so obviously poses no threat
to the order that the *popolino* struggle to establish in their lives. As we
know, there is no condemnation here of profit made among one's own
group (let alone in the quarter) as opposed to permissible profit extracted
from 'others'. Given this important (Nelson 1949) fact, the basic discriminative criterion – arbitrary in this case, as in any case – is *moderation*
vs. *usury*, intended not only in the restricted sense of 'the abuse of a certain
superiority at the expense of another man's necessity' (Vermeersch
1912:237) but, more generally, as 'credit transactions carrying excessive
charges' (Salin 1949:193). The selective symbolism by which the 'sellers of
money' are internally differentiated and its underlying rationale make a
fascinating case for the idea that money (particularly its use) and profit

generate not moral uncertainty (through confusion between good and evil) but a sharp distinction between improper (but tolerable) and evil action.

The usurious lenders are loathed, despised and marginalized. They deal in large sums (usually over £10,000), charge high interest[12] and allow no flexibility in repayment. In this culture they are the providers of an important service, allowing people to raise substantial capital for high-profit-making investments, even though they can offer only unorthodox security (such as local backing and 'informal income', which are not accepted by the banks). But they are also *strozzini* (money-grubbers, loan sharks; literally, stranglers),[13] dangerous and antisocial parasites whose moral excommunication and social marginalization is made worse by their use of criminals' 'persuading' intervention, which costs them 10 to 15 per cent of the money thus recovered.[14] These *strozzini*'s pitiless entrepreneurship, like that of the equally disruptive drug dealers, extends well beyond the limits of the local idea of moneymaking and the accumulation of capital as legitimate goals. They represent so real a danger of profound corruption of the moral and social order that, despite their recognized usefulness, the *popolino* and the petty bourgeoisie alike exclude them from ordinary social relations only slightly less severely than they do the Camorristi.

These evildoers – as opposed to wrongdoers, whose sinning is reparable – make evil *real*, not simply the absence of good. In many ways similar to drug dealers and criminals, they embody the *concrete evil* of prevarication and abuse and the *abstract evil* of their treachery in extending a hand that so often leads to economic and psychological ruin. And, like drug dealers and criminals, they make a powerful case for evil-mindedness's 'drying up' people's energies and good fortune not only symbolically and psychologically but also factually. They are the objects of the most imaginative curses based on the belief (of which they appear to be aware) that their work destines them to the 'true death' of eternal damnation (Landsberg 1953). They are imagined in (and wished to) a hell strongly reminiscent of Doré's representations of Dante's poem which is anticipated (Hertz 1922: 20) by the 'hell' of their marginalization in this life. This extreme condition, we know, contrasts sharply with the (purgatorial) afterlife that most *popolino* expect for themselves and which is anticipated by the earthly purgatory in which they describe themselves to be. It seems to me that, by so arguing, local people place these issues of evil, as embodied by the consequences of usury, at the very heart of their interpretation of the Christian concept of salvation. Eternal cosmic punishment at once embodies an extreme condition that contrasts with their commitment to negotiation in life and after death and, regardless of the ecclesiastical view, entails the symbolic exclusion of usurers from the interaction between sin, suffering and atonement. In their case, the evil suffered constitutes no compensation for the evil committed (Ricoeur 1969) because, it is believed, no compensation is conceivable.

In contrast, the moderate (or 'reasonable', 'fair') price of money involved in small- and medium-scale moneylending makes a case for reparable transgression.[15] The widespread tolerance of this kind of moneylending brings the local culture of borrowing and repayment of debt – and the related profit – strikingly in tune with the persistent ambiguity of Christianity (Nelson 1949), particularly since the Reformation, when a trend traceable at least to Thomas Aquinas (Dow 1921:551) became predominant. The medieval-style intransigence about charging interest *tout court* was gradually replaced by an obscure casuistry regarding especially the definition of excessive, therefore usurious, interest rates (Vermeersch 1912:235–6). If until recently, Catholicism has been indecisive and ambivalent,[16] the attitude of Protestantism can be roughly seen as established by reformers caught between moral zeal and the practical considerations pressed upon them by a changing society (Salin 1949; also, on different lines, Vermeersch 1912, Dow 1921 and Groethuysen 1927).

This culture recognizes the link between lending at interest and sin against the Christian principle of charity implied in the First Commandment and made more explicit by the Apostles (e.g., Luke 6: 34–5 and the Lord's Prayer as reported by St Matthew). But it also takes into account the facts that moneylending is the inevitable ancillary of commerce and entrepreneurship in general, that investment is the best use for money, and that money invested in credit (instead of somewhere else) ought to be *reasonably* productive. In this light, the fact that informal credit accounts for a very important part of local people's access to capital points to a problem of broad significance.

Financial experts and operators and trade-unionists in this sector share the view that credit is subjected to unfair conditions in the South. The establishment, and development, of enterprise at all levels, they say, is unjustifiably frustrated by exceptionally long procedures and high interest, to which excessive collateral expenses are added. These conditions are imposed by the banks with the excuse that business in this part of Italy is exposed to particularly high risks. The material discussed in this book and the evidence from research in progress in Naples and elsewhere in the South indicate that this line of argument may be convenient to specific interests (see also Pardo 1993), and may serve partisan politics in the country. My own observation of small-scale entrepreneurship would agree with the belief, widespread in the banking community, that, as more people have access to formal income, official sources of credit are increasingly approached. However, it is also obvious that no priority is given in my informants' strategies to these difficult sources of credit. Seeing little difference between moderate moneylenders and banks, as between *rammari* and the shopkeepers who sell goods on instalments (an ancient institution in Naples), actors appreciate that the services of moderate moneylenders may be marginally more costly,[17] but, unconstrained by overregulation and bureaucratic demands, they broaden access to credit and also save time and avoid hassle by circumventing lengthy procedures or payment of bribes. To put it simply, in this complex economy borrowing is not merely a need of the poor who would otherwise starve but, through debt, fall even deeper into deprivation. As part of the local entrepreneurial way of life, borrowing marks the establishment – or improvement – of small-scale business.

There is a less visible aspect of debt and repayment that deserves a momentary digression because it directly bears on the nature of the *popolino*'s capitalist spirit. People often borrow from several moneylenders at once, in the quarter and outside it, knowing that not only is timely repayment always economically advisable but also prevents the destructive effects of public quarrels on the borrowers' reputation and future attempts to borrow. Perversely, as this accumulation of debts (which may also include money borrowed from formal sources) forces borrowers to improve their productivity, those who manage to get out of debt (especially when they use credit wisely) may well borrow again, but they are also left with considerable experience of how to improve the financial output of their entrepreneurship. For instance, my observation of Lino documents how, having repaid his debt, he kept on working hard, and with the profits and a mortgage on his stipend he was able to assemble all but a small part of the capital necessary to start the new shop.

The sinning and transgression of moderate moneylenders does not completely escape the resentment inspired by usury, but unlike usury it is not so problematic as to be destructive of the social order in the way described by the Classical philosophers (e.g., Aristotle, *Politics*, 1.10) and seen by many as a major problem of modern capitalism. Moreover, while people so strongly condemn the usurers' unscrupulousness and are cynical about bankers, they also broadly accept that the 'fairer' lenders can be generous only occasionally, and only regarding delay in payment or interest. It is, finally, only cases of 'pressing need' (e.g. serious illness) that justify lending money with insufficient security. The exceptions to such restricted generosity raise interesting issues. Mario, for example, has mortgaged his modest stipend as a manual worker in order to pay for the marriage of his pregnant adolescent daughter. He admits, however, that his family has had 'proper holidays'[18] and celebrated important events[19] anyway by borrowing from a local moneylender. He explains that he pays very low interest but does not say why. Observation and a systematic review of his case material suggest that, although neither Mario nor the moneylender has clearly stated the transactional character of their relationship, the moneylender's generosity is motivated by Mario's spiritual powers, particularly his 'faculty' to communicate with the good souls on their relatives' behalf. Mario does not accept money, but he does welcome alternative expressions of gratitude – in this case, easy terms of repayment.

In brief, moderate moneylenders may well be ambiguous and controversial, more tolerated than approved. However, like other useful but problematic people (e.g., prostitutes), they are not marginalized through a rigid interpretation of moral and religious values. Instead, their restricted generosity helps to improve their business and to identify them as morally acceptable resources. Let us concentrate on the relation of these principles for codifying and structuring morality and meaning to religious belief, personal identity and social position.

Religious belief, identity and integration

In negotiating the morality of the profit extracted from the sale of money, the petty moneylenders have certainly been less successful than their medieval forefathers, the powerful Italian bankers described by Le Goff (1980; also Salin 1949: 195). Given the general rationale of the *popolino*'s attitude to work and entrepreneurship, they in fact have much in common with the laborious process by which the newly born eighteenth-century French bourgeoisie eventually managed to construct a capitalist identity that was financially sound and acceptable to God, though not to all of the clergy (Groethuysen 1927). The key point is that, as long as they are 'fair' (and moderate) they are regarded as persistent but venial sinners. Their religiosity, unlike that of usurers, is not regarded as offensive to God and society. Like prostitutes, they are believed (and believe themselves) to be destined to an uneasy relationship with the sacred and to a long and difficult but not eternal stay in purgatory, a painfully purifying step towards the sight of God. This reachable goal of salvation makes them ardently religious in private. They never fail to erect the sacred space of the household shrine and, far more emphatically than ordinary people, they use the protective symbols – such as sacred images and religious jewellery – that characterize popular religiosity in Italy. Things are much more difficult in public.

The contrition of petty moneylenders and *rammari*, like that of prostitutes, has to reckon with ecclesiastical ambiguity and with their own difficulty with the institutional sacred space. The restriction formally imposed by the Church on their penitence is generally considered unfair, but they are also seen as having reason to feel uncomfortable attending church services. Their religious acts, unlike those of local pre-eminent villains or other local well-off but not apparently dishonest persons, are correspondingly low key. They rarely involve grand gestures (showing-off, people say) such as restoring a street shrine or giving large sums of money for the various celebrations.[20] It is mainly in the context of 'collective' pilgrimages[21] that they publicly express their ultimate faith in forgiveness as a characteristic of divine grace. In many ways these pilgrimages involve more than emotional and religious experience. These highly ritualized ways of approaching the sacred are at the same time 'concretizations' of penitence[22] that help to alleviate guilt and unhappiness and manifestations of the desire to re-establish the order (mythically) pre-existing transgression. It is in this profound sense that these religious expressions should be seen as complementary to the strategies of reparation examined above. Like most popular rituals, their 'moral reality' (Hertz 1922: 27) for the most part dispenses, emblematically, with an ecclesiastical authority considered distant and only formally necessary. They require limited use of ecclesiastical premises, and they are only partially controlled by the Church. As in other cases, the latter, well aware of the issues of power involved, acquiesces with the usual disdain but this time also with an eye to the conspicuous offerings. People of all ages and various social position and power consistently take part in these pilgrimages and other communal events (e.g., religious celebrations). Taking advantage of the temporary relaxation of boundaries of social and, in part, symbolic taxonomy, people establish and strengthen new relations, particularly in terms of 'intermediary networks'.

Giovanni's *rammara* relative exemplifies these special workers' religious beliefs and perfomances in relation to the issues of sin, good-heartedness, reparation and integration. Her customers call her ''a Zia' (the aunt) in affectionate recognition of her good treatment of her customers.[23] This corresponds with the belief that, since there is nothing evil about 'reasonable' *rammari* and moneylenders, their sin is mitigated by their active efforts to obtain the pardon of their living fellows – and, ideally, of the supramundane – through *observable* (but only to a limited degree *public*) sacrifice, devotion and occasional generosity. However, forgiveness does not exclude punishment, or guilt. 'A Zia feels guilty, I was told, and makes sacrifices to punish herself. For example, believing that her chronic illness is God's punishment for her job, she has offered money, candles, silver *ex votos* and innumerable solitary and collective pilgrimages to the Volto Santo. Apparently, her anxiety about her destiny finds only limited relief in her family's commitment to sympathizing, even after her death, by keeping alive her memory.

The behaviour of Angelina, a petty moneylender and occasional *rammara*, is equally symptomatic. As a devotee of the Madonna of Montevergine, she organizes annual pilgrimages to the sanctuary, accepting payment in interest-free instalments. Many believe that the negligible profit that she denies she makes ('Everything goes to the madonna', she says) does not provide sufficient explanation for her hard work, which she does as 'un'opera buona' (a good action), to feel less guilty about her job, people say. We may accept that non-material motivations are pre-eminent in Angelina's action as, remarkably, they are in that of signora Pina. If invested in her business, the time and energy would produce better monetary results, though at the expense of her sense of self-worth. There is, I have said, an instrumental bias to the entrepreneurship of people like Ciro, Angelina and 'a Zia which, even when they do business with their kin or friends, forbids their 'doing things for nothing'. And, of course, their moderation, occasional generosity and involvement in pious activities serve the interest of their image and network (hence business) improvement. It is also obvious, however, that they extract implicit moral and spiritual benefits which directly address their concern with establishing order in their lives. Their devotion (private and public) is explained in terms of a religious rationale in which the positive disposition of the sacred supramundane may well not be associated with received grace but does signify the mitigation of guilt and encourage hope of God's forgiveness. In this hope, Angelina has walked in solitary barefoot pilgrimage to thank St Ciro for miraculous healing when a specialist eventually dispelled her fears about a cyst which her doctor had suspected was cancer.[24]

This difficulty is at once recognized and criticized by the local community. As in some ordinary cases (e.g., Lina), these people's financial success is not believed to derive entirely from their ability. Typically, 'a Zia's business is said to have improved considerably since she saw the Monacello. In a sense, envy and condemnation of these special workers appear to be reduced to acceptable levels by the belief that the sinful nature of their business, which makes it particularly difficult for them to achieve God's grace, also endears them to the spirits, who help them. This, my informants believe, is also why they are so concerned with showing their motivation for redemption.

A dialectic relationship, instead of an equivalence, is thus established between the meanings of liminality and ambiguity and those of marginality through appropriate negotiations over action and thought at the various levels of the unspoken. These venial sinners are thus factually normalized while remaining symbolically liminal. When monetary achievement exceeds acceptable limits and accusations of greed are judged inappropriate, local morality assigns such achievement to the domain of liminality explained by sin. This interlocking of liminality and sin suggests that the repentant behaviour of these people, their pursuit of forgiveness, does much more than establish a rational balance between transgression and order. This symbolic edifice both allows the incorporation of their ambiguity (like that of other ultimately forgivable moral transgressors) into the established order and makes worthiness part of their image and identity, thus encouraging their own and others' entrepreneurialism.

Mundane liminality as a point of entry to unorthodox supramundane domains

The analysis given suggests that it is the condition of liminality in its various forms, not these forms as such, that justifies the ambiguity of certain persons. The significance of liminality in the construction of roles which allow so much that is out-of-the-ordinary to be explained (and to some extent controlled) inevitably places liminality itself at the centre of attention.

While human syntheses of liminality such as the prostitutes and the moneylenders are relatively common and approachable resources, the experience of supramundane liminality is more unusual and problematic. In various degrees of strength and consciousness, this involves both ordinary people and ambiguous people, both the non-sacred and, in a sense, the sacred. Paolo shares with many locals a perceptual experience of spirits marked by the *feeling* (sometimes physical) of their presence. It is, however, when these dead are *seen* that two very different conditions of liminality are believed to be brought into contact. Such extraordinary involvement of the non-sacred supramundane distinguishes the actor from others. With a 'vision', the numinous experience of the non-sacred supramundane becomes *existentially real* in the sense of Otto (1950).[25] A degree of liminality is thus revealed in an ordinary person's life, implying at once danger and opportunity. The *mysterium* of such numinous experience is laden with both of the fundamental aspects conceptualized by Otto. It bears the disquieting, potentially threatening element of *tremendum*, but, provided that it remains unmentioned, it usually also includes, syncretically, the desirable element of *fascinans*. The revelation of personal liminality implicit in such a vision acquires an almost unqualified advantageous meaning. It becomes an opportunity to establish extraordinary relations with this aspect of the supramundane – within the limits imposed by its arbitrary character.

According to local culture, certain otherwise ordinary persons see spirits because their ritual initiation to Christian life, baptism, was improper. For Lévi-Strauss (1969) the mispronunciation or misuse of language may be classifiable, along with incest, as a cause of aberrations that can upset the natural order. The *popolino* attach great importance to the situation of structured disorder which they believe to be brought about by the imperfect wording of the sacramental formula of baptism. Such alleged unaccomplished purification makes actors the objects of an inversion of the framework of meaning of important 'natural symbols' (Douglas 1970). Placed outside the ordinary taxonomies, they become 'unsettled', numinous concretizations of moral liminality. When such a vision coincides with other extraordinary events (positive or negative), it produces awareness that this existential unrest contains powerful symbols different from those attached to the liminality (acquired later in life through actions that can be repaired) of, say, prostitutes, moneylenders and *rammari* and the temporary liminality of children. Although such symbolic synthesis does not make the persons concerned abnormal or strange, it does have (domesticated) significance in their perception and management of the spiritual in their lives.

The experience of Anna provides a comprehensive account of local beliefs and ambivalent attitudes in this area. Embodying the early signs of the important changes in the rhetoric of womanhood and gender relations which we have examined, Anna used to 'answer back'. She now says, without regret, that her frequent clashes with older people over what she saw as a new, more emancipated mentality and behaviour were bound to cause her serious trouble. On one occasion, her irreverent reaction to what she describes as unjust accusations of frivolity by her mother-in-law-to-be provoked a train of events which Anna considers of primary importance in her life. Harshly rebuffed by her opponent and, later, by her parents, who saw good neighbourhood – and, potentially, kinship – relations jeopardized, the angry Anna went to stay with her widowed grandmother, who lived alone in a flat she owned nearby. Doing so at once and in broad daylight, Anna says, pre-empted false accusations of her having run away with Luigi and, in those days, the inevitable consequence of a reparatory marriage – something she was determined to avoid.

Anna stayed with her grandmother until she married Luigi some years later. Meanwhile, under her grandmother's supervision, she continued to meet him in a neighbourhood now more inquisitive than ever. This pressure and the desire to avoid unpleasant consequences were the explanation she gave Luigi for her decision, soon after the crisis, to play safe and go no farther than the building's main entrance after dusk. Luigi thought that she was exaggerating the problem but acquiesced. There were other reasons for her decision of which he has learned only recently, finding them 'laughable'. These reasons require attention because they illustrate an important aspect of the interconnection between different levels of rationality in local people's explanation of action. Anna believes that the unnegotiated move to a darker and relatively unfamiliar house in a building where 'things were said to happen' and, especially, the emotional unrest prepared the ground for the extraordinary experience of visual contact with what she called 'supernatural entities', using the word 'spirits' only twice in our frequent and lengthy conversations.

Her grandmother left to open her local business early, while Anna was still asleep. One morning Anna was roused by the sensation of the duvet slipping off her body 'like a caress'.[26] From her bed, in the early light, she saw two bodyless hands rummaging in a drawer. 'Frightened to death, I rushed to our neighbour still in my nightdress,' she said with obvious uneasiness, 'but when we went back the room was empty.' Anna and her hastily summoned grandmother checked the house carefully and determinedly, only to find that what she had seen was unlikely to have been a burglar, for nothing was amiss. Perhaps it had been her imagination, they concluded, unconvinced. Anna reacted like Lino and others in similar circumstances. She says she did not generally compromise on her independent-minded attitude but, feeling exposed in a new, much less controllable way, she dared not continue strolling with Luigi after dark as she had done until then despite the risk of gossip and the possible consequences. Moreover, she experienced other traditionally recognized signs of a haunted house; she recurrently felt a weight on her body ('like somebody dancing on me') while asleep, finding herself alone on waking up; she kept finding coins in the house which belonged to no-one; and both her family situation and Luigi's business suddenly improved.

She and most of her significant others link what they regard as clear evidence of her experience of the non-sacred supramundane with a similar episode years before, while she was still living with her family in a large flat in her grandmother's building. She had been left with the task of feeding her baby cousin while her mother and her aunt chatted with a neighbour in the hallway of the floor above. Amidst the child's cries and her own shouted exhortations, she heard a loud noise from the bedroom. On investigation she discovered that a clay statue of St Anthony had fallen off the family shrine, breaking its glass dome. Rising from the floor after having cleared up the mess, Anna saw 'a handsome middle-aged man in black' staring at her from the far end of the room. The man resembled her – living – grandfather as a younger man. More frightened, she says, by the coincidence of this vision with the accident to the sacred icon than by the vision itself,[27] she picked up the baby and ran. As her mother pointed out to her from the window, her grandfather had been playing cards outside for some time. At this point Anna realized that to get out she had had to unlock the door from the inside.

More recent experiences all seem to have occurred in places Anna does not regard as 'home'. Anna feels good in her home and thinks that the Bella 'Mbriana likes her family. 'Things have happened' instead, she says, in the recently built holiday flat that they rent in the summer. Anna has repeatedly found money, has won in the lottery and has become 'generally luckier'. Moreover, she stresses, not only is their business flourishing but 'everyone in the household enjoys good health despite living in an unhealthy environment and being casual about what and how much we eat'. She has discovered that a young man died in the holiday flat soon after it was built. *Mors certa, hora incerta*, Landsberg reflects (1953: ii); by overemphasizing the second part of this philosophical truth, a premature death (in this case, the interruption of a full but unaccomplished life) critically upsets the intimate dialectic of death. It typifies the *popolino*'s idea of a bad death as opposed to a good one – peaceful, processual and accepted by the group and the dying (Pardo 1989: 113–15). As Landsberg asks us to note (1953: v), death makes human existence by definition incomplete. The wide recognition of this ontological fundamental among the *popolino* does not seem to contrast with the fact that sudden, accidental, or indeed unquestionably 'premature' deaths have strong connotations of resistance. Given the powerful negative symbolism of *forced* and extraordinary incompleteness, a death like this young man's is therefore believed to remain unaccepted. It produces an *eternally unsettled* – liminal – spirit that can intervene in this life *as it likes*. These meanings are even more unequivocally attached to the old building in which Anna's grand-mother lived.

An otherwise 'daring woman' (as she describes herself), Anna is ambiva-lent about 'these things'; she is only a 'half-believer'. But, as she cannot find another explanation for the 'strange' events she has experienced throughout her life, she accepts that they may have something to do with (benevolent) spirits. And, although she does *speak* about them, her care-lessness is only apparent; she has never discussed current events and reported those occurring in her holiday flat in the 'symbolic security' (Pardo 1992: 261–3) of her home. True believers behave differently. For instance, Luisa does not claim to have seen spirits, but the fragmentary information I gathered from an uneasy Lino and from her sister suggest that this possibility is contemplated – and basically welcomed – among her significant group. Fearing negative consequences, Luisa adheres to the rule that such experiences must not be discussed while they are occurring. This careful behaviour is seen, however, as a tacit admission. Interestingly, events such as those described by Anna are said to have occurred in Luisa's holiday flat as well. This is perhaps less problematic because the experience of the liminal is necessarily occasional and physically remote from home and ordinary life while retaining symbolic importance. Lacking the psychological and emotional pressure of events that occur in one's home, this kind of experience of the non-sacred supramundane produces impor-tant extraordinary meanings in the existence of these two women and gives them access to a powerful explanatory domain including spiritual as well as tangible facts of life.

Luisa, who was upset when I appeared to know, refused to discuss the issue. Unlike Anna, she appears to be more worried than embarrassed. She does talk about other similar beliefs, particularly her 'instinct' for fore-seeing future events or 'feeling' things that are happening elsewhere, but even in this case there are difficulties. Believing that claims of divination are sinful, Luisa qualifies her 'instinct' by saying that it works only occa-sionally. Moreover, because her divination is not recognized (by her or her group) to coexist with other extraordinary qualities, it is not linked to any interaction with the dead. Luisa's, or her significant others' recognition of her *current* experience of the non-sacred supramundane would upset this balance, despite her otherwise ordinary image, and despite the fact that she does not *interact* with these spirits[28] but simply *enjoys their benevolence*. The problem seems to be that Luisa's divinatory 'instinct', though occa-sional, is not sufficiently dissimilar from the powers attributed to recogniz-ably liminal persons to set her apart from the extraordinary in this life.[29]

As I have said, despite her extraordinary experiences, no aura of strangeness or liminality looms about Anna. She *sees* spirits and therefore uneasily accepts that 'something must have been wrong' with her baptism. She does not, however, perform any special work activity, her good fortune is not so exceptional as to justify allegations (or claims) of liminality, ambiguity or special powers, and she has none of Luisa's special 'instincts'. Thus she apparently makes no secret of the presence of the non-sacred supramundane in her life. On a different level, sometimes this kind of relationship is attributed to and claimed by persons who have been so close to death as to require 'extreme' unction.[30] These survivors are believed to have ambivalent symbolic power over other living people. They are supposed to have gained a glimpse of the sacred, but instead of creating holiness in their lives their unaccomplished death – their 'unlikely return to life' – makes them liminal, opening them to the evil aspect of the personality of the liminal dead. Through them this evil can affect others, whose misfortune they are said to foresee or even provoke through curses which 'coglien' semp'' (always hit their target).

Throughout the social spectrum Catholicism poses no real challenge to the convenient complexity of this framework of thought or to the entrepreneurial capitalism linked to it. Even the petty bourgeoisie, whose beliefs remain low key, refer to important aspects of the popular re-elaboration of the theology of human relations with the supramundane. Although many evade the issue of spirits, they do not deny their existence. Moreover, they make no secret of their devotion to powerful dead persons unquestionably located in the sacred supramundane by popular piety and towards whom the Church opportunely maintains various degrees of ambiguity. Regardless of the ecclesiastical position, dead intermediaries such as Padre Pio, Madre Flora, Angela Jacobellis and the souls in purgatory are central in popular cultic expressions and in the related culture of the sacred supramundane.

Among the *popolino* in particular, *miracolati* epitomize an important aspect of this complexity and relative religious independence. They are relatives, neighbours or acquaintances who have been the recipients of what the local community recognizes as a miracle, especially regarding health. They become the living proof of supramundane powers, to which they are believed to be closer *because of* this miracle. Unlike the survivors described above, they are liminal in a 'sacred' sense and are asked to pray on other people's behalf, despite the fact that they carry no holiness and are not regarded to be true mediators with the supramundane.

We may reasonably say that liminality (sacred and non-sacred) is an important explanatory field with regard to so-called inconsistencies in the relationships between morality, religion, money and entrepreneurship, but this definition is still too vague. With various degrees of significance depending on the nature of their liminality, certain (liminal) persons are points of entry for unorthodox exchanges and resources and unorthodox aspects of actors' spirituality, and as such they attract the most ambivalent attitudes. The ethnography of *assistiti* and, at the opposite pole, of homosexuals emphasizes the extent to which the significance of mundane liminality reaches into this cultural and social fabric, becoming, at the same time, the object of sophisticated strategies of control.

Persons who are called *assistiti* are strange and liminal and therefore potentially threatening to the ideal order. The issue of control (of the numinous they bring about in this life) in their case, however, develops prominently around the spiritual desirability of their controversial identity. Instead of being stigmatized as disorders, their shabbiness, physical weakness (and often poor health) and melancholy are associated with an aura of purity which explains their 'faculties' but also almost completely neutralizes them erotically and as performers of orthodox work activities. *Assistiti* are treated with a mixture of heed and expectation, for they are believed to have the extraordinary power of *communicating* with the good souls, particularly the near dead. In line with the complicated relationship between the sacred and the non-sacred, it is common belief that their speech, enlightened by the good souls, can be transformed into winning numbers in the lottery.[31] Numbers can be extracted from all sorts of events, including dreams. However, those extracted from the *assistiti* are regarded as a better option, in spite of the fact that, as happens with sorcery, magic and divination, their (often nonsense) statements are open to different interpretations, producing a great variety of combinations.[32] Their powers hold only for distant others; they cannot communicate with their own dead, nor can they and their close relatives place bets, for they would not win and would risk the good souls' punishment and withdrawal of communication. However, because of their special condition of purity they are said to have little interest in material life. They are therefore in no danger of establishing a transgressive (direct) link between the spirituality of their communication with the supramundane and the materiality of monetary pursuit.

The condition of *assistito* is essentially a male one. The impurity of female disordering sexuality and, especially, of the periodic pollution of menstruation makes it inconsistent even with the spiritual and moral purity of women like Maria. Luisa exemplifies, in a sense, the female equivalent, for her sensitivity towards the supramundane sometimes finds expression in foretelling and providing good numbers, but unlike the *assistiti* she bets and occasionally wins. Probably because of the impurity attached to certain aspects of womanhood, this kind of transgressive behaviour is unlikely to pollute and therefore invalidate her faculties. The psychological instability associated with the melancholy of the *assistiti* (complementary, in a sense, to the weakness and sensitivity associated with menstruation) endorses their symbolic closeness to the dead still in transition towards the stability and grace implied by the sight of God. However, although the *assistiti* feel and are considered different, they bear no *mysterium*, and they serve not as true mediators between the living and the dead but as translators of the sacred into a relatively comprehensible and useful form. For the *popolino* and for many petty bourgeois, they are one of the alternative routes to important psychological and spiritual resources. Establishing good though indirect relationships with the good souls improves actors' sense of well-being and may bring good luck and monetary gains.

Mario – who is employed, healthy and well connected in politics and the trade unions and at the same time communicates with the good souls[33] – stressed his satisfaction in being good to people and in receiving their affection. A local *assistito*, who, more in tune with his 'faculties', is sick-looking and unemployed, also expressed his gratitude for people's (often expensive) gifts. Many informants say that the physical weakness of *assistiti* makes them unfit for work and thus, excused from fulfilling basic requirements of *sapè fà*, legitimately dependent on their wives' and children's incomes and on gifts. However, in line with the discussion of work and entrepreneurship given earlier, these 'jobless' people's activities may not conform to an abstract view of working life but are, nevertheless, entrepreneurial – if unorthodox – forms of work. These exchanges, like many other important ones, are always unspecified and deferred. Gifts are given without explicit reference to the *assistiti*'s powers. Actors' relationships with and investments in them draw strength from collective beliefs and (unspoken) individual expectations, practical and spiritual, much less than from the actual returns. An *assistito*'s credibility is not questioned, even though it is seldom supported by successful prophecies and/or wins. Losses and wrong predictions are generally explained by mistakes in interpretation.

Certain monks display a holy version of the *assistiti*'s liminality. My informants associate their retired way of life with a spiritual purity unmatched by other clerics. It is priests and nuns who participate in the popular iconography of purgatory (observable, for example, in the street shrines (Pardo 1994a)), but monks' occasional begging humanizes them. Their presumed better understanding of the human condition is said to be supported by their more secular manners and, despite the contradiction (particularly with their supposed purity), by their 'tendency to harass women sexually'.[34] They are regarded as more 'human' and closer to their flock than other clerics. Their 'holiness' crucially balances their symbolic ambiguity. Many locals visit Padre Celeste, a monk popular among *popolino* and petty bourgeois throughout Naples and the region, describing him as a holy man close to good souls. Through symbolic association, the hieratic air surrounding Padre Celeste produces beneficial emotions in his visitors. Reminding us of Giovanni's experience of Maria, they say that the joy and peace they feel there they do not feel at mass. Informants' rationalization of their periodic visits gave me a lead into the complexity of this issue.

One early-spring evening I joined Lino, Michele, Salvatore, a stall-holder, and three others in the street just under my window. They were discussing what to take Padre Celeste on the morrow, spelling out processes and values of exchange with which I was by now familiar. The dominant argument was that the spiritual value of their relationship with the monk ruled out money while allowing good-quality food and wine or spirits. The discussion moved onto much less familiar ground with the group's reaction to Salvatore's decision to give him "nu bellu regal" (a nice gift), meaning an expensive one. In a mixture of reproach and scorn for Salvatore's unspoken motives, they asked, 'What's so special between you and the monk?' 'What are you expecting to buy?' 'Don't you see that he may get used to expensive presents and, then, poor us!?' The last comment clearly indicated an interest in keeping what the group regarded as a positive balance in their exchanges with the monk. The other comments conflicted, however, with the fact that it is usually left to individuals to decide independently how much they want to invest in an exchange, especially in one of such highly symbolic value. And yet, those comments obviously had an accepted rationale, and they were not posed as questions that Salvatore was expected to answer. Apparently only I needed answers.

A remark of Lino's was particularly interesting: 'Salvatò, I know you feel obliged, but you're overdoing it.' Salvatore's reply that he was not such a rascal and that he really felt affection for Padre Celeste was met with scepticism and sarcasm. As the angry Salvatore left, the party broke up, and I could grasp only Lino's grumbling about Salvatore's being 'interested', and about some wins in the lotteries and at a raffle.[35] Back in my lodgings, I kept feeling that there was more than just inconsistency to the quarrel, and, anyway, by then I had learned to take 'inconsistencies' seriously.

Recollection of an old novel written by the controversial Neapolitan novelist and journalist Matilde Serao (1902; also 1973 [1884]),[36] helped to make sense of this episode and of other scattered information. Serao devotes pages to *lotto* and to the *assistiti*'s relationships with the good souls, and with people who believe in their powers, and she mentions monks among the *assistiti*. This places the group's behaviour in a new perspective.[37] Salvatore had felt so confident about the numbers he had extracted from Padre Celeste's speech that he had placed several bets on them. The connection between the monk's holiness, the lottery and people's gifts clarified not only Salvatore's excessive gratitude but also Lino's linking that gratitude to the monetary value of Salvatore's gift (and to his successful bets) and the resentful Salvatore's inability to deny that link. Such a connection, unethical by these people's explicit standards, is very central in their practices. They may well tend to identify clerics almost exclusively with liturgical formality, but they also believe that Padre Celeste's 'faculty' for communicating with the good souls and the value of his speech are strengthened by his 'holiness'.

Having got through the crowd of visitors on the monk's weekly reception day, people are quiet, respectful, and listen carefully. Money is offered to the church, but it is excluded from people's exchanges with the monk as inconsistent with the concept of holiness, with the spirituality of any event in which the *popolino* approach the sacred and with the purity that is required of their intentions. Banned as a motivation, money must play an unstated, indirect role. There was probably an (unacknowledged) element of envy in the attitudes towards Salvatore just described, but his behaviour was criticized mainly because gifts should remain credible complements of the actors' devotion and affection rather than part of specific exchanges involving the calculation of desirable returns. Even supposing that Padre Celeste was unaware of what was being transacted, Salvatore's expensive gift would have violated this unspoken logic by asserting his gratitude for something of material value.

This domain of belief is not immune from potential conflict. When questioned, my informants express an awareness of wrongdoing in their 'using', as they say, 'spiritually gifted people for monetary purposes'. Moreover, many understand *assistiti*'s accepting gifts because 'they're poor, ill and can't bet themselves' but resent what they describe as Padre Celeste's pretension of ignorance ('Why does he think people give him so many presents?'). However, these themes (and the underlying cynicism) normally go unmentioned on both sides of the exchange. Obedience to this normative rule helps to prevent the damaging effects of cultural and practical tension; it also protects the monk's presumed holiness and, most important, his 'unawareness of his faculties'.

This belief that the holy *assistiti* lose their powers if they become aware of their monetary value or concerned with making a monetary profit suggests that the *popolino* have extrapolated the legitimacy of the deliberate pursuit of monetary interest from this domain of exchange. The monk's holiness – stressed, in the eyes of my informants, by his popularity among people who are not interested in the lottery[38] – helps to make their monetary investments (the gifts, that is, and the bets) meet their sense of worthiness. In contrast, the secular *assistiti*, who are aware of their powers and legitimately extract material returns, are an interesting case of liminality in which the transactional aspect is acceptable as long as it remains moderate, indirect and unmentioned. This case of mundane liminality, more problematically than others (e.g., prostitutes and moneylenders), illustrates the relationship of the *popolino*'s entrepreneurial attitude to a moral rationale that allows flexibility in the affairs of this world and the other world without pre-empting social norms or the (however unspecified) terms of exchange.

While my bourgeois informants are casual about their hopes regarding the lottery, saying that they have nothing to lose in trying, the *popolino* often describe their betting not simply as vice or leisure but as a risky activity performed in the hope of *radically* changing one's life. However, their explicit admission that this is why they bet regularly – which in some cases explains indebtedness – lends little or no strength to the argument that they behave irrationally in this field. Certainly, it does not make it any easier for us to sympathize with the view of rationality by which, for example, Gramsci, who mentions Serao's work, describes lotto as 'the opium of the poor' (1975: 402–7, esp. p. 406 and, more generally, 1950). Instead, people's activities in this field warn us about recognizing that received categories, such as the opposition between the spiritual and the material, may well be inventions of our understanding that get in the way of grasping what others are doing. Quite in agreement with the contextual situation of exchange studied thus far, relationships with the *assistiti* are an aspect of these people's bringing together diverse aspects and meanings of their lives. In this rationality they are seen to have practical relevance, in the sense of reducing risks in a highly unpredictable domain of action, at the same time contributing to personal identity through good relations with the sacred supramundane. However strange and liminal, the *assistiti* are thus integrated into local life even when, by (indirectly) extracting monetary returns from their faculties, they place themselves at the limits of normality. Their role is a sublimation, in purity, of that of moneylenders and *rammari*. In contrast, homosexuals and transsexuals represent further steps towards marginalization.

Sexual ambiguity, like ambivalence, is part of the transcendental self of this city. St Gennaro, its protector, is the friend and foe in whom, traditionally, Neapolitans place their devotion and hope. He also symbolizes this quintessential form of ambiguity, as his holy maleness is periodically transformed into femaleness through the ritual liquefaction of the blood of his martyrdom.[39] This is a powerful symbolic equivalent of the periodic flow of the menstrual blood – the very arbiter, that is, of life but also a pregnant symbol of impurity. The event has miraculous, ambivalent power, involving simultaneously a powerful collective supplication (in the sense of Hertz 1922: 15) and a forecast of the city's fortune or misfortune, life or death.[40] At the receiving end of such ambivalence, the *popolino* use a carefully balanced mixture of pleading and berating when they ritually address the saint.

In religious terms, the obvious ambiguity of homosexuals (male, *ricchiun'*; female, *masculill'*) challenges the established taxonomies of sex and gender. Some contemporary writers argue that this challenge is, in fact, a symbolic dissonance that confirms the complementarity between male and female (Moberly 1983: 29). Traditionally, homosexuality is condemned by Christianity as contrary to the will and purpose of God for mankind. With minor differences, scriptural references treat it as sinful sexuality unmitigated by reproductive purpose. By transgressive sex, homosexuals are destined to an unsettled life and a troubled afterlife but not excluded from redemption. They are described as abnormal (physically and psychologically) and liminal, and an embarrassment for their significant others (especially their kin). Like prostitutes (and ex-prostitutes), they have access to ritual situations from which 'ordinary' men and women are formally excluded,[41] but they are not regarded as absolute abominations or treated with unqualified condemnation. Also in this case there is no evidence in the attitudes of my informants of the harsh biblical treatment of this subject.[42] Instead, probably because this form of ambiguity brings to mind transcendental powers (e.g., St Gennaro) which are central to their collective consciousness, their attitudes contradict the common stereotype of Neapolitan and particularly *popolino* machismo.

Transsexuals (*femmeniell'*) represent extreme sexual ambiguity and transgression. They play no relevant part in ordinary life, and, despite being described as 'unfortunate', they are marginalized through mockery and contempt. In contrast, homosexuals are described as 'different' persons with disgusting sexual habits but also as *brave persone* (good persons). Normal people would not go out with them but also would not offend them without good reason or refuse to interact with them *in public*. During the case-studies I asked questions about homosexuals as problematic only to discover that, except for domains of meaning and activity specifically concerned with physical power and (lack or excess of) masculinity, they are widely integrated. In Giovanni's universe they are tailors, hairdressers, cleaners, sellers of smuggled cigarettes; in that of Lino they are shop assistants, council employees, tradespeople, and so forth. Like ordinary women, they may be mediators in social relations and exchanges. But they may also perform other forms of mediation that are unorthodox even by local standards.

For example, homosexuals are often believed to *interact* with spirits.[43] This exceptional quality makes them imperfect members of their fellows' universes, links at once *creative* and *numinous* between the ordinary and ordered side of everyday life and the extraordinary, liminal, non-sacred and potentially dangerous but powerful supramundane. Giulio is a middle-aged unmarried businessman widely admired for his wit, joviality and humanity; his homosexuality is widely known but seldom mentioned. He is said to welcome contact with spirits. Various informants explained his 'immunity' to their evil will in terms of a causal relation between his absolute ambiguity and liminality and his unsettled and troubled ontological condition. The fact that he is unmarried makes the label *squitat'* (without quiet; unsettled, or restless), normally used for bachelors of a certain age, particularly fitting.[44] Above all, his homosexuality is a cause of permanent, serious sin. He feels unaccepted and unprotected by the Church in doctrinal and spiritual terms and in terms of his relationships with its ministers. However, as in other cases of mundane liminality, this does not affect his private informal devotion to St Gennaro or his participation in pilgrimages to Montevergine. Nor does his ambiguity jeopardize his integration into the local community. His homosexuality is seen alternatively as a weakness or as an illness. However, as the *popolino* always sympathetically forgive human weakness and never take advantage of illness, not only does his condition go unmentioned but he is mainly described as good-hearted and friendly. Moreover, because of that condition, he is sometimes mobilized as a resource option.

As we know, the behaviour of spirits normally eludes the control of the living. The local priest, carefully kept in the dark regarding the real reason for his being summoned (he would otherwise refuse to come), may be called to bestow the relative protection of his formal blessing on a house believed to be haunted by spirits. At a very different symbolic level, the visit of a homosexual may make the inhabitants 'feel safer'. On two occasions reported to me Giulio has played this role. In both cases there was only a superficial similarity with Mario's checking my house, for the ritual and symbolic power attributed to Giulio seems to have provided an alternative way of establishing control over these spirits' arbitrary influence over this life. According to an informant, as a last resort Giulio slept alone in his flat for one night, 'fighting away' the spirits that made it 'difficult to live in': 'My wife got hurt with all sorts of things: the red-hot iron, slippery ladders and floors; children were constantly ill, and the younger one was hit by a car. I fell seriously ill and lost my job. Moreover, I couldn't move because I couldn't afford to pay more.'

The unusual power of certain homosexuals to *interact* with the supramundane further challenges the relatively standardized Catholic system of supramundane intermediation, protection and favour-bestowing and the related themes of enlightenment, miracles and exorcism. Although indirect, this challenge is, in a sense, far more substantial than that posed by other popular forms of interaction with the mediatory, favour-bestowing sacred. These religious expressions, I have noted, are contemptuously tolerated and only partially controlled by the Church. In this case of sexual ambiguity the idea of extraordinary sinning produces meanings and values that escape almost completely the official religious rationale but nonetheless have crucial importance in actors' practical and spiritual lives.

Those who relate to the irregular sides of the supramundane appear to be basically united by their common liminality. The sexual habits, physical appearance, special work activities, etc. that create their mundane liminality also explain the practical and moral advantages that ordinary people derive from it, but these peculiarities do not in themselves justify special faculties or their significance in ordinary people's lives. Expanding on an earlier point, I would argue that it is, rather, through these symbolic dealings with the liminal in life and death that the *popolino* exert some control over aspects of existence that have the potential to threaten their establishment of order and security.

Intermediary networks

The study of extraordinary persons has clarified not only the processes of moral, symbolic and practical control over specific situations and resources but also the power structure to which they belong. Apart from earning their group's gratitude, these people establish relations of friendship and respect with powerful individuals such as favour-bestowers, criminal or not, thus becoming part of changing and rather flexible intermediary networks. This concept of an intermediary network is quite distant from the idea of horizontal ties among patrons instrumental to a hierarchy of patronage relations (Silverman 1965). Transactions and favour relations involving local people – liminal or ordinary – are too flexible, shifting, and multifaceted and the resulting networks too negotiable for them to belong to a fixed hierarchy or to have real filtering power (Boissevain 1966, 1977; Blok 1974; Silverman 1977).

With a few exceptions, the relations of the *popolino* with the supramundane are decreasingly mediated by living agents such as clerics or holy persons such as Padre Pio and Madre Flora. At the same time, they strongly emphasize the role of dead intermediaries with other, more powerful dead. Their relationships with these sacred supramundane beings are profoundly religious relationships of devotion between individual living and individual dead which circumvent a Church increasingly called to play a formalistic, well-paid legitimating role. They include protection in (unspecified) exchange for memory and care and symbolic, moral and perhaps psychological sublimation.

Something similar applies to mundane relations of mediation. We have seen that ordinary people's growing cynicism about traditional favour-bestowers like Ciro and Pasquale has corresponded to the decline of this kind of entrepreneurship, while that of ordinary people like Michele, Lino and Giovanni has evolved into more flexible, individual and complex forms. Cases like Ciro's provide, however, significant examples of the power of an entrepreneur who can develop contacts in the bureaucracy, politics, the Church, local associations (religious and lay), the social services, etc., and pull these resources together in a career strategy characterized by professional brokership. In such cases, one person becomes a crucial 'junction' between different networks, enjoying relations of alliance with other powerful locals, ordinary and extraordinary.

It would be difficult to see the relatively new kind of entrepreneurship performed by Michele and, particularly, Giovanni as specialized intermediation, or as replaceable by formalized intermediating agencies (in the sense argued by Boissevain (1977)). We have discussed how different networks and spheres of power are connected through a person via marriage, ritual kinship or relations of friendship and neighbourhood. It is equally indicative that a non-professional and occasional favour-bestower like

Michele draws on his contacts in the workplace, in politics, and among people like Mario and Padre Celeste as well as on his friendship with the chairman of a local religious association who controls the organization of official rituals and the association's relations with the church, the neighbourhood and other associations. The important difference between Michele and professional favour-bestowers like Ciro is that, in the case of Michele, the junction is embodied not by one person but, rather, by a temporary and shifting alliance between two persons, neither of whom has exclusive control over resources.[45] These alliances are an aspect of the agency/structure relationship that influences not only the communication process between levels of urban life (at the neighbourhood level and between the neighbourhood and the rest of the city and beyond) but, more important, the structure of relations of power and imperfect competition.

Liminality and the broadening of options

Our study of ambiguity and liminality has shown that certain persons are often excluded from the 'stage-representation' (very broadly in Goffman's (1959) sense) of ordinary life despite their factual importance. The unspoken exchanges in which they are involved emphasize the point that individuals' control of important resources – and, basically, of the interests of successful entrepreneurship – depends on their ability to elaborate morally acceptable reconciliations between events and meanings which are potentially conflicting in moral, religious and practical terms. Equally crucial is management of the relationship between personal identity, norms and the pursuit of interest which meets the complex requirements of the interaction between the non-material and the material in this culture of fulfilment.

The domains of bureaucracy, politics and power, supposedly impersonal in the West, tend to be personalized in Naples. It can be safely argued that this corresponds to a more general erosion of the impersonal that makes (relative) secrecy – and, more generally, the relevance of the unspoken – dependent upon the very activities and operations of thought that secrecy generates. Even in the most problematic circumstances, these dynamics of secrecy do not result from the unbridgeable split of the personal into the socially 'objective' and the socially 'subjective' that Simmel (1964) regarded as characteristic of depersonalization in Western society.

Unspoken resources and exchanges do not simply coincide with acquiescence, retreat into the private sphere, or marginalization. Instead, actors use privacy and confidentiality as negotiable resources in coping with problematic relations and redefining them in acceptable and useful ways.

Offering stimuli for separate comparative analysis, the management of secrecy has emerged, more generally, as a central aspect of *public* (but unspoken) communication that affects social discourse as a whole. Indeed, this social system would probably collapse if it were truly 'incorporative' (Paine 1976) or *Geimende*-oriented (Allum 1973, after Tönnies 1955), and it would probably become totally uncontrollable if these transactions remained unexplained and liminal instead of being, in fact, ordered through normalization. When secrecy is untenable and seriousness dangerous, joking, laughter and the negotiated use of the liminal become functional to such normalization.

This control of the relationship between the obvious and the hidden in religious and social morality and in exchange and entrepreneurship supports the public reconstruction of certain (ambiguous) individuals' positions. Secrecy is not a product of alienation, nor does it merely shelter actors from external pressure (Simmel 1964, pt 4: chs. 4 and 3). Instead, the ethnography of domains such as the extraordinary and the ambiguous suggests that the management of the unmentioned and secret addresses the rational balance between exchange and morality and among transgression, control and order in a way that takes into account the ecclesiastical rationale but is not restricted by (or to) it. Thus liminality is controlled, and the inherent activities and meanings, combined and recombined, become part of the recognized order. More precisely, thus the rationality of liminality broadens options in terms of the pursuit of personal betterment for, through the entrepreneurial management of the liminal, viable resources are constructed in the domains of personal identity, inner life, contacts and monetary gain.

6

The mass diffusion of contacts: redefined power relations, values of representation

Throughout European history, the importance of personal contacts has taken many forms and labels, the best known of which are nepotism, patronage and clientelism. The concept that contacts are crucial in coping with legal and bureaucratic organization is one aspect of the combination of group and individual interests that has profoundly influenced urban life (Weber 1978, esp. ch. 16) and, in fact, the rationalization of civil society.

Neapolitans say, 'Chi ten' sant' va 'mparavis'' (Contacts with saints get you to heaven). Our study of strong continuous interaction between resources of very different kinds has suggested that the *popolino* are bearers of a culture that links this maxim with values such as cleverness (*sapè fà*), 'God helps those who help themselves', 'I don't want to be subject to anyone', and 'If you behave like a sheep, you'll become a wolf's meal.' The political framework of this aspect of the agency/structure relationship in Naples indicates a complex moral conflict between different purposes, expectations and values.[1] An outline, however rough, ought to address at least two major issues: first, the dichotomy between ordinary people's entrepreneurial spirit and the left's strategic interest in the formalization of social relations and the state-sponsored industrialization (and the related proletarianization) of the South and, second and more important, the historical bias generated by central-government assistance implemented through local potentates (Lepre 1963; Graziani and Pugliese 1979; Gribaudi 1980; Mingione 1985; Pardo 1993). This policy, particularly abusive because unsupported by structural investments,[2] is resented by many Southerners as undignified benefaction (see also Prato (1995) and, with reference to different ethnographies, Hann (1996)). It has long been inspired by the relationship between political power and bureaucratic, financial, ecclesiastical and criminal powers (Villari 1979 [1885]; De Giovanni 1983; Garofalo 1984; La Palombara 1987; Allum 1973).

Apart from criminality and political corruption, a well-known by-product of this policy of assistance is that *rights* have been traditionally presented, pursued and granted as *favours*. However, control over resources and benefits – licit and illicit – has become diffused throughout Naples society; it is no longer the prerogative of specific groups. Nowadays, ordinary people are generally not isolated, dependent on specialized favour-bestowers and subject to the despotism of the system. A corrupt and powerful element of the ruling élite may well have imposed the restrictions of political clientelism on 'those below', often forcing into illegitimacy people's commitment to personal relations and individual entrepreneurship. It is a mistake, however, to regard bureaucracy as polit- ically and morally above human agency. The empirical evidence suggests that 'those below', accustomed but not reconciled to the situation, have become active agencies capable of redefining it by making choices which, aware of the 'social character of self-interest' (Herzfeld 1987: 154), chal- lenge this logic of power from the inside.

In the light of the background situation studied thus far, I shall argue here that these social and political relations belong to a 'moral climate', a 'way of doing things', that cannot simply be explained by the Neapolitans' supposedly predatory instinct and proneness to succumb to corruption and clientelism (Allum 1973; Graziano 1980; Altan 1986) or by the improper use that politicians, trade-unionists and bureaucrats make of their public offices (Altan 1986). We need, instead, to develop a per- spective that, drawing the line as carefully as possible between fact and fiction, accounts for the constraints on individuals' action but does not underestimate the complex relationship between identity values, norma- tive flexibility and personal interest and, I stress, 'disinterest' (Parry 1986) that allows their strategies to cut across crucial spheres of public life.

Entrepreneurialism vs. dependence: the urban case

As I have pointed out, the anthropological study of largely urbanized European countries such as Italy has focused on the rural dimension. It is fair to say that recent research avoids describing peasants (and people who live in small towns more generally) as disadvantaged by a critical shortage of power and resources. The mainstream argument has been, however, that as 'clients' they are basically constrained into long-term relations of depen- dence, unbalanced exchange and, according to some writers, class exploita- tion with resource-controllers ('patrons') who, drawing on ideological

(Li Causi 1975; Littlewood 1977), mythical (Silverman 1965, 1977) or. factual (Boissevain 1966, 1977) bases intervene between citizens and the state (see also Blok 1974; Eisenstadt and Roninger 1984). More recently, it has been argued that these relations redistribute social responsibility through a deliberate and conscious exchange of exploitation for protection, constituting successful forms of manipulative collusion to extract spoils from the state (Korovkin 1988: 123–4).

I have advocated an approach that avoids a conceptual reduction of power to exchange[3] and of exchange to monetary and political transactions. This is particularly important in the urban field, where the categories of power outlined above are historically inconsistent. The control allowed by the relatively more rigid social organization of rural areas (Bloch 1949) is inevitably restricted in the city (Weber 1978: ch. 16. 1). To cite a Classical example, Fustel de Coulanges (1980 [1864]) has shown that when clientship was urbanized in ancient Rome, it lost its moral (particularly religious) credentials – clients (themselves without property) stopped being the property of their masters. They acquired information about other clients and patrons, established new contacts and, most important, developed a new culture of clientship.

Our analysis ought to account for the adaptation, or maladaptation, of dependent clientship to the flexible and multifaceted (by definition) urban situation. Clientship was a key problem in the medieval city. The new urban situation jeopardized the power relations (Bloch 1949) that marked the feudal distinction between those with political responsibility, who held almost complete power over things and people, and those with little or no power, responsibility, or scope for choice. Increasingly attracted by the new cities, people found themselves without patrons, work or identity. In the absence of the urbanization (and modernization) of the old system of patronage (Cohn 1957) and of effective protection against banditry and warfare (Bloch 1949), those former villagers became 'free' people with little freedom of choice (see, e.g., Elliott and McCrone 1982: ch. 2).

In their pursuit of an urban niche, these rural–urban migrants were drastically restricted by their lack of the culture necessary to construct strategies for acquiring essential resources (Cohn 1957). This question of survival soon transformed them into a mobile threat to a young social organization, the precursors of a devastating series of revolutionary movements. Attacks on the system with religious themes became widespread as various 'heresies' challenged the closed predicament (in the sense of Horton 1982) of the order the Church had established jointly with sovereigns. In Naples the Church and the state apparently enjoyed firm control, but in fact individuals quietly practised their unorthodox ideas (Ambrasi 1980) according to a distinctive pattern in the history of the city and its traditionally urbanized inhabitants (De Rosa 1987).

Davis states that patronage exists 'whenever men adopt a posture of deference to those more powerful than they and gain access to resources as a result' (1977: 132). Anthropologists who specialize in rural Europe might want to ask whether the concept of patronage explains even rural-based relations of power, particularly nowadays.[4] Regarding this urban case of Naples, we need to understand the complex issue of the 'power of the powerless' in other terms. My contention is that actors' basically negotiational (rather than confrontational) approach should not mislead us into believing that their actions are inevitably manipulated by patrons (or patron-brokers) who hold financial power and useful contacts, extending to government agencies at the regional and national levels (see Silverman 1965: 178). This would make it necessary to treat command over resources and benefits and command over people and actions as a single category when maintaining the separation of these aspects of power (Ortner 1984) is crucial to our investigation of the relationship between actors' entrepreneurialism and observable cultural and socio-political change.

Getting through the labyrinths of power

In a bureaucratic organization, Gellner notes, 'the individual should act or refrain from acting in a systematic and orderly manner, in accordance with what stated and known rules prescribe: indeed it is plausibly argued that such organizations are only possible if staffed by men who understand and respect this ideal' (1969: 91). This ideal and the way in which the system actually works are two, not mutually exclusive (Stirling 1968: 51), aspects typical of Western bureaucracies. In contemporary Italy, the all-pervasive bureaucratic process has two levels, the formal and the informal, sometimes illegal or semi-legal (Graziano 1980; Ferraresi 1980). Officially, in accordance with the main characteristics of modern bureaucracy (Beetham 1987; Weber 1978: 956–8), communication channels, authority, spheres of competence, responsibility and career prospects are well defined, technical and hierarchical; personal interest in the office and favouritism are banned, and written orders are the rule. In fact, despite the guarantee of continuity (the office is a full-time and secure salaried occupation) and technical expertise throughout the system, things are made notoriously different not just by the informal negotiation of hierarchy and procedures that is necessary (Blau 1972) to a working bureaucracy, but by the gaps engendered by illegitimate political interests and corruption. The inherent connection between public services and profit (monetary and otherwise) and the related competition both among bureaucrats and among members of the public may be problematic and technically unsustainable, but it is recognized as a fact (not necessarily always convenient or favourable) throughout the system.

The basic question lies in the link between politics and bureaucracy in democratic society (Smith 1987; Beetham 1987). Throughout Europe, bureaucracy and the civil service are increasingly controlled by politicians. This control takes various forms. In Italy all too often the bureaucrat as a person, especially when connected with (or dependent on) political bosses, prevails over the office (Aliberti 1987). Thus, all too often both the office and relations with the applicant are personalized, privatized. It is an apparent paradox that this bureaucratic practice restricts the scope for intransigence and justification of arbitrary actions among bureaucrats. On more orthodox levels, in this situation it creates advantages for bureaucrats, their political connections, and citizens who seek favours instead of claiming benefits by allowing them to achieve their goals faster. It belongs to a general pattern of personalization of politics and use of the public domain which raises important issues regarding ordinary people's conceptualization and management of bureaucratic and political relations and the extent to which they and those who operate the system share a culture. Case materials on the bureaucratic and political dealings of the *popolino* and the petty bourgeois will help us to address these issues of value, organization and power.

Having lost her husband shortly after he became formally employed, Michele's cousin Carmela and her teenage children lived in a local *basso* on a small pension and occasional help from relatives. Carmela's life-style degenerated further when the 1980 earthquake seriously damaged the building where she lived, forcing her to move to a post-earthquake camp. She remained there until she was granted a purpose-built council flat almost five years later. Other local *popolino*, we know, coped differently.

Soon after her arrival in the camp, Carmela began selling smuggled cigarettes, soft drinks, sweets and household goods; thus transferring to the new situation a traditional skill practised by her neighbours in the quarter. She did this, she says, in order to survive, and yet once she had obtained a council job with Michele's help she refused to sell the goodwill to a drug-dealer neighbour. Instead, she entrusted the unlicensed business to her children while continuing to manage it herself. Having obtained the favour, Carmela severed the links with Michele, who believes that she wanted to avoid the long-term moral implications of obligation.

Keeping in mind the nature of these *popolino*'s entrepreneurialism, let us now focus on its political significance. On this occasion, local contacts introduced Michele to a right-wing member of parliament with power over council employment. The meeting produced only half-promises. However, far from feeling lost in a hostile or uncontrollable world (Allum 1973: 10), Michele adopted an alternative strategy. He knew that he could do without a protecting (and dominating) political boss, and he knew that he had time, because the council is notoriously slow in dealing with job applications.[5] He contacted Caiazza, an *assessore*'s secretary to whom he had been introduced years before by Papele, a local tradesman and 'well-connected' council clerk who exchanges his contacts for cash to speed the council's dealing with files, applications, etc.[6]

Writing on Central Italy, Silverman (1977) has pointed out that favours may be effectively presented as signs of benevolence and generosity. My experience suggests that, while this may be *said* by both parties in the transaction, the favour-seeker normally regards the benefits he obtains as direct results of his ability and investments, not as concessions from pseudo-friends or protectors. From the beginning, Michele's relationship with Caiazza was consistent with this rationale of contacts and favours. For instance, having learned that Caiazza needed some expensive medicine, he managed to obtain it free by giving a small present at his own expense to a friend. Caiazza was not yet very powerful, but because Michele thought that his career was promising he continued to keep in touch. As we have seen, he has made other such investments, with contrasting results, by linking the concept of friendship with the culture of 'One never knows' which, throughout Naples, motivates all sorts of people to establish links with those who control 'public' resources and benefits.

Since the job for which Carmela had formally applied fell under the jurisdiction of an *assessore* belonging to another party of the centre-left ruling coalition, Caiazza gave Michele a letter of introduction to Giordano, a clerk in the secretariat of the correct *assessore*. This man's allegiance to a different party was irrelevant both to Caiazza, for whom he was 'a friend', and to Michele, who shares most ordinary people's pragmatic view of formal political taxonomies and rejection of their associated potential stranglehold on the individual. After much stair-climbing, two missed meetings, long waits in vain outside Giordano's office and several tips to the usher who knew Giordano's whereabouts and schedule, Michele 'finally managed to catch the man and give him Caiazza's letter'. Giordano, Michele says, was courteous and helpful. Carmela had not, he found, been shortlisted, but, 'considering the needy case', he promised he 'would do his best' when the committee met again, to please his friend Caiazza. Michele continued to visit Giordano's office regularly 'just to say hello, bring him Caiazza's regards and see whether there was any service I could do for him'. The list of successful applicants published some weeks later included Carmela.

The grateful Michele declared himself 'at Caiazza's disposal' and bought him a painting he knew he fancied, anticipating the return of the half million lire (about £200) that it cost from Carmela. This was an inexpensive gift, for such favours notoriously cost millions of lire. Sometimes it is agreed that, having given an advance, the favour-seeker will pay the rest of the money in instalments from his future stipend, but this provides no guarantee; the transaction may well end in the favour-seeker's losing the 'deposit'. Michele valued the favour he had received. Above all, he knew from experience (direct and indirect) whom he owed and how soon and in what form gratitude should be expressed, and he knew that, following their dealing with his case, the two secretaries' relationship had become closer.

This episode illuminates important issues of morality and action in this domain of power relations and, more generally, in the relationship between individuals and the system. The bitterness occasioned by Carmela's ingratitude was largely compensated for by the various benefits resulting from Michele's performance, a show of both good-heartedness and prestigious and useful connections. We know that even as a neophyte to the system Michele had been a discerning entrepreneur. Instead of fatalistically bowing to patronage, he gained manoeuvring space (and a better position in his group) by using the politician's patronizing attitude to transfer obligation to more promising normative ground. Specified obligation, we have observed, demands reciprocation in the relatively arbitrary terms established by the favour-bestower. However, this recent performance of Michele's exemplifies what has become a dominant pattern in favour relations. Obligation often becomes a vehicle whereby the entrepreneurial favour-seeker extracts satisfaction from the exchange. The transactional balance depends, of course, on the nature of the relationship that the agents have established. But obligation generally opens up options in social relations, its effects extending beyond the accomplishment of reciprocation.

These changes only marginally concern the traditional, clientelistic favour-bestowers, who are gradually losing their power. Instead, they mark the entrepreneurship of Andrea and of 'non-professional' favour-bestowers such as Michele. Referring again to the case presented in Chapter 4, it seems clear now that Michele's learning and achieving more despite Pasquale's greater experience originated a process whereby, quite in line with medium-term changes among the *popolino*, he takes advantage of the diversification of spheres and relations of power. I have argued that the results that Lino obtains through a matter-of-fact use of his skills and experience are obtained by Michele (and his family) through an emphasis – not necessarily instrumental – on normative themes. This is, however, a *difference* not a *polarization*. The case just presented exemplifies the process by which Michele now draws on his knowledge of the logic and relations of *sottogoverno* to approach relevant bureaucrats without having to see his enterprise limited by their declared commitment to different parties.

It would, I think, be simplistic to interpret this motivated cynicism as pure instrumentalism. Instead, it corresponds to the positive interaction between these Neapolitans' rationality, their groups' expectations and their changing conceptualization of their relationship to the system. That such interaction increasingly runs counter to the culture and motivations of clientelistic politicians and administrators may complicate the situation from the latter's viewpoint, but it also underlines the sociological value of the entrepreneurialism that marks the mass diffusion of contacts and favours.

It is difficult to assess the significance of non-professional favour-bestowing in contemporary relations of power. We know that this domain of the favour system is complicated by widespread offers and promises of help. This form of generosity is obviously less instrumental and exploita-tive than that of the clientelistic *pezzi grossi* and their professional brokers, but it does not completely relieve the 'beneficed' of the cajoling and manoeuvring so abhorred by the young. Nor does it prevent competition; it is, instead, one of its subtlest forms. Non-professional favour-bestowing, I have argued, is a rational form of investment that enhances self-esteem, power and reputation. A good network also allows actors to *offer* assis-tance without direct returns, thus helping to make their entrepreneurship more moral and therefore more rewarding. And when they do not want to – or cannot – mediate, they circumvent the risk of losing face by belittling their contacts. It is deliberate unwillingness to help that is an important exception to their group's general disregard of inconsistency between what they do and what they are supposed to do as favour-bestowers, for such unwillingness violates the culture of mutual help and good-heartedness that marks significant local relations. And yet, regardless of their fre-quency, such violations do not seem to have much effect on the belief that ''a ggent' do quartier' ten' 'o cor' buon'' (people of the quarter are good-hearted). Only apparently does this important moral theme in exchange and competition fly in the face of these people's generally flexible approach. In fact, it provides an illustration of the explanatory redundancy of the concept of irrationality.

This invites reflection. Non-professional favour-bestowing, we know, is an internally differentiated category whose main unifying elements are good skills and a culture of fulfilment based on the concepts of personal ability, local standing and sense of worthiness. Liminal people are extreme expressions of a situation in which moral and spiritual themes, especially when unstated, are crucial in the relationship between different levels of value and action. Even when such themes merely affect the appearance of the situation, they are much more than disguises for instrumental motives, for they are crucial in the symbolic defence from envy and ostracism. This is complicated by the shifting nature of actors' roles. In this situation of mass diffusion of contacts roles may well be reversed, for the one-time favour-seeker may have better contacts than his old favour-bestower.

Lino's actions while a young man have provided a processual example of the incompatibility between the *popolino*'s entrepreneurship and culture of personal independence and the despotism of patronage-oriented *pezzi grossi*. We know that, having severed his links with the instrumentally minded politician through whom he obtained his social-services job, he has partially succeeded in staying away from the political world. Like many other *popolino*, he says that he does not depend on any particular favour-bestower and praises 'anyone who can say the same'. Far from being restricted by this attitude, he has drawn on the diffusion of contacts to construct a relatively successful entrepreneurship that meets the moral demands of his identity and social environment. His management of a serious crisis provoked by clientelism and indiscipline in the workplace highlights central issues of bureaucratic organization in industry (Gouldner 1954; Harris 1986) and political relations.

It all started with Lino's decision to confront Nando, a fellow deputy supervisor and right-wing trade-unionist, also of *popolino* origin, with whom he shared responsibility for the service. In the overheated atmosphere created in the city by the combined effects of administrative inefficiency and social-services workers' wildcat strikes, Nando was encouraging workers' absenteeism and poor production. Lino said he could accept a degree of tolerance because he is one of the many who benefit from (informal) flexibility to look after their businesses. But Nando's behaviour was totally immoral, even considering that a significant proportion of public- and semipublic-sector employees retain the instrumentally interested protection of the *maniglie* through whom they have obtained their jobs and who obviously want to retain their support but know that they cannot take it for granted. As we know, Lino sees in his career prospects an opportunity to better himself in the long term. Improving the dignity of his job, he says, may help him in this task. Moreover, he shares with many *popolino* a strong motivation to 'see Naples improved' and believes that better services would help to check its deterioration. Nando's interests lay, instead, in obtaining the workers' support to climb the hierarchy of his trade union. He found an ally in the branch manager, who belonged to an opposed centre-left trade union but shared his interest in the workers' support. Because Lino's resistance jeopardized their plans, they and the undisciplined workers joined forces in boycotting him, thus adding practical difficulties to the misery of the administrative sanctions taken against him and Nando after their branch was caught red-handed by inspectors.[7] He did, however, receive moral support, advice and practical help from various senior workers and from relatives and local friends.

Lino found naïve my suggestion that he could have taken action through formal channels, including the service's bureaucracy and the trade-union protection to which he was entitled. Instead, through a social-service bureaucrat to whom he gives occasional presents, he obtained information on possible new locations to which Nando could be transferred. In line with the processes of resource mobilization discussed in Chapter 4, he also approached a friend's brother, who is a leftist trade-unionist, for advice on how to cope with the formal measures taken against him and to engineer Nando's removal. Finally, I witnessed how, having invited Nando, the manager and various senior workers to lunch, Lino negotiated an unspoken agreement with the manager, who obviously realized that by continuing to punish him he would antagonize those senior leading figures and the workers whose support they would be able to mobilize. Later Lino legitimated this new situation more broadly through a party given for all the workers. This event completed a strategy for resolving the crisis that would address the formal situation but would also be well received on the shop-floor. The senior workers who had helped him before did so again. Nando moved to another branch and later joined, as a middle-rank activist, the manager's trade union.

Lino's rejection of political clientelism in resolving this crisis raises interesting issues. In the conflict with Nando not only did he prove to have a better knowledge of his human environment, of normative behaviour and of work practices, he also proved to be a better manager of his resources – Nando's formal position in the trade-union hierarchy (and the related network) proving to give him no advantage. He characteristically mobilized trade-unionists, clerks and professionals through local and non-local contacts instead of resorting to the politician through whom he had obtained the job or to his party.[8] Similarly, using the above-mentioned bureaucrat and Andrea, he has obtained the necessary qualifications for a promotion, reciprocating mainly on the moral grounds of friendship (he has given only small presents). Electoral support, he says, was never asked. These transactions associate him with the not strictly instrumental rationale of the mass diffusion of favours. They emphasize the moral value of the gift in relations of unspecified, deferred exchange (Mauss 1966) rather than the favour-seeker's opportunist (or forced) submission. For the occasional favour-bestower such symbolic acknowledgement of his power (and good-heartedness) is a matter of satisfaction that, apart from non-material profits, may yield various kinds of indirect material returns.

The decision to mobilize a politician, trade-unionist or bureaucrat tends to be entrepreneurially rather than politically or emotionally motivated. Actors' strategies in this domain suggest that, with limitations, they make revocable but morally consistent choices in a situation in which it is increasingly difficult for the favour-bestower to retain control or withdraw the favour previously given. It would, of course, be hypocritical not to recognize that such strategies are formally incongruous and from the clientelist perspective inconceivable. But it would be equally hypocritical to ignore the fact that these people are sufficiently discerning to identify and expand resource spheres that have certainly not been created for their benefit. Their informed disregard of the formal taxonomies of politics does not make them unreliable opportunists. It may be instrumentally motivated, as in the case of Nando; more generally, it belongs to the qualified realism whereby the actors expand their resource systems by overtly supporting candidates of different parties. For example, in an interpretation of the logic of the competitive party model of this parliamentary democracy (Bobbio 1987, Prato 1995), Luigi, who now supports the PDS, in the past has often voted for a Social Democrat deputy and a Christian Democrat senator, having indirectly received a favour from the former and having been asked by a friend to support the latter. As it is well known to observers of the processes of *sottogoverno*, Italian politicians have traditionally used this situation to their advantage, often in an obviously distorted way. However, although this attitude of the *popolino* does not match the requirements of historical materialism it cannot be explained as 'false consciousness'.[9] On the contrary, it is no accident that it agrees with Beetham's (1987: 100) concept of a defence of individual choice in opposition to the demands of the expansion of the political sphere.[10]

The professor and the silly broker: elements of trust and independence

As I met Andrea, early in the fieldwork, it seemed important that he had acknowledged my task by calling me professor and, having said that he knew about and approved of my research, by making an open invitation to visit him at work, meaning the social service, and at his local office. This quasi-ritual legitimation by so prominent a local man had quickly produced results; Lino and the other *popolino* had not only begun to cooperate more willingly but become overtly interested in my friendship. However, it had soon become clear that even this form of trust is rarely blind faith. When Andrea found himself in the midst of the career crisis described in Chapter 3, he withdrew his cooperation. I learned of this sudden change in our relationship indirectly. One afternoon I arrived at his office only to find, instead, his assistant, who informed me that Andrea could not see me that day and was, indeed, too busy to continue the interviews with me. I was more disappointed than surprised. Andrea had been a precious source of information, but he had shown some reluctance and was not the first informant to behave in this way. Days later, when I bumped into him, he said that he was worried about who would have access to my notes. This change of attitude soon became widely known but found no sympathy among other informants. Andrea's previous acceptance had helped some of them to make the risky choice (I might still be dishonest in my purpose) of cooperating with '*o prufessor*', which was paying some dividends in terms of satisfaction and information. Thus, knowing me and my task better, these informants now made a new choice which endorsed the previous one, dismissing Andrea's fears as 'silly' and motivated by 'excessive anxiety' – implying scant judgement.

This typical example of the *popolino*'s independence of judgement in morally problematic situations emphasizes the discerning sense of trust and sentiment that marks the morality of their interactions, especially with favour-bestowers (religious, political or other). Their attitude towards Andrea bears no sign of the caution they show in dealing with Pasquale and Ciro and with the *pezzi grossi*, but even in Andrea's case trust remains a rationally controlled value which, like affection and loyalty, lacks the necessary strength to support the 'patron's' (or his agent's) exploitation of 'clients', as perhaps it did in the past. Instead, far from being institutions or emotions, these values are made to respond to the requirements of a rationale that closely relates risk to the expected results. This significantly affects the economics of social relations. In modern Naples, the moral aspects of social relations may help to explain transactions throughout the favour system, thus playing an ordering role. But it is also clear that, as actors' resource options improve, their dependence on the generosity – or ruthless speculation – of specialized favour-bestowers decreases, and so does the scope of inequality.

I have observed that when the bourgeois are favour-seekers the *popolino* favour-bestower obtains, beyond obligation, the satisfaction of having helped someone who is socially superior. There may also be improvement in the favour-bestower's position in the significant group, but there is no social identification or uplift. While negotiating distance, the *popolino* believe that social difference remains, beyond appearance, but they also say that it can be redefined through access to money, qualifications and 'privileges' (see a later section) and that what they learn from personal relationships with the socially better off contributes to such 'redefinition' by allowing them to better themselves. We know that these themes become particularly significant among the young, who also express greater social frustration.

The apparent erasure of boundaries can have various results including co-optation. In this market-oriented urban situation people are sufficiently sophisticated to recognize such apparent erasure for what it is and let it affect only the way the transaction is represented, not its essence. However, the fact that different relations occur between socially different people at different times helps to keep the balance of inequality in power relations unstable. This opens up options across the spectrum.

Entrepreneurial morals across social organization
This rationale is part of a framework in which self-interest may well not be necessarily unscrupulous but does inform important variations in actors' performance of social duties. The varied interest of many in this way of doing things gives new meaning to the point made earlier that when exchange extends into illegality actors do not need to be real criminals to acquiesce in it. In examining different attitudes in this regard, it will be helpful to recall that individually negotiated degrees of morality, tolerance of the illegitimate and management of the interaction between the material and the non-material play a discriminative role in actors' life-styles and careers. In addition, the construction of viable resources depends more on each individual's experience, motivations and ability to comply with the entrepreneurial rationale that informs this culture of a good life than on pre-existing opportunities in terms of personal history and universe. Social and financial achievement is, we know, cast in this interplay of facts and values.

The complexity of this situation of imperfect competition is emphasized by the petty bourgeoisie's relation to these issues of moral and practical control. Unlike signora Pina, most of them appear to be cut off from their *popolino* origins and the associated culture and, to a certain extent, network. Typical examples are provided by Umberto (a semiprofessional relative of Lino, now in his forties), my landlord Gino and his fiancée, Patrizia, and Patrizia's sister, Flora, and their parents.

Patrizia and Flora's parents, who run a small local shop, are of popular origins. Like most of the local bourgeoisie, they have kept their children almost totally segregated from the *popolino* and their culture and language.[11] The *popolino*, the two sisters were taught, were ignorant, superstitious, dangerous and corrupt. A major theme in their education was that they should avoid being caught in what was called 'the vicious circle of favours'. By a similar interpretation of moral righteousness and management of risk, Umberto refrains from using his powerful contacts in the administration to obtain favours. Much more zealously than young people like Giovanni and Lucia, he strictly associates manoeuvring with corruption but also avoids asking favours of his superiors for fear of losing their esteem and appearing undignified.

This attitude is scorned by Lino, whose idea of undignified behaviour has different bases. He responds to Umberto's accusation that he is 'too much of a wheeler and dealer' by calling him *fess'* but giving the word a half-joking meaning which was tellingly absent when he (and others) applied it to Paolo. As in other cases examined earlier, given Umberto's higher status and resources, his attitude is seen as a questionable but legitimate choice. Umberto, however, stresses that he has gained employment through 'regular *concorso* [competition]' and that he is happy with his lifestyle, despite what he calls sacrifices, because his household lacks nothing essential and his children will go to university. In contrast to most *popolino*, he also says that he does not feel less fulfilled because his family can have only one-week holidays or because, unlike his *popolino* relatives, he does not have a VCR, a hi-fi, or a personal computer.

Gino exemplifies an important variation on this view of proper behaviour. Only recently has he obtained a steady job, after a long period of occasional employment and part-time studies during which he managed his and his brother's properties. Having behaved only marginally more entrepreneurially than Umberto, he explains in terms of his lack of contacts both his employment situation and his failure to obtain 'necessary benefits' such as speeding an application for a council grant to which he was entitled. He found it frustrating that his *popolino* acquaintances should be so obviously undeterred by what he regards as a Kafkaesque bureaucracy, but he rejected my suggestion that he might ask their help in extracting the benefits he needed from that bureaucracy. He said he wanted 'nothing to do with corruption'. However, I have reason to think that avoiding 'mingling with the *popolino*' for fear of his peers' disapproval was a strong motivation too.

Since I first met Gino and Patrizia, they have married and become fully employed. With the help of a friend who kept him informed of future vacancies and introduced him to the director of the institution, Gino has become a mid-level manager in the social services: having gained part-time employment and, thus, access to the necessary information and experience, Gino had an advantage when the permanent position was eventually advertised. Despite the modest pay, he is proud of his job because it gives him responsibility and prestige. Through a similar process, Patrizia has become a fully employed teacher. Having graduated brilliantly (though with some delay), she did some part-time teaching, hoping to find a job in a school where she could do 'something constructive'. She fulfilled this ambition when a contact in the Associazione Cattolica[12] introduced her to the headmistress of the private school where, having proved her ability and qualifications, she stresses, she later became employed. Patrizia also teaches at home and is reading for a second degree. In contrast to the 'embourgeoised' Giovanni and Lucia, Gino and Patrizia offered a nuanced account of this change in their lives, referring to 'explanations' such as their qualifications and professional ability, their friends' sympathy with their predicament, and God's will. They never conceded, however, that they had skilfully managed contacts and that their new employment situation could be explained, at least in part, in terms of favours.

Whereas Flora not only strictly abides by her parents' views but is also taking up their local business, Patrizia has distanced herself from those views and, with the support of Gino, fought for her right to have an independent career that interests her. She says that she has benefited from the material and psychological independence provided by her marriage. As part of what they call 'personal development', Patrizia and Gino have also changed their attitude towards the *popolino*. They now say that they 'appreciate their resourcefulness[13] – as equals'. This may be patronizing, but it is nevertheless quite remarkable, given their socialization. They explain this newly found sympathy in terms of the combined effect of their relationship with a local young priest with progressive ideas and their voluntary work in the local church (they organize recreational and educational activities), which involves daily contact with the *popolino* and, especially, their children. Gino also says that he has become especially aware of the *popolino*'s humanity and drive by dealing daily with them as part of his job. However, despite having extracted obvious benefits from the favour system, they continue to reject on moral grounds the *popolino*'s attitude to the mass diffusion of contacts and favours. This indicates that the relationship between the morality and action of these bourgeois individuals may be superficially close to Paolo and Enrica's unwillingness to seek favours but bears no resemblance to the approach – at the same time selective and syncretic – to *popolino* and bourgeois expectations and concepts of ability and self-respect that is found among the locals of their own generation with *popolino* origins. Their explicit zealousness about the 'vicious circle of favours' generates a tendency to make self-defeating individualistic use of personal resources, perform specified exchanges, and resort to money in transactions in which the *popolino* (even those who are 'embourgeoised') have managed to reduce its direct significance.

This attitude of the local petty bourgeoisie may allow a degree of improper behaviour that does not too seriously violate the normative demands of their identity but it does not appear to be sophisticated enough to encourage the negotiated relationship between action, identity and norms that characterizes the honesty of the *popolino*. Above all, their case material shows no evidence of the highly diversified resources and exchanges found among the *popolino*, including those who are pursuing embourgeoisement through the Church network among others. Nor do they endorse (and perhaps forgive) those aspects of the *popolino*'s entrepreneurship that consistently help to redefine social relations.

Gino and his peers are probably more genuine and less complaisant when they castigate the blurring of boundaries between the legal and the illegal in local life. In theory they are quite unlike, say, Paolo and Giovanni, who also refuse to deal with villains but pragmatically accept degrees of semi-legality in their lives. However, most do compromise to a certain extent. For example, reminding us broadly of the unspoken – even secret – exchanges involving special persons, Umberto uses his *popolino* network to do things that he is ashamed or unable to do personally, such as buying 'bargain' merchandise, betting in the clandestine lotteries and, more important, coping with the crises caused by criminals' presence in local life. A minority, like Flora and her parents (and the Gino and Patrizia of some years ago), are restricted even in these exchanges by their contempt. This petty-bourgeois notion of shameful behaviour has other implications. For example, the *popolino* bitterly resent a stereotypical view of them as poor, ignorant and backward but they may decide to use to their advantage such a view. Far from seeing such behaviour as an expression of the resourcefulness which he claims to admire in them, Gino contemptuously says that he would never 'humiliate himself' in that way to reduce a professional's bill or smooth the way to a favour or benefit. This rationale underpins Umberto's idea of dignified behaviour and the remark of a young accountant of *popolino* origins that 'the *popolino* live at the margins of legality and when caught beg the judge's pity. Is that fair? Dignified?'

Gino and Patrizia also seem restricted in their management of existence by their religious beliefs and, more generally, by their attitude towards the supramundane. They are unlike the Socialist Umberto, who 'doesn't care much' about 'saints, madonnas and clerics' and recognizes only 'lay' values.[14] They strictly abide by the ecclesiastical teachings, dismissing most of the *popolino*'s beliefs as animistic and backward. Apparently their relationships with the dead conform to the official liturgy and representation of the hereafter. Sacred icons are discreetly placed in their homes, as in those of most bourgeois families, but one notes the absence of the family shrine and the symbols of protection ('pagan and superstitious', they say) that are central to the *popolino* culture of the house. Similarly, they dismiss, uneasily, the symbolism of spirits, claiming to refer exclusively to doctrinal forms of expiation, redemption and achievement of grace. These locals appear almost unanimously motivated to play down flexible modes of action and thought which they partly retain but associate with 'being *popolino*'. Only by devious verbal routes or through moral sublimation do they admit the necessity of contacts and of 'illegitimate' beliefs and behaviours. This obviously advises caution in interpreting the recent change in attitude of Gino and Patrizia as evidence of a general trend. We can say only that, when the *popolino* are compared with their petty-bourgeois neighbours, the inexcusable simplicity of arguments about their social, cultural and political marginality (or submission) becomes, if possible, more obvious.

The *popolino*'s familiarity with the favour system suggests that they have developed an entrepreneurial approach to all sorts of problems that absolves many of them from clientelistic dependence – though to a lesser extent, given the situational constraints, from clientelist dealings. Moreover, the *popolino* are certainly not the only users of the system. The careers of Gino and Patrizia exemplify the petty-bourgeois version of dealings in the favour system, a much more sophisticated form of which is found among the élites.[15] The bourgeois share with the *popolino* the feeling that the public sector is 'inevitably like this' and that 'formal complaints are useless', but they prefer to conceal (or deny) such dealings. While complicating social relations and competition, this poses no threat to their underlying logic. Indeed, thus the bourgeois contribute to Naples's image as the apotheosis of 'privilege' – a world of people 'who can', from the poorest to the better off. The crucial question, then, is not *whether* but *how* and *how overtly* privilege is pursued.

Rights and privileges in the economics of control

Frank Parkin has pointed to the importance of privilege-holding in the establishment of social closure (1979). His argument is that, depending on who has access to it, privilege may play a functional though ambiguous role in social organization. Davis argues that people 'can attempt to control the activities of the powerful centre by turning its rules around and against it' (1977: 80). As members of the same state, he continues, 'they can assert that what they want – a job, a passport, medical treatment – is theirs not by virtue of their personal loyalty to a particular magnate, not by virtue of their ability to vindicate their claim by mass action, but by right' (ibid.). The responses of many Neapolitans to the situation in which they find themselves conform in part to this model. They also open up alternative possibilities.

There are important processes by which superordinates reinforce domination 'by rendering subordinates unaware of their subordination' (Martin 1977: 165). We have explored this notion of awareness among local people, and we have assessed how both the *popolino* and the petty bourgeoisie draw on direct experience when they describe the public sector as overcomplicated – by neglect or by design – and polluted by the logic of favours. When questioned, they effortlessly offer examples of attempts by politicians, bureaucrats and professional favour-bestowers to impose themselves as indispensable resources and to transfer to the domain of favours services and benefits that they know are about to be implemented or, more generally, which are formally alien to that domain. Among the *popolino*, this awareness, vividly illustrated by case material, is linked directly to the widespread belief that loyalty to one particular favour-bestower is useless and counterproductive. Regarding the establishment, actors' independence of mind translates into their discerning use of the contrast between the poor quality of public social services and bureaucratic performance and the quality available to those who have developed the right skills and contacts.

Let us reflect on this aspect of the mass diffusion of favours, bearing in mind that, though all the necessary benefits are there, they are made difficult to obtain. In the quarter, the system of connections and favours is endlessly debated with emphasis on the injustice of 'having to struggle', as one informant put it, 'to get the inadequate benefits you're entitled to'. Taking a closer look, one discovers that people emphasize equally strongly the irony of feeling, at the same time, that generalized respect for rules would be preferable only up to a point, for in such an unlikely (it is stressed) situation it would be necessary to give up hope of obtaining better results, privileges in the sense given above. This attitude is motivated in part by actors' relatively successful entrepreneurship, in part by their disillusionment with the formal routes to benefits, and in part by their experience of a rigid application of 'honest administration' – particularly under the left, when personal initiative was often frustrated on basically ideological grounds (see Pardo 1993). As I have suggested, the years of leftist administration may have helped to strengthen – though certainly not to generate – people's social sense and awareness of their rights, but they have not persuaded them to give up individual strategies for the pursuit of goals.

Lino's view of rights and privileges illustrates an important aspect of these issues of collective vs. individual action and of deferred investments. 'Take a bed in hospital,' he said. 'If I can't get it, it could be because the doctors judge that I don't need it urgently, but in this situation I can't be sure that it isn't because I haven't got the right recommendation. It's all right to protest against corruption and disservice, but would you blame me if I started pulling strings?' This is precisely what he pre-emptively chose to do when Luisa needed specialist care. He used the public health service, but he also mobilized his contacts. Through a local GP to whom – 'just in case' – he periodically gives presents, he reached a specialist who hospitalized Luisa where he works. Thus, Lino says, he avoided unnecessary risks, bureaucratic hassle, 'and didn't have to beg to obtain what I'd the right to: that is, a bed in a room rather than in a corridor, speedy diagnosis and therapy, clean bedlinen, proper nursing, etc.' Lino has cultivated the specialist as a potential alternative resource.

The *popolino* have learned quickly that in this situation rights are relative: they must so often be fought for that they become, in fact, privileges. Perversely, obtaining privileges of all sorts gratifies the obvious desire of many – across society – to hold some prerogative, to appear 'privileged'. The multiplication of contacts in each field allows people to use a right or privilege repeatedly (even on others' behalf) without having to negotiate increasingly inconvenient terms with the same favour-bestower. For instance, most locals know more than one doctor willing to certify nonexistent illness (for sick-leaves and other reasons) in exchange for gifts, simply to be kind or sympathetic, to keep his practice in favour, or to obtain their votes. It is when problematic contacts such as politicians (or criminals) are involved, as we have seen, that actors become more selective, specify exchanges and sever links as soon as possible.

It could be technically argued that if people had traditionally had access to resources and benefits through formal and impersonal bureaucratic agencies, informal or illegal channels would probably have had a more limited development. This is a problematic issue in mainstream political philosophy (Lukes 1991a: 265 ff.). Clearly, this socially pervasive culture of privilege-holding not only encourages illicit transactions but is unfair to those who cannot cope. Having said this, I remain quite unconvinced that the widespread pursuit of favours imposed upon ordinary people necessarily makes them subaltern, dishonest and corrupt. A difficulty is posed, of course, by the importance given to informality and personalization of formal roles. The period of Communist-led administration (1975–83) through a series of coalitions is illustrative.[16]

Most Neapolitans were understandably bewildered when, during the early days of that administration, they obtained benefits without having to wait for ages or manoeuvre and pay their way to them. Conflicting analyses find common ground in recognizing the beneficial effects of the Communists' drive and organization. They rose to prominence and were widely applauded primarily on the strength of their commitment to administrative honesty and accountability. However, despite the open-mindedness, competence and charismatic authority of part of their élite, the administration began to lose popularity as ideology inched its way into its policies (Pardo 1993). To cite a classic example, its critics raised an important issue in the theory of bureaucratic organization in relation to politics (Smith 1987) in pointing to the introduction into the administrative process of newcomers who though politically loyal were technically inadequate.

There is another important aspect of this issue that needs attention. The central location of most public offices typical of Italian cities facilitates people's access to notables (and institutions) of all sorts. The case material discussed earlier is corroborated by direct observation of people's 'seasoned skills' in the council, the courts, hospitals and so on. Those who are not public-sector employees have kin or friends who are and act as favour-bestowers. Alternatively, trade unions notoriously reach almost anywhere, directly or indirectly. The Communists responded to this situation, typical of what they called 'the clientelist mentality', by making the self-damaging

choice of drastically depersonalizing the relationships between administrators (politicians and bureaucrats) and citizens (including employees,
ordinary people and favour-seekers of all kinds). Thus, citizens' relationships with the administration became perhaps more fair, while access to
those in power was not more objectively restricted than before. Before,
however, the powerful person was said to be available to all. He (or she)
could be seen, touched and spoken to. It was apparently irrelevant that
seldom would he care to answer and would often be 'busy' and surrounded
by too many of his people to be directly (and usefully) approached. Now
there was no soothing language and, above all, the barrier was stressed –
symbolically and factually – by a new formality, impersonality and drastic
restriction of indirect routes (such as Giordano and Caiazza). This policy
of correctness obviously conflicted with people's entrepreneurialism and
their (tacit, perhaps unconscious) resistance to alienation. It was also
implemented in a situation in which Italians had reason to feel that formal
relations with administrative powers were useless.

Some Communists also indulged in favouritism and relatively minor
forms of corruption, while their party pursued both overhierarchization in
decision-making and tactical alliances with old political enemies (Pardo
1993: 80–1). These alliances were in part made necessary by their insufficient electoral strength. Most rank-and-file comrades and the larger public
interpreted this unexpected combination of what they regarded as alien
forms of political behaviour as a further betrayal of distributive promises
which the party now seemed to be abandoning for selective policies in the
style of the Christian Democrats. Such political sins were too obviously
inconsistent with the party's traditional stress on moral righteousness and
censure of *sottogoverno*.

Moreover, in a way metaphorically reminiscent of the experience of the
young Lino (Pardo 1993: 86), the Communists were plagued by two
serious problems: the clumsiness of the parvenu (Blau 1972) and the lack
of the necessary network (Smith 1987). Indeed, the elevation of old-fashioned opposition politics to the level of (local) government highlighted
serious limitations. One was that the Communists had restricted access to
central-government resources and were distrusted in crucial financial
circles. This compounded with the ramified control established by the
centre parties, and especially by the Christian Democrats, through the
negotiated allocation of jobs in the council, the social services, etc.
(Valenzi and Ghiara 1978; Cappelli 1978; Valenzi 1987; Chubb 1981),
emphasizing the simple fact that electoral success and moral claims may
well not coincide with the power required to govern. The Communists

were increasingly spurned by many of the dissenting Catholics, young people, bourgeois and *popolino* who had switched their votes to them in the hope that the city's prospects in terms of jobs and quality of life would benefit from their clean hands and efficiency without having to suffer the accompanying ideological zeal and operative rigidity. In the wake of the administrative, financial and logistic disruption caused by the 1980 earthquake and amid accusations of involvement in *sottogoverno* the PCI was made to pay the price for the disenchantment of a large part of its electorate, old and new, who already resented its weak government and failure to implement structural intervention.

The legal and ethical ambiguity of the mass diffusion of favours is of course beyond dispute, but we should recognize that ordinary people, in their awareness of the *persons* who make up the domains of bureaucracy and politics, extend beyond the formal categories of politics and organization of civil society their idea of honesty and their concern with successful entrepreneurship and the pursuit of the side benefits of favour-seeking/bestowing (such as esteem, prestige and social position). Practical experience of the leftist view of them makes most *popolino* stress that it allows insufficient space to manoeuvre.[17] And they touch on an important aspect of the left's mismanagement of values and control when they say that they have unpleasant recollections of the Communists' rigidity and later partiality in social and industrial relations.

In other words, the favour system may well have been imposed from 'above' in the prevailing interest of a 'political bossism' (Allum 1973: pts 3 and 4; Zuckerman 1977, 1979; Gribaudi 1980) that managed to represent its own omnipotence as unchallengeable. The evidence suggests, however, that a reworking from 'below' – whatever its conscious or declared ends – has gradually transformed it into a *diversified* resource domain for many. My informants work very hard at improving their lives without having to submit to the powerful and, instinctively wary of the formal, the impersonal and the anonymous, they show a strong motivation to get round these aspects of power when they deal with the establishment. But they have also developed interests, values and modes of action that are generally aware of but in many ways run counter to those of the politicians who are traditionally involved in clientelism and corruption. The *popolino*, in particular, having coped in a pragmatic way with the paradox of being forced to seek rights as favours, capitalize on the resulting experience to use the system and remain honest, by their own standards, through consistent defiance of the basic principles of electioneering.

People's perceptions of bureaucratic culture, Collmann (1981: 106) says, determine their response to it. Actions like those of Michele obviously contribute to the reshaping of this domain of civil society and the associated economics of control as they find an active response in people like Papele (and indeed Andrea) or Caiazza at various levels of bureaucracy and administration. The *popolino*, like the many Italians who interpret entrepreneurially their relation to the ambiguities of the above-described bureaucratic culture, have developed the capacity for knowing what is best for them and wanting it. Their awareness that, in this situation of diffused privatization of public goods and services, costs can be reduced through mediation has had great heuristic power for the system of social relations. It has observably challenged their political submission, helping to expand their options beyond the limits established by decades of corrupt and unfair administration. Let me stress that this inconsistency is an important change from the past, when the bureaucratic and political machine could count on the mediation of prominent locals such as Pasquale and Ciro and of the local priests and their lay agents.

Beetham notes that one of the characteristics of bureaucracy is a bourgeois identity and approach (1974: 66–7). In Naples there is probably no strict association between the structure of formal power and the interests and values of the established bourgeoisie, moral or corrupt. This structure has been affected by the improved access of the non-bourgeois to education and other traditionally bourgeois resources. Caiazza is one of the many who have contributed to the social and cultural diversification of bureaucracy and administration and the increasing sharing of culture with 'the people' (see also Pardo 1993: 85). In this situation, whatever the rhetoric of power, favour relations do not prevent or replace bureaucratic organization, but, reminding us of recent arguments in anthropology (e.g., Herzfeld 1992), they do significantly affect its internal (arbitrary) taxonomies and output.

To sum up, four crucial aspects of clientelistic dependence are deeply challenged in Naples: the isolation of individual clients, people's need for protection against precariousness, the myth of the ineluctability of clientelistic submission, and the constriction of favours of all kinds into relations monopolized by a particular political machine. 'What politically and analytically distinguishes "clients" from non-clients', Collmann asks us to note, 'are the processes of making them objects . . . "Clients" are to be acted upon, bureaucratically moulded, mass produced' (1981: 110). Of course, these relations of exchange – flexible and multidimensional as they may be – remain influenced by an imbalance of power, but the empirical situation suggests that the *popolino* in particular pursue their goals in a fashion that deeply contrasts with the criteria for submission just listed. The culture of social exchange that corresponds to their entrepreneurialism is dynamic not simply because the power of resource-holders has become less exclusive. The fact is that, in a city, people more quickly and thoroughly recognize the factual value of the reduction of what Boissevain (1975: 9) calls 'power differentials' between groups and persons, and they are more aware both of the process of objectification and of their options for improvement of their goal pursuits. Whether they are *popolino* or petty bourgeois, actors belong to several social, economic and political domains in relations of interdependence, mutual influence or conflict with each other and with the wider state. They move among these domains without regard for abstract (and technical) models of social structure and organization but instead according to their own skills, motives, experience and identity requirements. It is not only the relations between the local and the broader context of the city but those between agent and system that are especially affected.

The Communists probably lost support among the *popolino* mainly because of their ideological zeal and cultural misunderstanding, but their clientelistic opponents (and successors) have certainly not been better-off. They and their local agents have lost control of the *popolino* as the latter have improved their access to information and to diversified resources. In this scenario, the younger generations are combining *popolino* entrepreneurialism with better education and a less obvious management of contacts, and this gives them advantage over people like Gino and Patrizia (let alone Flora). More broadly, given favourable conditions, this development has the potential to influence the future of the city. And it is important that, apart from being objectively not anti-society, actors' benefiting from the favour system is moral, in their view, because it implies distrust of the powerful who run the institutions though not necessarily of the institutions as such.

Given that trust is always relative, it is difficult to say whether it is such distrust that motivates my informants to expand their informal and personalized paths to resources or whether the two processes are interrelated. People's trust may well be generally tempered by a blend of pragmatism and disenchantment, but, as in most of Italy, this attitude is abundantly motivated by a political scenario wherein corruption and collusion with crime are clearly a matter of degree, no political party having a monopoly of the illicit. Lino and his mates emphasized this question when they provided an embarrassingly long list of reasons, making no exception for the politicians they elect, for their distrusting professional brokers and the favour-bestowing establishment. It is on terms of equal distrust that they prefer personalized relations with useful persons, such as Andrea, who identify with the common value of flexibility. There is no inevitable circularity in the fact that their participation – and sometimes omission of participation (electoral or other) – in the political process raises serious difficulties, because most of these relations occur outside institutional legitimacy. However, there is strong political significance in the fact that this, in turn, encourages their belief that the establishment has a vested interest in keeping the system as it is – even in collusion with criminals.

The establishment's unholy alliances: a diachronic view

Urban-based criminals have traditionally participated in some of the most problematic alliances in the history of the Neapolitan structure of power.[18] We have examined the processes which, at the micro-level, make favour-seeking sociologically independent of crime and political corruption and the culture which restricts the significance of criminals in ordinary people's resource systems. Let us now briefly consider the role of these alliances in the nature and form of citizens' relationships with their rulers.

The competition over the misappropriation of funds after the 1980 earthquake has only increased a phenomenon fuelled by the systematic policy of central-government assistance. Certain politicians, originally of the centre but increasingly diversified across the spectrum, have greatly benefited from this process, drawing on the illegal bias in the flexibility of the system. These relations are quite different from those of a 'Mafia type' (Pardo 1994b). In Sicily and in Mafia-type situations in general, clientelism developed in a rural context based on land-ownership and control in which personal relations and transactions drew heavily on loyalty and trust. The Mafiosi's use of a symbology linked to popular values has traditionally been a powerful palliative (Gambetta 1991) in such harsh conditions. The present generation of urban Mafiosi has developed modern and effective ways of using this background (Falcone 1992). In the urban complexity of Naples, real crime has traditionally enjoyed no ideological basis or popular consent. Moreover, feudalism ended earlier here than in Sicily (Lepre 1963: 142), partly as a consequence of influential ideas and the resulting short-lived movements (Cuoco 1966 [1806]; Croce 1967 [1944]: ch. 4) and then of the French decade (1805–15: Lepre 1979, 1963; Galasso 1978: ch. 7), and partly as a consequence of the state's (also legislative) intervention (Lepre 1963). By the time of the Unification in 1860, a large – if loosely identified – bourgeoisie had formed in the continental South, but 'institutional brokers' barely existed (Gramsci 1971).

Believing that no setting is insulated, I have serious reservations about the hypothesis that under the Bourbons local rulers and notables (lawyers, accountants, teachers, priests and others) played some sort of 'filtering' role.[19] After Unification these people lost some influence but were granted recognition and public office by the new rulers. 'The state', it is argued, became a sort of impersonal 'super-patron' (Gribaudi 1980), managing to penetrate the micro-level and control this part of the country by dispensing civil rights and benefits through local notables opportunely bribed into 'loyalty'. However, in contrast to what has been said regarding Sicily (Blok 1974; compare with Schneider et al. 1972; Schneider and Schneider 1976), it would appear that local rulers did not become 'keepers of the gates' between the state and the citizens. After a quickly negotiated opposition, they became functional to central-government control in the interest of the Northern industrial bourgeoisie. A new, punitive fiscal policy was implemented and the competitive Southern industrial system (e.g., Lepre 1979) was consistently undermined to the advantage of the comparatively lagging agricultural sector and, later, of the long-lasting policy of assistance without long-term structural investments, some aspects of which we have examined earlier.

The 1901 parliamentary inquiry (known as *Inchiesta Saredo*; see, e.g., Aliberti 1976: 545–8) shows the evolution of this situation from the first, limited enlargement of the franchise in 1882, when the system of favours controlled by the élites was strengthened by an effective – if unlawful – alliance between local notables, government ministers and prominent popular figures (*popolino* and bourgeois, criminal and law-abiding).[20] I use the term 'alliance' to define these relations because in this urban setting it would be difficult to argue for the *identification* between political power and criminal power that characterizes organized crime with a rural background (Pardo 1994b).[21] After the enlargement of the franchise in 1913, popular leaders and leading criminals organized shows of support for the best-paying politicians. The *popolino* remained at the dependent end of relations of power in which these politicians, elected by large majorities, continued to use their dubious brokers to establish a long-lasting grip on vital areas of administration and civic life.

It has been claimed that the co-option of the population by the élite of the right has thwarted attempts at revolution in Neapolitan history.[22] However, there is reason to believe that the 'populace' has acted in its own interest[23] and not, as some argue (e.g., Chubb 1981: 121), in a truly anti-statist drive. The situation during Unification is indicative. The Naples administration employed scores of Camorristi to police the city – according to the *Prefetto*, Liborio Romano, the only possible way of controlling the mass disorders subsequent to the downfall of the Bourbons and allowing Garibaldi's 'peaceful conquest' of the capital (Villari 1979 [1885]).[24] In a display of 'control', Camorristi and popular leaders physically joined the 'unifier politicians' in addressing the Neapolitans. The *popolino* applauded under duress, hoping that the new rulers would bring about an improvement in their miserable (e.g., Villari 1979 [1885] and White-Mario 1978 [1876]) livelihood, but remaining culturally marginal and politically and economically subject. Bluntly, the point is that they had not yet developed the crucial resources (i.e., the entrepreneurial use of the system and independent attitude) that relatively recently have begun to affect their relationship to the structure. As for the Camorristi, they were initially repaid with a degree of tolerance of their business (see Monnier 1965 [1863] and esp. Villari 1979 [1885] and Garofalo 1984) and later prosecuted. They had nevertheless gained experience, information and contacts that would prove invaluable in the years to come. The above-mentioned parliamentary inquiry finally proved that this 'political' recruitment of villains was an aspect of dubious politics which reached far into central government and which, despite some notable opposition (Ricci and Scarano 1990; Monnier 1965 [1863]), had been upgraded under the new rulers but with which ordinary people had little involvement. Several Camorristi, in part of *popolino* origin, became the protagonists of one of a long series of mega-trials starring prominent criminals which have helped to nourish a rather sinister folklore but have barely affected the grassroots situation.

Such an alliance between spurious forms of power, certainly not unprecedented in Italian history, has been replicated many times, though on basically different terms. These urban criminals generally stay away from politics, to which they feel they do not belong, but most willingly 'work' with politicians. Older locals bitterly remember, for instance, that Camorristi were directly employed by the fascist regime as 'men of order' and could therefore perform their criminal deeds arrogantly and without scandal.[25] After the war, criminals ran a lucrative illegal business in undercover cooperation with the Allies and became instrumental in providing micro-level assistance in governing the city.[26] Later they organized both electoral support and rallies for various postwar candidates and shows of hostility against their opponents. This input of criminal power into politics produced huge returns during the postwar reconstruction of the 1950s and 1960s,[27] and, together with clientelism, it typified a number of local administrations up to the mid-1970s, when various factors combined to bring the Communists to power.

Nowadays, fraud-prone sectors of finance and the political establishment are involved in criminal enterprises in specifically modern ways. This collusion – in the opinion of some, only temporarily checked by the current judicial inquiries – extends into murky domains of power relations well beyond financial and political competition and, alarmingly, well beyond the kind of low- and middle-level connivance discussed earlier. This apparently justifies the widespread belief that professionals and politicians – and their services – can be bought.[28] But corruption and embezzlement are only some of the questions raised by the contemporary role of criminals. I have argued that the villains' interest in local support is irremediably crippled by their increasing need to expand their business and territorial control.[29] The consequent murderous action rarely, if ever, affects ordinary people, but the ensuing anomy and violent atmosphere do harm their everyday lives too significantly for them to be truly acquiescent. At the same time, there are far-reaching implications in the oblique alliances and dealings between criminal power, political power and, more generally, sections of the élites (in Naples and outside it), as there is much political capital to be extracted from the 'presence' of criminals. Some politicians have notoriously obtained electoral support from criminals, while others have constructed their careers on the powerful rhetoric of 'fighting organized crime' – administrative sabotage, criminal activity, character assassination and alarmist campaigns in the media invariably increase as elections approach.

Corruption and clientelism vs. ideological rigidity: a truly inescapable dichotomy?

For a long time corrupt politicians have thrived by expanding the clientelist system created by their predecessors. However, their interpretation of pragmatism has recently begun to backfire as the links between clientelism, electoral success and administrative power – which they unequivocally embody but which depend on people's support or indifference – have been visibly weakened by the widespread demand for adequate political programmes and policies. We have studied important changes in a situation in which, as recently as in the 1960s, religious, political and economic brokerage often combined in the persons of local priests, who, with the active help of the Associazioni Cattoliche, upheld the relations of dominance established by the Christian Democrat Party. Equally significant are the effects of people's experience of the left.

Superordination and subordination are not sociological constants. The Naples situation makes it plain that the economics of power and dominance depend on the economics of imperfect competition and must therefore be understood in the light of the processual redefinition of actors' moral and socio-economic positions. In this context, the demise of 'alternative rulers' in the past is probably attributable less to their attitude to politics or the people's so-called predilection for clientelism than to their own difficulty (some say unwillingness) to come to terms with the complexity and the implications of people's values and commitment to informality, personal relations and individual initiative beyond any ideological preconception. Such values and the related expectations disagree with leftist politicians' traditional idea of what is good for the masses and with their preference for formalized and institutionalized social relations. Having associated such values with an addiction to corruption and clientelism, these rulers set about the task of controlling and educating the people to proletarian values with which they did not identify. Thus, they may have been faithful to Gramsci's theory of political leadership (1971) but they have arguably failed in a major task of the political party in pluralist society (Weber 1970) – establishing the in-depth understanding of and genuine link with ordinary citizens that are indispensable to true representation.

The entrepreneurialism and capitalist spirit of ordinary Neapolitans – especially but not only the *popolino* – has obviously been distorted by a corrupt political and bureaucratic machine. It is hard to assess causes and effects in these processes or even to judge which is which. The task is not made easier by these people's individual-oriented cooperative spirit, market-oriented mentality and sense of solidarity and their historically grounded distrust of their rulers. An empirical investigation of them does, however, raise several questions. It suggests that in this urban situation individuals with limited resources do manage to develop an attitude to life that may often conflict with the rationality of formal law but, in fact, allows them to escape criminality and corruption. They construct a strong identity with a collective image of themselves, their quarter and their city that does not conform to the stereotypes of marginality and deprivation. And, taking advantage of the negotiable relations of power which inevitably (Martin 1977) characterize this capitalist democracy, they make long-term investments circumventing in many important ways the logic and conditions of clientelism.

Above all, this ethnography offers a sobering warning about interpreting their entrepreneurialism as flawed by a grassroots susceptibility to the injustice, corruption and coercion that traditionally go with clientelism. It gives us reason to think that it is a matter of inadequate – or dishonest – political will not to recognize that such entrepreneurialism and culture effectively contrast with the powerfuls' 'power over' (in Weber's (1978:941–8) sense) and that they can and ought to be encouraged to express themselves in ways that are legitimate to a basically moral civil society. The non-materialist understanding of man in society argued here has addressed the sources and nature of the moral conflict that marks the difficulty of this socio-political situation. It has shown that ordinary people's rationality of action and thought substantially contributes to the reshaping of social relations by shunning the extremes of rigidity and corruption, dominance and apparent anarchy, which have traditionally characterized their rulers' management of the links between agency and the system.

The citizen, the state and the credibility of representation

This urban case emphasizes that the issue of power – the core issue, that is, of the agency/structure relationship – is too complex and multifaceted to be addressed in polarized terms, even those – however dialectic and complex – of hegemony and subalternity. This is especially true in contemporary capitalist society, where relations of power may well be unbalanced, but, borrowing from Martin, 'exchange relations are more symmetrical than under either slavery or feudalism, and power relations are based less upon coercion – although coercive elements continue to exist' (1977:163).

It could be argued that urban life makes more immediate what is latent in rural settings. In Naples, where the mass diffusion of favours places considerable pressure on the organization of society, ordinary people are not necessarily caught in categories of exchange or, indeed, in relations of power where they have no (or only a complacent) say in how they are structured. The diversification of relations between seekers and bestowers of favours has corresponded to a transformation of the bases and nature of crucial exchanges and choices encouraging new forms of negotiation of the presence of the state at the local level.

In democracy, power resides not in the state but in governments (Parkin 1979), and it is governments and their *personae* that are elected rather than the state, which is the independent variable of Western democracy (Beetham 1974). Building on ethnographic evidence, I have grown convinced that, contrary to common views, the attitude of ordinary Neapolitans towards the persons who embody politics and administration jeopardizes not democracy – or the state – but, less dramatically, the power of traditionally hegemonic groups. It generates forms of active participation in civil society that elude traditional forms of control and dominance, licit or illicit, defy corporate, bureaucratic and institutionalized forms of brokership[30] and are basically unsympathetic to part of the political field's overt cynicism about clientelism, corruption and embezzlement. Most of my informants, regardless of social position, share with other Italians a qualified trust in the 'radical changes' that are apparently occurring in the country's political system. Among the *popolino*, this suspension of judgement – extending to the new progressive administration – is strengthened by suspicion of political and electoral adventurism and by a tendency to give priority to a principle that is fundamental to democracy – freedom of personal initiative and action.

The following pages address some of the complex and difficult issues raised by this moral conflict, making sense of which may well be crucial to the liberal political order. Here it is important to note that this empirical study indicates the need for a political perspective which, without renouncing the great moral ideals of social justice and the common good, is unambiguously aware of the significance of the individual in society. At this critical moment it is certainly the task of the basically honest, society-oriented and institutionally committed in Italian public life to recognize the vanity of reifying either the individual or society re-establishing the legitimate link between citizenship, politics and administration. If past mistakes (Cuoco 1966 [1806]: esp. 140–1 and 299–305; Marotta 1991: 674–8; Pardo 1993) are to be avoided, this means recognizing that the 'sane forces' determinant of democracy are found throughout society and that an ethical understanding of the continuous interaction that informs ordinary people's lives may give crucial strength and credibility to representation. Within the framework of an enlightened moral and political philosophy, people must be addressed with well-defined and recognizable propositions that correspond to their motivations and levels of entrepreneurialism, rather than being asked to commit themselves to abstract ideologies and aspirations that are foreign to them. Correspondingly competitive structural policies with a clear sense of purpose – moral as well as practical – rather than the short-sighted 'solutions' of political expediency should follow.

Fulfilling this important requirement may mean the difference between losing and winning elections. More important, it will play a discriminating role in providing adequate and practicable answers to people's demands for a satisfactory degree of moralization of public life, never again to be frustrated by politicians' empty preaching (or boasting) of morality.

7

The relation of agency to organization and structure: deconstructed polarizations at the grassroots of democracy

Contextualizing the micro-level in the complexity of power relations has helped us to understand more about the problematic of structuring (Abrams 1982; Giddens 1979). We have assessed the significance of ordinary people's purposive action in the redefinition of important aspects of urban life. We have studied the relationship between morality, belief, norms and self-interest that informs individuals' management of existence. More specifically, we have addressed the significance of this relationship to the strong continuous interaction between material and non-material aspects of life and the way in which this interaction affects their relation to the system, strengthening their factual – if not always wilful – defiance of a political status quo (La Palombara 1987) made of 'polarized pluralism' (Sartori 1987) in which they would have little to gain. This defiance is deeply rooted in political and social disenchantment.

The documentation on these issues of value, control and representation has directed us to recognize the empirical state of basic democratic values. The following pages address this point in greater detail, suggesting that the actions 'from below' that characterize the Naples case in many ways counteract democracy's tendency toward self-destruction (Lively 1975; Stankiewicz 1980). This does not, in my view, result in a democracy at significant variance with those of the rest of Europe. It does, however, highlight a certain irony in the fact that thus far the sophistication of ordinary citizens' entrepreneurialism has corresponded to (relative) diversification of control over resources and benefits and mitigation of the alienating effects of the rationalization of society but not to observable improvement in civic life.

We have found that the mass diffusion of favours is linked (perhaps causally) to processes that go far beyond the bending of bureaucratic rules, challenging crucial processes of domination. Of course we need to know more about the precise relationship of the ('new' and 'old') élites' moral universes and actual practices to the democratic system. It is most telling, however, that the effects of ordinary people's new understanding of 'electoral auctioneering' (Beetham 1987:100) and improved access to important resources have built up in a way apparently unforeseen by the profiteering, clientelist-oriented potentates, who have seen their mediating role and dynamics of control begin to deteriorate. It would, in fact, be reductive to explain the decline of old patterns of clientelism in terms of the hypothetical development of new forms of professionalism in machine politics (Zuckerman 1979) and/or mass patronage (Graziani and Pugliese 1979; Gribaudi 1980) as opposed to relations of personal dependence between members of different 'classes' (see, e.g., Scott 1977).

Inequality is a condition of clientelism. As inequality is redefined in significant areas of exchange and action, I have argued, the associated power relations (and their internal imbalance) also become open to redefinition. Thus entrepreneurial performance is encouraged in people who express a distinctly individual-oriented identity both as workers and as individuals enmeshed in the bureaucratization of society. The corresponding modes of action, profoundly incompatible both with ruthless (and rootless) individualism and with organized collectivism, belong to a culture of fulfilment and personal betterment centred upon the pursuit of symbolic, moral, spiritual and practical control – however relative – over one's own life and construction of personhood.

It should be clear by now that an individual-oriented understanding of rational choice and action in a given structure need not be bonded to an instrumental (or marketistic) view of motives. We have observed that pursuing fulfilment means pursuing ends that are profoundly moral, deferred and real. The study of ordinary people's motives, expectations and actions has demonstrated that purpose implies a meaningful orientation in which material interest is only one aspect of broader strategies for the long-term achievement of existential security. Thus, work, production, consumption, investment and favour-seeking/bestowing (in this world and the other world) become fields for choice, individual initiative and diversification of socio-economic positions – not for mass action or for the 'inevitable' (Crompton 1993; Bourdieu 1977, 1991) reproduction of inequality and of the encroachments of class through social closure (Parkin 1979). Thus, individuals' actions acquire the observable power to influence social structure.

This situation is, I believe, not peculiar to Naples. The Neapolitan case provides a significant example of the internal instability of power and social closure characteristic of the development of European urban settings. In view of the sweeping changes that are occurring on the Old Continent, I shall argue in conclusion that the line of conflict between the rulers and the ruled cannot be drawn according to social class (Lukes 1991a: chs. 14 and 16). This ethnography suggests that a class perspective, even when it is wary of vulgar materialism, provides us with an interpretive model that, however sophisticated, remains too deterministic and abstract. It does not account for the entrepreneurial negotiation of objective restrictions (and inequality) that characterizes the processes of value and action and of exchange and power in the complexity of real life.

Entrepreneurial morality and religious value in the relationship between bureaucracy, democracy and the market

The significance of the individual in this democratic system stimulates a reformulation of the concept of rationalization of power and politics in direct connection with the fundamental question of the relation of bureaucratic efficiency to democracy on the one hand, and to the market, on the other (Beetham 1987: 97 ff.).[1] Ordinary Neapolitans' commitment to the exercise of personal initiative and independence as individuals appears to be crucial on three levels. First, within limits it increasingly defies the active interest of certain *pezzi grossi* in reproducing personal relations of clientelistic dominance (Chapter 6). Secondly, it helps to contain the impersonal bureaucratization of exchange, society, and the related forms of control (Chapter 2 and Chapter 6). Thirdly, it is instrumental to the Church's failure to bureaucratize access to the hereafter, sacred and non-sacred (Chapter 5). People's relations with the powerful – dead or living – remain distinctly individual-oriented and entrepreneurial in the broad sense employed here.[2] Among the *popolino*, in particular, they tend to be private and to involve the privatization of what is supposed to be public and collective.

The accent in the order of life is accordingly placed on informalization and personalization rather than simply on individualization. This process, profoundly significant to the rational organization of this democratic system, raises issues which are central to the ambiguous (Brubaker 1991) interplay between Weber's social thought and his moral reflections. Given that bureaucracy, as a general set of administrative features, is 'a universal requirement of modern industrial society' (Beetham 1987: 111), important questions are whether the Weberian relationship between Protestantism (particularly Calvinism), industrial capitalism and the rational organization of democratic society is automatic and should be taken for granted and what degree of mutual tolerance is possible between bureaucratization of social life and of the market and personal freedom,[3] however relative this concept of freedom may be.

The complexity introduced to these questions by the Naples material is thought-provoking, especially in relation to the Puritan orientation in the Weberian notions of morality (and rationalism and rationalization (see Eisen 1978; also Brubaker 1991)). Money, we have seen, is made and seldom wasted among the *popolino* and there is no stigma placed on monetary profit extracted from kin, friends and neighbours, as opposed to 'others'. Moreover, their sense of capitalist enterprise may well not be dependent on or specially linked to a specific ethic marked by a direct (if difficult) approach to God, and by the need to prove to oneself one's own election. Among them, the development of 'the spirit of capitalism' may well not be centred, as in the Weberian model, on ploughing profits back into a fund of capital because luxurious living is incompatible with a godly life. Finally, their capitalist entrepreneurialism has developed relatively independently of industrialism, especially heavy industry, and its rationale, profoundly influenced by a morality of merit, is more in tune with the market, small-scale production, independent work and, nowadays, the tertiary sector (e.g., services). It is, in fact, committed to a culture of personal achievement through mediation, negotiation and flexibility. However, we have found that in this scenario consumption is important, and part of the surplus goes into the consumption necessary to satisfy the symbolic and moral requirements of the construction and representation of a good life.[4] Even on this important level, however, consumption is basically secondary to the values of enterprise, for most of the surplus is invested in existing or new entrepreneurial ventures or in medium- to long-term goals such as education, the acquisition of property and the accumulation of capital. The ability to borrow through informal and, increasingly, formal channels and to raise money through various kinds of exchange further complicates the correspondingly competitive social relations across the urban spectrum, indicating that moral action is a choice, more often normatively negotiated than dictated.

The need to move beyond the Weberian model is stressed on another level by the relationship between these people's entrepreneurial culture and the organization and structure of the social system in which they operate. In particular, this morphology of power is, I suggest, far too problematic to be explained by a causal relation between a 'weak state', mediation and patronage, and Catholicism (see, e.g., Boissevain 1977). The study of negotiation and mediation suggests that a connection of a Weberian type (1948) may exist, to a certain extent, in the ways in which people construct their relations with the powerful living and with the powerful dead, but careful scrutiny raises several objections. First, as I have noted, it would be unhelpful to explain these urban relations of power as relations of patronage. Secondly, mundane and supramundane domains of mediation are characterized by highly diversified and shifting liminal (and ambiguous) positions which, unaccounted for by the causality hypothesis, are determinant in actors' purposeful action in the pursuit of fulfilment. Thirdly, the relationships of the living with the dead are basically different in value, form, and norms from those among the living. Mundane and supramundane contacts are approached simultaneously but in profoundly different ways and with substantially different expectations.[5] Most important, observably aware of their behaviour (political, religious, etc.), people exert various amounts of control in their transactions with their mundane contacts, and they do so without resigning themselves to subjugation. Instead, because supramundane protection must be spiritually deserved through a complex interplay of practical actions and moral commitments with self and the others, it can to a certain extent be *symbolically negotiated* but not *transacted.*[6]

My contention is that, in order to understand this relationship between culture, entrepreneurial spirit and the organization of society, we must recognize the significance of actors' almost systematically linking their operations of thought to the moral and normative value of their actions. This is important because personal fulfilment (even after death) is subordinated to the successful negotiation of such value. According to this rationale, the concepts of accomplishment in life and the achievement of grace are mediated through profoundly individual symbolic and behavioural statements which transcend the official Catholic idea of intermediation as a (formal) strategy for achieving supramundane protection. The entrepreneurial actor benefits from the ability to adopt a morally and normatively manageable version of the (Catholic) concept of mediation of the human condition. This process is linked to important aspects of the democratic system of values (Stankiewicz 1980:98–100), for, quite unhindered by theological casuistry and doctrinal ethics and ambiguities, it is *rationally determined* (Runciman 1991; Lukes 1991b) by the symbolic and moral investments made by the actors as they combine very different resources in their management of existence. The ecclesiastical institution may find it difficult to tolerate the (relative) moral autonomy inspired by this culture[7] and may stigmatize the underlying rationale and behaviours as an unholy mixture of superstitious and animistic beliefs. But this is akin to a political élite's expediently stigmatizing the *popolino*'s culture as predatory and fatalist.[8] The Church may profit, in a limited way, from these people's approaches and actions but it is observably incapable of controlling or even modifying them.[9] And, like the lay potentates, it appears incapable of influencing significantly the role played by such actions and culture in their explanation (and redefinition) of their place – and perhaps their role – in society.

It ought not to surprise us that such moral and spiritual values and entrepreneurialism should strongly interact. As Bernard Groethuysen has demonstrated in his masterpiece on the eighteenth-century French up-and-coming bourgeoisie (1927), a very similar situation marked the development of a 'revolutionary' model of capitalist entrepreneurship which would later deeply affect social relations and organization. This accomplishment was characteristically made possible by a negotiated rela-tionship between entrepreneurial and capitalist drive, religious belief and ecclesiastical interests. Most intriguing, this process of negotiation was basically inspired by St Alphonsus Liguori's moral philosophy of a medi-ated relationship between doctrinal requirements and the values of indi-viduals' pursuit of interest. Significantly, this religious leader had chosen to apply his philosophy to the urban populace of South Italy in the first place, finding wide response among the *popolino* of Naples (De Rosa 1987). It is by referring to principles that were central to his theological teachings that the Jesuits managed to provide a suitable point of reference for the needs and desires of the new French bourgeoisie (Gruerber 1973).

In northern Europe, a corollary to the negative values attached to inter-mediation by the Protestant ethic (Landsberg 1953; Michel 1939; Le Goff 1984) has been the impersonalization of people's relations with formal power. Emphasizing the ironies of Weber's vision, the correspondingly characteristic interpretation of the rational organization of society has generated overbureaucratized welfare schemes which, in accordance with modern theories of liberal democracy, 'can be better understood in terms of their promoting conditions necessary to "rational" behaviour than as manifestations of democratic norms' (Stankiewicz 1980: 7).

There are, of course, many variations on this theme. In Sweden, for example, the driving force has been a value system based on the concept of a pure, new man (Frykman 1981). This model rational citizen is meant to belong to a society founded on a strictly technical (rational) organization of the state (Fred 1984; also Fred 1979: 159–61) and, ultimately, of civil rights and individual freedom. The pursuit of this ideal has been as thorough as the promotion in the 1930s of the complete embourgeoisement of that society (see Frykman 1981; Fred 1984; Frykman and Löfgren 1987).[10]

The flexible modes of thought, exchange and action that inform rational organization in Naples would be unthinkable in terms of the taxonomic puritanism that marks strongly bureaucratized social systems. They would be regarded as time-wasting, irrational and disordering pollutants of the bureaucratic order as the perfect order.[11] Perhaps they would be seen as evil and dishonourable, for the widespread negotiation of bureaucratic rigidity that they bring about contrasts too sharply with the ideal of efficiency, equality and impersonal righteousness that informs the bureaucratic model and the correspondingly inhuman order of existence. The observable costs of approximating such an ideally unpolluted order bring to mind the Nietzschean nightmare of an objectified modern society. To the extent that it is successful, the pursuit of a technically perfect and hierarchized organization reduces the scope for individual influence on social structure, raising virtually unresolvable issues in political theory (Stankiewicz 1980). Whether the superordering entity is an authoritarian (political) individual or a strongly formalized bureaucracy, this pursuit appears to further a kind of rationalization of social life, with restrictive effects on individuals' autonomy (Beetham 1987: ch. 3) and, therefore, on democracy (Weber 1978: 983–6; Blau 1972: esp. chs. 10 and 14; Tocqueville 1945). The case of Naples introduces stimulating variables into this discussion.

Equality, liberty and rationalization of power: an anarchic representation of democracy?

In contemporary democracy, authority, like freedom and equality, is distinctly relative.[12] In arguing that any effective leadership must include elements of more than one ideal-typical kind of authority, Weber (1978, Pt 1: ch. 3) was aware that Western bureaucratic organization, weakened by an overemphasis on technicality, fatally restricted individual initiative and the development of democracy (esp. 225–6). In today's Europe, widespread levelling in the guise of the egalitarian promise of an ideal impersonal apparatus in which the office is thoroughly objective may give a more democratic appearance to systems in which the individual dimension has less and less influence on the organization and structure of society. This situation highlights the problem of distinguishing egalitarianism from levelling (Lukes 1987; Martin 1977), which remains debatable and susceptible to self-contradiction (see Weber 1978: 983–6; Beetham 1987 and, from different perspectives, Habermas and the Frankfurt School

(Ingram 1987) and Lukes 1991a). Certainly, a highly rationalized world raises the classical question 'whether humankind is able to cope with this environment without losing its uniquely human character' (Stauth 1992: 232), and it carries to its logical conclusion the conflict between equality and liberty (Lukes 1991a: ch. 4).

The categories of domination, equality and objectification are problematic and ambiguous, and so is the nature of the relationship between democracy and the rationality of formality and impersonality. I have suggested that bureaucratic precision and formality are inconsistent with the culture of negotiable achievement of fulfilment which we have been examining here. This broadly agrees with Weberian views of rationalization as a problematic – not automatic – development (Weber 1948; 1978: chs. 11 and 10). However, the fact that fulfilment is measured in direct and problematic relation to the significant group is in no contradiction, I have argued, with the entrepreneurial commitment of many Neapolitans to individual manoeuvring and negotiation.

This ethical relationship of bureaucracy to democracy and the market must be understood in the light of the important principle that, whatever form democracy may take, the *sine qua non* for its social basis is a (relatively) discerning, self-determining and creative individual agent. Of course, the distorted form assumed by people's discernment and self-determination under the adverse conditions of Naples underlines the fundamental relativity of this ethical relationship and the (natural) imperfection of both democracy and the market (Lively 1975; Higley and Gunther 1992: Introduction). However, we cannot afford to interpret one aspect of a situation as its cause. The role of individual independence and creativity in the dynamics of the social, economic and symbolic order bears, ultimately, on relations of power and political authority in this democratic system. We have identified ordinary people's manoeuvring their way to important resources as part of an individual-oriented rationale which cannot be explained as a form of amoral instrumentalism – or of solipsism (Nietzsche 1966) – because it works against the bureaucratization of the market and society. More precisely, it has emerged that actors' motivation to situate their lives in a recognizable (and relatively controllable) moral order finds expression in a variety of competitive activities which cannot be dismissed as functions of social and moral fragmentation simply because they do not serve the interests of rulers or prospective rulers. But there is a further complication which needs attention.

It must be recognized that the entrepreneurial culture of fulfilment and betterment which we have studied inspires dealings with the establishment which defy the rationale of a rigid structure, especially because they factually if not always deliberately contrast with the tendency of politics and bureaucracy to become irresponsible powers separate from civil society.[13] This contrast is strengthened by the tendency to resist subjugation to the more powerful. Resistance is an important aspect of the individual's power to influence the structure, because this subjugation is characteristic of the degeneration of modern bureaucracy into despotism (Beetham 1974). The style of administration, politics and civil society created by the subordination of bureaucracy to political interests, only superficially in tune with Neapolitans' preference for personal relations, may have met with uneasiness on their part. The evidence suggests, however, that many ordinary people have gone beyond expanding their scope for choice and finding ways of getting round the traditional restrictions of clientelism (Chapter 6).

Regarding, in particular, the relationships of the *popolino* with the system, we have observed that, given the mass diffusion of favours and the non-professional provision of services and information, they cannot be reduced to a mere modality of the management of power. They occur on two levels: *formal* democratic participation via elections and the *informal* (even illicit) driving of a coach and horses through its 'unfair organization'. Representative agencies (trade unions and political parties) and bureaucrats of all sorts are key facilitating elements in this process. The personalization and informalization of the organization of society is thus explained by spurious interests more than by incompetence,[14] or by the injection into bureaucracy of non-bureaucratic values and behaviours. That the negotiation of the bureaucratic ideal produces delay, inefficiency and Kafkaesque frustration for those who lack access to the necessary resources is evidence of such spurious interests rather than of irrationality or chaos in the system. Pointing to the 'factual inequality' inherent in democracy (Stankiewicz 1980: 247–8), the pursuit of favours and privileges rewards individual initiative, but it is also so widespread that in many ways this 'society of privilege' becomes perversely egalitarian, though unlevelled and perhaps unlevellable. This entrepreneurial understanding of bureaucracy and *sottogoverno* actually ends up challenging a perverse feature of democratic power – levelling status and rank (Tocqueville 1945; Stankiewicz 1980). It also forces the establishment to come to terms not with class differentiation (which might still allow some surface representation of such levelling) but with the differences between individuals engendered by the relation of entrepreneurialism to value.

Judgemental biases apart, it would be unhelpful to write off this social system as essentially anarchic and ungovernable. It is better to recognize that distinguishing dominance and control from power helps us to understand power as a sociological category that works in multiple directions – not just between above and below, let alone from above to below. As has happened with the supramundane, intermediation between ordinary citizens and their rulers has been quietly redefined in such a way that vertical relations of dominance and technically objectified organization fail to be practicable strategies. Let me be very clear: it has been argued that a state which is insufficiently co-cultural with significant parts of society and fails to provide widespread affluence cannot expect to retain the trust and loyalty of all (Gellner 1969: 33). The fact that, as I have indicated, democracy is not weakened by people's distrust of their various governors is explained by the problematic relationship between the motivations for such distrust and the sense of having the power to influence the system, and extract benefits from it.

In particular, the *popolino* have conceptualized their relations with the more powerful in a way which, appearances apart, does not lead them to acquiesce in their received rhetoric. Their awareness of the concurrence of socially diversified bureaucracy and the mass diffusion of favours has visibly informed their transactional power in exchanges with resource-controllers of all sorts. They have developed modes of action which help to mitigate those aspects of modern society – among them formality, compartmentalization and the elusiveness of bureaucracy as a form of power in the state – that especially conflict with their entrepreneurship and identity. This popular conceptualization of the system recalls the point made earlier (Chapter 6) that the culture and action of ordinary Neapolitans underline an important aspect of the moral conflict generated by actors' negotiated approach to the corrupt personalization of administrative power associated with the centre parties, the 'honest' but rigid and ideological government associated with the traditional left, and the ruthlessness of the hybrid positions midway between these extremes. As recent political events suggest, the *popolino*'s morality could be said to agree in principle with some basic requirements of a society in which fundamental civil rights are guaranteed by administrative action, through political choice, but sufficient room is left for investment in personal initiative.

All my informants say that they desire better communal living. The relationship between this desire and their actions and role in the democratic process exemplifies the normative difference between democracy and anarchism (Stankiewicz 1980: ch. 4). It will appear to be supportive or even generative of anarchy – as speciously opposed to bureaucratic rationality –

only if we fail or omit to penetrate the processes of 'tolerance' underlying the stage-representation of life which differently motivated individuals across the social spectrum seem to have an interest in upholding (Chapters 4 and 5). The kind of popular participation in control which I have described – and indeed the current political climate – suggest that opposing participatory democracy to representative democracy in the Italian situation begs the question of the credibility, accountability and representativeness of democratic institutions.[15] Given that the conception of the good life in democracy is not a matter of technical knowledge[16] or objective rationality, it is well beyond formal rules and principles. I suggest, therefore, that individuals' initiative in the domains of work, entrepreneurship and exchange significantly helps to determine how democracy and its values are understood and practised. More precisely, it is the degree of normative and moral consistency of individuals' actions with their ideas of (short- and long-term) betterment rather than with superimposed 'values' that orders their participation – sometimes in forms that are 'objectively' unorthodox.

The doubts raised earlier about the equivalence that is often established between technically efficient bureaucracy and 'good democracy' now serve to emphasize the point that, in order to understand the nature of any democratic system, we must address the empirical combination of these two aspects. The case of Naples shows that since ordinary people's respect for rules is less a value than a negotiable symbol, 'normality' is susceptible to moral and normative redefinition. This complicated interplay between form and content in the political and bureaucratic fields is very close, in principle, to the processes that we have studied at the micro-level. Without making our task any easier, we have recognized that this interplay is entirely consistent with a style of management of existence in which individuals' negotiations of morality, thought and action make the (basically manipulable) form appear as the (shared, ideally ordered, and much less manipulable) content. This important and intriguing distinction between form and content helps us to address the difficulty of establishing the exact nature of the relationship between social norms and rational conduct, for we can reasonably say that the interplay between these two categories lends a degree of consistency to the relationship between individuals' actions, their identity and the general requirements of social organization.

Individual vs. collective aspects of purposive action
Current arguments in defence of the class analysis approach to modern society reiterate the significance of conflict, particularly class conflict, in

our understanding of structure and action (Eder 1993). From a strongly structure-oriented viewpoint, it is generally argued that conflict develops, rationally, in the specific context provided by organized collective action (Castells 1977, 1983; Crompton 1993: 197–208). Across Naples society, conflict occurs in various forms which include the collective but in a way that, I suggest, grants it no sociological determinance.

In a traditional leftist line of argument, the failure to 'mobilize the masses' (particularly the *popolino*) in a permanent and organized way is explained by the instrumental role of short-term central-government assistance in perpetuating clientelism (see, e.g., Graziani and Pugliese 1979; Chubb 1981) among a populace that is supposed to lack long-term goals, and to be more interested in consumption than in production. The evidence examined earlier suggests that this line of argument is weak. Here I question its logic further, focusing on the empirical relationship between individuals' purposive action and their collective performance. Purposive collective action, Castells (1983) argues, depends on the efficacy of 'systematized' behaviour, the sharing of interests, the binding role of mediation among the participants, and the dilution of individual agency in mainstream collective transactions entrusted to movement representatives. In many ways, these conditions run counter to basic aspects of the action and culture of the *popolino*, as of many other Neapolitans (Pardo 1993). In particular, they counter the *popolino*'s individual-oriented strategies, with their motivation to pursue goals that are recognizably consistent with their management of existence, their assessment of risk in choice-making, and the demands of their problem with 'representation' in the present situation.

Accordingly, even when collective purposes are identified, collective action tends to be short-lived. Of course *popolino* collective actions do not 'just happen'. However, although under given circumstances collective action is believed to provide support for the personal transactions of individual protesters/goal-pursuers, it remains an ineffectual – perhaps inaccurate – representation of a situation strongly characterized by a culture of socio-economic relations and relations of power that transcends the basic requirements of the collective. This, I believe, does not make any more credible the view that the *popolino*, like most Southerners, are fundamentally incapable of communal action (or perform it only randomly and chaotically) and need to be made class-conscious.[17] It indicates that they remain, instead, committed to individually significant and well-defined objectives.

Historical experience of abortive movements in Naples, we must

observe, finds part of its explanation in the trained ability of the establishment (local and national government, the bureaucracy, the Church) not
only to divide and rule but also to co-opt the motivations, aims and interests of the leaders into individual solutions and then discredit and prose-
cute the rest or simply let the protest degenerate into silence.[18]
Contemporary forms of collective action stimulate a more complex view,
however. A broadly representative example is provided by the Movimento
dei Disoccupati Organizzati (Movement of Organized Unemployed
(MDO)). The MDO, involving many *popolino*, was founded in Naples in
the mid-1970s (Massa and Raffa 1975; Ramondino 1977). It has been
described as a historically crucial – some say revolutionary (Lay 1981) –
form of resistance to 'the conditions of work and livelihood in the informal sector' (Pinnarò and Pugliese 1985:229). Only financially rewarded
activities were significant, it is argued, and the people involved, motivated
by the diffusion of trade-union values, resisted the informal in the fields of
labour and social affairs.[19] It is significant that this protest of the unemployed developed for the first time in European history in Naples. It is also
not surprising, however, that, after a short period of communal battles, its
organized action gradually atomized into individual transactions.[20]

The employing power of the local Christian Democrat-dominated
administration played a significant role in 'reducing tension', especially
among the many unemployed who had a non-industrial background and
values, and, of course, tactics reminiscent of old patterns of co-optation
and patronage were used. As in other such cases, however, collective action
lost its purpose as the majority of individuals' strategies reached their
goals or alternative ones. A charismatic MDO leader who had argued for
the 'proletarianization of the unemployed' became a Socialist MP and
then a consultant for the Ministry of Labour of the centre-left government. Later he successfully fought parliamentary elections, as an MP, for
other leftist parties. Some members became personal drivers or factotums
for powerful politicians of various parties. Some started training schemes
leading – they hoped – to 'proper jobs'. Others remained formally unemployed entrepreneurs or, encouraged by trade-unionists and politicians,
joined cooperatives of the kind described in Chapter 3.

These events may well have included an element of clientelism, but it
would be wrong to say that the logic of assistance played the decisive role.
It is precisely in the performance of unemployed *popolino* in competition
and cooperation with each other over benefits and jobs that we have found
early evidence of the discriminative attitude, increasingly independent of
both clientelism and collectivism, which nowadays is clearly observable in

this part of the population. As I have already noted, this and other collective experiences and relationships with leftist activists have undeniably contributed to this process, making people more aware of their rights and their options in the pursuit of steady jobs – which, quite significantly, often provide the secure (if inconspicuous) financial background for the development of free enterprise. It could be argued that collective action for jobs (or other benefits) does not normally include, for a sufficiently long period, the unifying motivation of the formally unemployed to maximize the sum of their assets. Our analysis of the way in which most *popolino* informants, including a few who are industrial (manual) workers, have obtained their formal jobs and other benefits shows that frustrated goal pursuit underlies many forms of communal action. These processes of collective performance become more complex when formally employed people are involved. They participate ('duly', they say) in organized trade-union action for better services, working conditions and pay, but we have seen that when it comes to more specific goals they prefer to act individually, negotiating their goals individually with the persons who run the relevant department or who are believed to have the power to grant the required benefits. That they do so without necessarily submitting themselves to relations of personal dependence, subjection and exploitation powerfully reinforces the point. In brief, the left's attempts to mobilize particularly the *popolino* (formally unemployed or employed) in long-lasting collective action with general political ends seems to have failed less because of these people's presumed shortcomings than because of Marxism's great 'difficulty in linking its monistic motivational requirement with the likely motivations of actual people' (Lukes 1991a: 310; also Bobbio 1987).

I have argued that opposing norms to self-interest is unhelpful and confusing. It is equally unhelpful to stress the collective aspect of the agency/structure relationship. The point is that, with a very few exceptions, there seems to be an awareness among ordinary Neapolitans that collective action – usually organized by trade unions (Mingione 1985: 35) – is appropriate when it is about services or benefits unambiguously identifiable as 'moral' goals of public interest, such as prevention of epidemics, clean water, housing and employment for all and better working conditions and pay. In these instances, competition gives way to a clear emphasis on solidarity, organization and collective identity, including the sense of belonging and of fighting together for a just cause. This kind of approach is supported rather than contradicted by the equally widespread belief that mass action is of little use when one is trying to redress unfair work relations or to obtain a job, a licence or proper medical treatment.

These attitudes are profoundly compatible aspects of actors' increased ability to manage individually and resourcefully their existence; they call into question the argument that urban change is inseparable from the construction of knowledge of previous (collective) struggles crystallized in history (Castells 1983; also E. P. Thompson 1978 and Eder 1993). Class formation depends on the recognition of shared interests and identity with others who are considered to be in a similar condition. People's actions and their views of their place in the system which we have examined help to *diversify* social relations through a process of definition and redefinition of personal entrepreneurship, resources and strategies. Of course, this process may be influenced by ascribed socio-economic position, bureaucratic buck-passing and corruption, and the manipulative strategies of 'the powerful'. However, considering also new patterns of social differentiation in the fields of administration and politics, there is strong reason to doubt that it is *determined* by these (relatively negotiable) factors.

The interpretive model of conflict set out by the Marxist historian E. P. Thompson,[21] and described as culture-conscious for its concern with the cultural determinants of (working-) class consciousness, emphasizes the significance of individuals' experience and interpretation of relations of power for the development of long-term mass action and, ultimately, class formation and social change. It is, of course, beyond the scope of this book to assess this culturalist interpretation of modern history.[22] It can be usefully observed, however, that in Naples as elsewhere in Europe it appears that it is the cumulative outcomes (in a diachronic sense) of these individual strategies, not the development of class consciousness and 'rationally organized' mass action, that produce significant changes in the social system (Leach 1977). This is, however, an uneven process. There is reason to accept, at least in part, my informants' claim that they would willingly fight for a common (society-oriented) ideal in which individual motivations could be integrated into shared values. It is also clear, however, that, given the right conditions for such forms of morally oriented collective action, their informed interpretation of power relations and qualified view of representation would crucially affect the nature of their participation. Both their view of 'honest administrators' and their direct experience and collective memory of the instrumental interest that politicians of almost all parties clearly have in them would probably encourage a kind of participation which would pre-empt the control normally ensured both ways by organized mass action. Whether this relationship between participation, representation and control could be less problematic must be addressed elsewhere. In any case, I fail to see why the *popolino* should be condemned because, entrepreneurially minded as they happen to be, they have understood in their own way that the system is not a technically impersonal entity but made up of *persons* who do not enjoy unchallengeable powers and with whom – as things stand at the moment – it is wise to be cautious. As I have suggested earlier, it is up to their leaders – the 'new élites' – to engage in a constructive interpretation of this empirical fact.

The fact that these attitudes towards the establishment must be understood in other than political terms does not help to justify the labelling of the *popolino* as individualists and opportunists. Instead it highlights the relative independence and power of the 'powerless', particularly to influence social structure. Moreover, this style of individual entrepreneurship prevails even when action appears to be collective and organized. To paraphrase Pareto (1935), among the – unproletarianizable – contemporary *popolino* 'foxes' may play collective 'lions', not sheep. And they appear not only to be doing so with good results but also thus to be participating in the controlled defiance of formal organization and social polarization which may well underlie the new political approach that marks this critical phase of Italian democracy.

Values, norms and self-interest in agency's relationship to closure and structure

I have attempted to show that important changes in social relations and participation in civil society find no satisfactory explanation in ideological casuistry or in the categories of collectivism. They are better accounted for by the processual analysis of the strong continuous interaction between morality and action and between different resource domains which deeply informs actors' entrepreneurial drive towards a better life. Because the economics of this interaction do influence social structure, its empirical investigation has been crucial to our understanding of actors' positions in relation to work and employment, enterprise, property, housing, education and, ultimately, power. It is in these domains, I have argued, that social closure becomes relevant.

The empirical investigation of values, norms and self-interest in relation to exchange and representation has shed new light on the way in which urban dwellers deal with restrictions on their choices and actions. The combination of their entrepreneurial morality with the socially diversified and personalized organization of the social system to which they belong affects power relations in a way that contributes to the distance which, for Weber, exists between power and social class. The study of the *popolino* (the so-called underclass) and the petty bourgeoisie (the 'non-class') poses the question whether the abstract categories of the class perspective help us to understand the relationships between citizens and their rulers and to recognize the important variables introduced into these market-oriented relations by the not strictly materialist value attributed to material goals.

We ought to recognize that structural constraints in the crucial domains of social, economic and political life (Parkin 1979) are countered by people's motivation to improve their prospects. The *popolino*, especially, seek to do so resourcefully by doing more than one job, running more than one enterprise or expanding those already existing, becoming not only homeowners but multiple-property owners, and dealing profitably in the administrative and generally public arena. We have also observed, however, that among both the *popolino* and the petty bourgeoisie house ownership or tenancy – like the pursuit of a job, service or any other object of desire – is not simply an issue of consumption determined by actors' relation to production and their position in terms of subalternity. A house is not simply a place to be lived in and a financial resource, nor is a shop or workshop simply a place to work in or a job or enterprise merely a way of making money. Profoundly significant identity values are attached to these basic aspects of livelihood.

Elsewhere (1992) I have argued that the weakness of the abstract approach to culture that characterizes interpretations of urban social relations in terms of class is made obvious by the analysis of 'housing consumption'.[23] I find this concept questionable because it refers to a materialist-based view of value to argue that the cultural background of part of the population (immigrants and generally those 'marginal' to the system) determines the choices that crucially disadvantage them in socio-economic competition, driving them into segregation and submission. This view of urban relations owes much of its reductivism to the concept that popular culture is instrumental to the interests of the socially superior and to the Chicagoan view of the city in terms of socially, spatially and culturally segregated areas which this study of Naples has encouraged us to reject. The comparative value of the Naples situation in Europe must be addressed in a separate discussion. Here I would draw attention to the fact that the culture of the house (and property generally) which we have found in Naples, like the culture of work, success and well-being, draws on a relationship between morality, inner-life, belief and action which may well not produce class consciousness but is not for this necessarily functional to people's suppression.

Actors' controlled negotiation of practical and cultural values in the pursuit of such basic goals suggests that concepts such as 'housing classes', 'socio-economic marginality' and 'backwardness' are culturally and socially relative. More importantly, it suggests that, by overlooking (or oversimplifying) the role of values, beliefs and expectations in the normative framework in which they pursue their self-interest, the class perspective ends up reproducing some of the rigidity it seeks to avoid. The significance of culture in actors' relation to production and consumption is much more complex and significant than is suggested by the mainstream culturalist approach to class. Work, property, consumption location and accumulation and management of money and privilege are important in the definition and redefinition of status and social relations, but they are too flexible to be principles of closure. For example, the local petty bourgeoisie, even when they are landlords, no longer derive pre-eminence from access to (and control over) money, property, education, contacts (especially in the Church and the administration) and public-sector resources, or to income earned without 'toiling'. Instead, these traditional areas of bourgeois privilege must come to terms with the pressure brought about by significant changes in socio-economic and cultural relations.

In broad agreement with Saunders (1981, 1984), we have observed that social position does not determine consumption. A very similar principle applies to formal economic position. Life-strategies cross-cut economic and social interests in factual disregard of the formal (or, more properly, abstract) categories of relations of production and the rational organization of society. Most importantly, the terms of imperfect competition are observably not fixed in a more or less historical dialectical relationship or 'class tension'. Instead, they change profoundly over time as they are informed by changes in the material and non-material aspects of people's lives and, more generally, in their understanding of their place in society and in their moral and spiritual universes. Neapolitans are quite aware of the existence of social differences, and they do not see these differences as easily bridgeable. But there is also a strong correspondence in their personal histories between their entrepreneurialism and their belief that these differences are not unchallengeable. Their management of existence draws on a sense of shifting boundaries (geographical, political, economic, social, administrative, moral and cosmological); it is not confined to (abstract) categories. Regardless of employment status, their action cuts across these boundaries and, within limits, transcends closure. They display an ability to move from one socio-economic pigeon-hole to another without incorporating the characteristics formally ascribed to any of them so completely as to identify themselves either as deprived and ignorant people or as professionals, businessmen and people of property.

Lino, Antonio, Michele, Domenico, Paolo and the rest call themselves *popolino* and identify with the quarter – its social relations and culture. But they are also low-ranking clerks, semiprofessional employees, freelance entrepreneurs and, in some cases, trade union representatives, political canvassers and so on. Often they are more than one of these things, which suits them very well indeed. In the quarter they are clever, respected and successful entrepreneurs or, alternatively (sometimes simultaneously), poor fellows who must make sacrifices to survive. In any case they are (or try to be) and represent themselves as good-hearted people, strongly motivated to establish moral, symbolic and practical order in their earthly purgatory, where, as in purgatory after death, personal betterment can be negotiated through ability, worthiness and the support of significant others.

They may consider it appropriate, or useful, to present an image of themselves that is the opposite of their self-image. Outside the quarter they may be seen as amoral opportunists. From a less contrived viewpoint, their entrepreneurship, resources (including monetary ones) and values (such as, for example, their views about their and their children's future) would place them somewhere among the middle classes (Weber 1970, 1978). They have traditionally known the importance of money. They now also understand the importance of education up to university level. They pursue emancipation in a way that nods both to their direct experience of the bourgeois and to their understanding of the media's message. An analogous process, particularly obvious among the young, marks their pursuit of betterment. One wonders, for example, whether Giovanni is an averagely well-educated businessman with good political contacts who is motivated to improve his manners, speech, clothing, etc., and has some power to create job opportunities or a poor, unemployed and dependent client who superstitiously holds animistic beliefs. And what about Umberto, Lucia, Enzo? Or the children of Lino, Luigi, Michele and the others?

Are these individuals alienated, marginal and subaltern as has so often been claimed, or does their control over skills and resources (including work, property, information and education) identify them differently? And how are we to account for their increasing interest in bourgeois values, identity and points of reference? Pursuing this line of questioning would be approaching the situation from the wrong end, and any answer would be too partial to be useful. Raising issues of a refreshingly unorthodox character, the social relations in which these people are involved are basically unaccounted for by concepts of false consciousness and models of predetermined and institutionalized domains of exchange and control over resources.

The comparative study of the *popolino* and the petty bourgeois supports the argument, powerfully formulated from different disciplinary viewpoints, that the concept of class is inadequate to the study of the contemporary West. Calvert (1982) concludes his review of this 'essentially contested concept' by suggesting that it be abandoned altogether, and Lukes argues for a social analysis 'unencumbered by wishful and anachronistic notions of class and class structure' (1991a: 293).[24] This view is echoed in the growing scepticism of a class analysis of our society that has found its way into the criticism of the left across Europe. I have suggested that not even 'modern' class-related notions, such as social closure, provide much help in understanding crucial aspects of ordinary life in our cities. It is argued that this notion may help us to account for new principles (credentials) which are being used to construct new social barriers. Particularly in the light of Gramsci's production and of current work on class (Bourdieu 1984, 1991; Eder 1993), this is an intriguing issue which is the object of empirical research now in progress (see Chapter 6: n. 15).

An outstanding example of recent work on the theory of class is that of Klaus Eder (1993). Eder argues that in modern society, where industrialism is vanishing, a hierarchical model is too simple to fit social reality (1993: 8–15) in that it opposes (anachronistically, he rightly notes) dominating and dominated classes, exploiting and exploited classes, etc. In partial agreement with the issues raised by the Naples case, Eder also recognizes the interdependence of rulers and ruled and points out that the inequality that marks their relationships does not preclude reciprocity (p. 11). He attempts to reformulate the concept of objective class by linking class to social movement, proposing a 'network model' in which power and interdependence are the principles that generate modern social structure. Eder summarizes as follows: 'Instead of giving up the notion of class, we only give up the notion of hierarchical relations between classes' (p. 12). In this line he proposes to adopt 'culture' as a mediatory level of analysis of 'structurally determined and culturally textured action space' (p. 12). His sophisticated attempt to categorize the uncategorizable ultimately seems to support the view, elegantly and unambiguously put by Furbank (1985), that class simply cannot be defined on the basis of any specific criteria – including material ones – because the concept draws on a theoretical ambiguity that has more to do with the language of ethics than with that of science.

Empirical analysis of the individual level of morality and social and political action in the constraints of a given situation has highlighted the weakness of a class-based view of man in society. One is reminded here of Leach's warning against imposing figments of thought on the facts of ethnography (1977: xvi–xvii). Given that our task is to penetrate the nature and forms of the agency/structure relationship, we might reasonably conclude that we have no business trying to force the variations in motivations, expectations and actions that mark the lives of real people into the more or less dialectical, objective, but inevitably arbitrary, categories of class.

Confronting the individual's management of existence in society:
theoretical pluralism

The study of the Naples case has suggested that understanding life in urban Europe compels us to go beyond the recognition of social and cultural tension and of the unequal distribution of power, authority and resources. Confronting the significance of the individual in society has brought to light a complex situation in which industrialism is not thoroughly rooted and democracy is based upon an apparently chaotic bureaucratic and political system. Without the support of polarized interests and identities, social boundaries tend to blur, and instead of links of mutual dependence there are various sorts of shifting alliances. Detailed, in-depth analysis in the anthropological fashion shows that imperfect competition at various levels of society is not characterized by moral fragmentation. On the contrary, the moral, spiritual and emotional aspects of existence are determinant in the normative and practically significant construction of action. This key fact gives a distinctive character to urban life.

One lesson to be learned from empirically based analysis is certainly that there is little to gain from opposing agency to structure. As long as our task remains the study of the individual in society (urban European or, indeed, any other), our understanding may be made embarrassingly difficult by the multiplicity of real life; nevertheless, it has everything to gain from avoiding abstract and generic references to culture and to action. There is, in other words, an incomparable advantage in coming to terms with the moral and spiritual complexity of people's lives in its multifaceted relation to practical aspects such as work, transaction, choice, risk, investment, capital, property, education, entrepreneurship and contacts – in brief, individuals' management of existence as the pursuit of fulfilment.

That individuals' construction of position and identity challenges

polarization and objectification suggests that it will be theoretically productive simply to consider people for what they are: rational, motivated
actors who have developed the ability to pursue fulfilment and relative
security through the redefinition of culture and exchange in the structure
to which they belong. And, in the course of doing so, they contribute significantly to affecting such structure 'from below'. There are, of course,
complex reasons that the Naples situation appears problematic. The
detailed study of these reasons has helped us to clarify the significance of
an entrepreneurial style that has thus far remained largely misunderstood.
This has, inevitably I believe, encouraged us to adopt a salutary pluralist
perspective on the questions to be asked about this urban European
setting. In the end, it seems appropriate for the ethnographer to conclude
that the translation of such entrepreneurialism into terms acceptable to a
truly open and legitimate civil society is one of the most basic conditions
for a better social order, and perhaps for the reconsolidation of this democratic system as a whole.

Notes

1 Issues of anthropological research in urban Europe

1 Neapolitans and other Italians often address persons with some knowledge whom they respect, regardless of their formal qualifications, as 'doctor'. The same is basically true of *prufesso'*[*re*] (professor). Neapolitans often omit the end of words, and sometimes the first letters as well.

2 Basically a council-employed traffic policeman who also performs various other policing duties.

3 The city continues to be described in such contrasting terms, to stress its supposed diversity or uniqueness (for recent examples see De Matteis 1991: 12; Dini 1990). Herzfeld offers some immunizing reflections on this kind of stereotyping (e.g., 1992: 72 ff.).

4 More detailed examples of this view are found in earlier chapters. For example, at the end of a chapter on 'Want', Belmonte states: 'Faced with the choice between morality and survival, the Neapolitan always chooses survival' (p. 121).

5 Specialists in the field have persuasively criticized Banfield's paradigm (see Davis 1970; see also Marselli 1962, Muraskin 1974, Colombis 1975 and, more recently, Prato 1995 and, from a comparative perspective, Herzfeld 1992: 35–6; also 1987).

6 This idea of segregation in the Western city is clearly set out by the Chicagoans of the 1930s (see, e.g., Park et al. 1967 [1925]; Whyte 1955; Zorbaugh 1929; and their critics, e.g., Hannerz 1980) and, more recently, in the work of sociologists such as Rex and Moore (1967) and Hobbs (1989).

7 Weber, in his essay on 'The City' (1978: ch. 16), established the important role of historical enquiry in this field (see also Elliott and McCrone 1982). Albera (1988) has efficiently criticized 'decontextualized' analysis. Recent works (e.g., Herzfeld 1987, 1992; Viazzo 1989; Holmes 1989; Prato 1995; see also Kertzer 1980) seriously grapple with this problem.

8 Naturally, as Tonkin notes (1984: 218; see also Jackson 1987: 8), unfamiliar circumstances need not be geographically remote. Strathern (1987: 16) argues that one should maintain an open mind in a 'spirit of honest difference'. Apolito (1987) reviews the issue from the point of view of Italian anthropology.

9 In an essay of some years ago, Lukes (1982: esp. pp. 302–5), bringing together thought-provoking views on the rationality debate, states the case for 'weak' perspectivism as opposed to 'strong' perspectivism. Eisen (1978) discusses Weberian perspectivism.

10 It is beyond the task of this book to examine the literature on urban Europe. For reviews, see Kenny and Kertzer (1983) and Sanjek (1990: esp. pp. 164–5). Hannerz (1980) raises this point on a more general level.

11 Such a tendency in anthropology has been convincingly criticized (see, e.g., Bloch and Houtman 1988). It is of course desirable that the results of anthropological enquiry contribute to the improvement of life in our cities. However, it seems to me good sense for application to follow academic research and for intellectual curiosity, not the economics of utility, to be its motivation.

12 Apart from the works on Naples which I have mentioned, my background sources include magistracy accounts, literary production and filmography, which will be referred to at the appropriate places in the text. The assistance of the researchers of the Ufficio di Statistica del Comune di Napoli produced detailed census figures on population, housing, employment, health, mortality, migration and electoral behaviour. Keeping in mind the problems involved in the production and use of official statistics (see, e.g., Bulmer 1986), quantitative information can be found in Comune di Napoli (1981, 1991), IRSES (1987), ISTAT (1994a, b, 1995).

13 The *popolino* who had cooperated years earlier in my research on death and the hereafter (e.g., Pardo 1989) saw a study of life in central Naples as inadvisable, and the contacts I had made as an undergraduate in Naples proved of little use in easing my relations with the bureaucracy. Helpfully, however, one may happen to find individual enthusiasm even where one would expect impenetrable opposition.

14 These maps concerned informants' 'kin/non-kin' and 'this world/the other world' universes. In using these empirical methods, I was originally stimulated by Wallman (1984) and by discussion with Andra Goldman. Mitchell (1983) discusses the logical rather than statistical relevance of case-studies.

15 The centre of Naples can reasonably be regarded as sociologically homogeneous.

16 Since the Second World War most of the bourgeois residents have moved to the suburbs, leaving their upper-floor apartments to the better off among the *popolino* for rent or sale. Thus provincial towns – such as Portici (see Map 1) – were abnormally expanded, gradually becoming incorporated into suburban Naples (see, e.g., Leone 1980; De Seta 1969, 1988). Popular housing built on the periphery for industrial workers, subsequently joined by some *popolino*, is characterized by poor services and poor environmental conditions (see e.g., CRESM 1986).

17 Local people say that they love the quarter and would like to see the streets better kept, the buildings restored, street crime reduced, drug-selling eliminated. They fear, however, that, because the place is very central, rich people and offices would move in and they would be 'persuaded' to move out. These issues have been long debated, and various proposals of urban planning (e.g.,

SCSN 1986; AA. VV. 1991; see also Bellacci and Rea 1989) have been the object of controversy. This is a complex problem that deserves separate attention.

18 They do not sell them or continue to pay the rent for them, leave them partially furnished, and regularly visit them.

19 (Neap. *Munaciell'*.) Informants use the Italian or the Neapolitan word interchangeably. A large number of reports collected over the years suggest that the spirits of people who have died violently or 'improperly' and linger between this world and the other world may take various anthropomorphic forms (the Pacchiana (female peasant) is another of these forms) but they never resemble people whom one knew when they were alive. This would imply, inconceivably, the admission of their improper death.

20 Otherwise, cars parked in the neighbourhood continued to provide some privacy, and 'private' ordered space was carved out on the pavement, shops, etc., raising issues which belong to a separate discussion of the local categories of space and time.

21 It was helpful that anyone not there could be easily contacted when necessary, or to stress a point when a conversation included a person of that 'type' or performing that kind of activity.

22 Apart from the ethical problems posed by the fact that this obviously affected the interplay of opinions and judgements (Gans 1968; Jarvie 1969; Pálsson 1992; Bourdieu 1993), strategic difficulties arose, for it was not always possible to prevent contrasts in our views from surfacing. However, people's reactions to my remarks were often rewardingly illuminating.

23 (Neap. *vascio*.) Over the past two decades many *bassi* have been converted for non-residential purposes.

24 Normally mindless of noise and casual body contact, *popolino* informants say, 'Unlike the high-noses of the Vomero (a bourgeois district) we don't like too much quietness. It's boring and reminds you of death and bad omen [*mal'aúrio*].' What they mean to emphasize is the contrast between bourgeois ('cold', 'aseptic') composure and *popolino* norms encouraging exuberance and communication. This view makes us think of the extremes reached, in a sense unsurprisingly, at the bourgeois end of this contrast in the West (see, e.g., *The Spectator* 16/26 December 1992, pp. 48–9).

25 Quite apart from folklore, one thinks of the Neapolitans' view of their football team's fortunes. A graffito celebrating the Serie A championship read: '1927–1987, *scusate il ritardo*' (forgive the delay), referring to a film by Massimo Troisi.

26 Of course, the opposite could also be true. A strong sense of dignity and self-respect seemed, in fact, to motivate some poorer locals (e.g., Paolo and Gina, discussed in a later chapter) to represent themselves as better off than they actually were.

27 For example, they and other locals (especially young people who had some knowledge of the English language and culture) showed a critical interest in Britain almost equal to that they showed in current events closer to them, in Naples and the rest of the country.

28 Significantly, some informants began to report or take notes on events that I

had not witnessed but in which they thought I might be interested. The way this happened was itself informative.

29 On a similar line, Lukes (1991b: 14) notes that the pursuit of profit is not merely the pursuit of material gain.

30 Such perspectivism raises problems. In his attempt to sort out the meanings and confusions of Weberian notions of rationality, Eisen (1978) suggests that there is a prejudicial measure of valutation to which they are traced – the Puritan schema on which Weber believed rational conduct to be based.

31 The work activities of the *popolino* have often been described in this way. For various angles, see Belmonte (1989 [1979]: esp. pp. 107–12), Allum (1973; see also Luongo and Oliva 1959), Lay (1981), Laino (1984), Pinnarò and Pugliese (1985: esp. pp. 237–8), and Becchi-Collidà (1984b: Introduction).

32 I originally used the expression 'continuous positive feedback' to describe this process (see e.g., 1992 and 1993). However, as an anonymous reader for Cambridge University Press has pointed out, this expression may be seen to carry mechanistic meanings (and implications of systemic equilibrium and nonequilibrium) which I certainly do not want to convey. 'Strong continuous interaction' is a better wording for what I want to say.

33 This line of argument could be usefully expanded in view of abstract claims about the 'anti-market attitude' of Southerners. (e.g., Pizzorno 1967; Graziano 1980; Altan 1986). Davis (1992: 7; see also p. 79) provocatively notes that 'embeddedness' to one degree or another is a universal characteristic of exchanges.

34 This point comes close in spirit to recent criticism (e.g., Herzfeld 1992: 9) of the misconceived logic whereby entrepreneurship and the related expressions of interest, virtues in the Protestant West, become immoral grasping when practised by others.

35 *Sottogoverno* refers to the favour exchanges, and backstage interpersonal bargaining between politicians and other notables linked to different parties and exerting power in various bodies (political, bureaucratic, economic and administrative) that pervade the Italian situation (e.g., Bobbio 1983; Prato 1993). The illicit exercise of power is also a component.

36 In Bourdieu's model, for instance, the 'dominated' basically (if unwittingly) contribute to strengthen the conditions of their dominance, or they 'react' to changes in objective circumstances beyond their control – they play anyway little or no part in bringing about such changes.

37 These themes of subalternity are variously expressed in the Italian mainstream literature on the South. A rough selection, with particular reference to 'popular culture', would include such works as De Martino (1977), Lombardi-Satriani (1974), Sanga (1980) and Altan (1986).

2 Beyond unemployment: work, morality and entrepreneurship

1 According to official estimates, there are huge numbers of unemployed in Naples (see, e.g., ISTAT 1994a, b, 1995). Similarly controversial figures have been produced in the past. Ragone and Clarizia (1985) have argued that only a minority of the thousands of officially unemployed are at a survival level. This has been debated (Massa and Raffa 1975; Ramondino 1977; Liguori and

Veneziano 1982, 1984; Pinnarò and Pugliese 1985). For other figures, see CENSIS (1984) and IRSES (1987).

2 These activities, it is often argued, help to reduce joblessness and tension.

3 Setting up a legal stall, shop, or workshop requires a licence, which can be obtained by taking an exam and then applying to the council for a place.

4 Throughout Italy, this is a hallmark of self-employment and trade that has resisted all sorts of legislation and is unlikely to be deterred by the existing laws or doctrinal injunctions such as the definition of 'serious sin' in the 1992 Catholic Catechism.

5 Regardless of status, many households employ unregistered plumbers, electricians, builders, carpenters, house-painters, hi-fi, television and computer technicians, etc. In the public sector as well (e.g. in hospitals, council departments, graveyards, etc.), unlicensed workers find ways to provide their services, charging their customers directly.

6 In this and similar cases the gender and number of words is indicated by the article, demonstrative adjective, emphasis, or context. Nowadays *rammar'* (from *ramma* (copper) because *rammar'* originally sold kitchen utensils (D'Ascoli 1979)) sell merchandise (usually linen, household appliances and jewellery) at shop price, without a licence, on credit and charge interest (5–10 per cent per month) on the instalments.

7 This job, made necessary in the past by widespread illiteracy, continues to be performed by some because people find it useful to delegate what is now merely a time-consuming task, willingly paying a fee (rarely less than £1.50) to avoid the long queues to apply for or collect a document.

8 This activity is performed by persons who are not formally qualified but have learned by experience and are locally trusted. Qualified nurses, who evade taxes on this extra income, may also be involved.

9 As authorized parking space is quite limited in central Naples, it is widespread practice for two or more persons (usually men) to select a piece of pavement in a busy area and invite drivers to park there for a fee. The drivers usually willingly pay the convenient fee and even leave the car keys with the 'wardens'.

10 This is not unusual in Europe (see, e.g., the *Sunday Telegraph*, 18 October 1987).

11 This category includes the Camorristi, drug-dealers and persons who have committed violent crimes and show no remorse.

12 These boys, called *muschill'*[i] (sing. *muschill'*[o], midges), are organized, with small motorcycles and a vast network of contacts.

13 In the Naples region, shop and business advertising is traditionally managed by local specialists (now including private television). In the past, these 'specialists' were called *pazziariell'*[i] (sing. *pazziariell'* [o], joker). They toured the neighbourhood performing their rhyming 'commercials', accompanied by a band of players, all in colourful costumes.

14 However, clandestine lotteries are discussed with perceptible uneasiness. For example, Antonio willingly cooperated in his case-study but only after elaborate negotiation did he agree to discuss his illicit work-activities in some detail.

15 My informants helped me to make sense of the whirl of activity and the

excitement at the local betting-stalls (*muschilli* came and went carrying messages, acolytes looked out for the police, bets and winning numbers were debated). This, I was made to note, was 'part of the huge business of clandestine lotteries . . . where very little's really clandestine.'

16 In the case of lotto, the regulations have recently been changed to make them more appealing to betters (see, e.g., Law No. 85, 19 April 1990). However, informants continue to say that they prefer the clandestine option because winnings are paid speedily and it is possible to bet large sums (bets lower than a pound are considered 'shameful', but there is no upper limit). Large bets are usually split up on several tickets to reduce the risk of theft and missed payment should the win be too large and to keep the total amount secret.

17 A high estimate has been made of this industry (see, e.g., Pinnarò and Pugliese 1985: 236), which is widespread throughout Italy. Many workshops have resettled in the hinterland, especially since the 1980 earthquake (Laino 1984; Diamantini 1984; Liguori and Veneziano 1984; SCSN 1992).

18 This phenomenon brings to mind the work in official workshops described by Wallace and Pahl (1985). See also Frey (1975: esp. pp. 1311–63), De Marco and Talamo (1976), Goddard (1977), Esposito and Persico (1978), Laino (1984), Cetro (1984) and Diamantini (1984).

19 Even in the public sector, an employee may enjoy privileges because he is protected by criminals. As we shall see, the protection of a political party or a trade union may bring similar benefits.

20 In Italy analogous affairs have occurred in various sectors. For instance, medical frauds have involved politicians (up to ministerial level), trade-unionists, academics, doctors, nurses, chemists and ordinary people.

21 Reburial takes place after about two years. This space-saving custom carries important cultural meanings (Pardo 1989).

22 A similar argument has been formulated regarding the British situation (Wallace and Pahl 1985; Pahl 1984). Wallman (1979) has emphasized the non-material value of work activities (paid or not) which substitute for formal labour.

23 The *popolino*'s general unfamiliarity with industrialism has been explained by the aristocratic feeling they are supposed to derive from being citizens of the former capital of a large European kingdom and from their traditional physical closeness to the bourgeoisie and aristocrats (Gribaudi 1980). This ethnography suggests a more complex situation.

24 Lino kept the stall, paying his brothers and sisters their share. Some of them used the money to open their own stalls.

25 In this kind of (widespread) arrangement, the profit of the figurehead consists in free merchandise (rarely money) and in a reputation as a good, generous and reliable person.

26 Communist Party-led coalitions governed Naples between 1975 and 1983. In 1991 the party became the PDS (Democratic Party of the Left). Splinter Communists formed a small party to the PDS's left called Rifondazione Comunista (Communist Refoundation). Communist intellectuals (see, e.g., De Giovanni 1990) have given an assessment of the problems underlying these changes in the Italian left.

27 Her task, Lino says, was made easier by the fact that she was promptly informed by a policeman-contact.

28 Lino has given priority to ensuring 'a proper home' for his family because, he says, he has experienced sharing a *basso* with his parents and siblings. Seldom having access to a mortgage, many formally unemployed locals use their savings and, when possible, they borrow money in the name of formally employed kin. It is indeed common wisdom that large sums of money should be borrowed from loan sharks only when repayment can be speedy enough to prevent the effects of exorbitant interest rates from becoming disastrous.

29 Michele concedes that he has only a minor health problem. Magistrates have exposed the widespread practice of obtaining bogus invalidity certificates for claiming civilian disablement pensions (D'Urso 1986).

30 By law a percentage of new jobs go to invalids.

31 These formally non-profit associations, found throughout Naples and elsewhere in Italy, are linked through informal networks. They serve religious and socializing purposes. Run by local devotees with the Church's approval, they are dedicated to a saint or madonna. They are often located in ground-floor rooms and are self-supported: the members pay an annual subscription fee, and money is collected in the neighbourhood for the annual celebrations. Surplus is supposed to go to charity. As in the case of gambling clubs, membership of these associations (where snooker and card-games are also often played) is predominantly male (though gambling is not in itself a male prerogative). Women play a prominent role in the ritual activities, including organization and fund-raising.

32 Apart from the Christian Democrats, until recently, the middle-ground of Italian politics was monopolized by the Republicans, Socialists and Social Democrats to the Christian Democrats' left, and by the Liberals to their right. The present situation is continuously changing and some approximation is inevitable. However, the main centre party is now Forza Italia and small parties involving former Christian Democrats have also been formed.

33 When money is involved in these transactions, it is usually paid part in advance and part after the successful accomplishment of the task.

34 In the early 1970s glue poisoning became a major issue (Maffei 1973; Esposito and Persico 1978). The health and environmental problems in this kind of industry have been widely debated (for recent discussion, see SCSN 1992).

35 In this setting, the nuclear family is usually made up of a married couple (Christian marriage is customary) and its children (nowadays, rarely more than four). Complexities in this issue are discussed in Chapter 4.

36 From informants' accounts, it would appear that the element of sacrifice lies mainly in the fact that they sleep little and cannot spend much time with their families.

37 She now emphasizes the social aspects of her work in the shop and of the raffles she occasionally organizes within her network.

38 Apart from selling cheap trinkets in his small stall, he sold goods door-to-door in the evenings.

39 Women dominate the organization of baptisms, confirmations and marriages; above all, they dominate the mortuary situation and a large part of the process

of healing the psychological and social disruption of death (Pardo 1989). Reminding us of Du Boulay's inspiring theological point (1991), they continue to play such a ritually redeeming role, even though they do not absolutely depend on men.

40 We are broadly reminded here of Herzfeld's (1991:96) argument that women's determined 'verbal articulation of resistance' is crucial 'to bring about a radical change in their social lives'.

41 See *Costituzione della Repubblica Italiana* (1948: esp. Arts. 3 and 4).

42 It has been argued, particularly in the honour-and-shame literature, that in South Italy such control is securely in male hands and that women have control over the relationship between the representation of their sexual behaviour and what they actually do. See, for example, *Anthropological Quarterly* (1967), Blok (1981), Schneider (1971) and Giovannini (1981). Herzfeld's critique exposes the survivalist bias of this paradigm (1987: e.g., pp. 7–12).

43 We should remember that in those days the legitimate places where a young woman could socialize were much more restricted than they are today.

44 Gina and her husband, who say that though they are not rich the larder is never empty, made a point of seeing me in the evening, when their recently redecorated *basso* was at its most neat and immaculate.

45 Elsewhere I have argued against the hypothesis that the Western approach is characterized by a process of 'repression of death' (Pardo 1989, 1985; see also Prato 1987). It is in these terms, beyond ecclesiastical values and beyond the view (e.g., Belmonte 1989 [1979]: 141 and Epilogue) that the *popolino* hold animistic beliefs, that we can understand the presence (in local houses, workplaces and places of socialization (bars, clubs, etc.)) of shrines including the images of dead relatives and friends alongside those of the saints most important to the actors and enlivened by lights and flowers (Pardo 1994a).

46 As I explain at length elsewhere (1989:115–17), in Naples the fundamental importance of purgatory in the Catholic rationale (Landsberg 1953:iv) finds expression in the cult of both 'near souls' (of friends and relatives) and 'forgotten souls'(of unknown dead). The *popolino* associate the unburied skulls kept in the crypts of various churches (Pardo 1994a) with souls in purgatory neglected by the living. Taking care of these skulls/souls and of the remains of near souls, is meritorious behaviour that gives the living hope of intercession.

47 The local priests 'understand', condone, and sometimes even encourage these and other expressions of 'popular piety'. The intellectual élite of the Church formally ignores and, when questioned, disdains them but avoids opposing them for fear of alienating popular devotion altogether.

48 The cult of this madonna is widespread, especially among the *popolino* and the petty bourgeois, throughout the region. To her are dedicated a sanctuary just outside Naples and hundreds of religious associations and street shrines. Over Easter the sanctuary becomes the object of huge, highly ritualized collective pilgrimages involving thousands of people and very large sums of money (see Pardo 1995b).

49 It is when these spirits are believed to exist in one's present home that their presence must not be mentioned outside the household for fear of provoking their ill will towards the inhabitants (see Pardo 1989:113–14).

50 The man who had the licence was not particularly sanctioned. In the opinion of many, he was giving Paolo 'a chance to earn his living'.

51 The theological debate on these issues is vast and complex. Apart from Paul VI's encyclical *Humanae Vitae*, standard reference can be made, for example, to O'Neil (1912), MacKintosh (1920), Von Hildebrand (1967: 148, 149–50), Gründel (1975: 1571–9), Sattler (1967), Levis (1967), Thomas (1967) and Molinski (1975).

52 He believes that although this combination made him a loser he did not deserve to be so downtrodden.

53 Objects such as horseshoes, horns, etc. (placed in strategic places in the house or work premises and worn in small reproductions) are part of the counter-measures adopted by people across society.

54 Beautiful 'Mbriana (Meridiana, from medieval Latin, according to D'Ascoli 1979). The word has connotations of 'shadow' (Cortellazzo and Zolli 1983).

55 Most people expect at least one of their sons or daughters to establish residence in their neighbourhood after marriage.

56 However, possible links with a point made by Campbell (1964: 325) seem to be suggested on the religious and moral levels by my informants' tendency to regard negative events in their own lives and those of their children more as the result of others' envy and of ill-disposed spirits than of their own sin. At the same time, in certain circumstances they tend to see similarly negative events in others' lives as evidence of sin. This appears to be so not only in cases like that of signora Pina, where the nature of such sin is known, but also in cases in which sin is suspected.

57 As Anna puts it, 'When I behave heartlessly, I feel very uneasy. It's a matter of good conscience. We say, "Fà bene e scuordate, e fà male e pienzace" (Forget the good you do, but remember the evil).'

58 Michele's role in the construction of Rafele's welfare, signora Pina's work on Paolo's behalf and the free and the sublet spaces provided by the locals, and Lina's helping the needy are significant examples.

59 An example of such reproduction of generosity is provided by Michele's action stimulating Rafele's shopkeeper employer to be helpful. Generosity is seen as particularly meritorious when possible monetary returns are not claimed, as in the case of 'o Russo's choice not to profiteer (he sold the goodwill for a 'reasonable price') and Rafele's generous treatment of his nephew-assistant.

3 Entrepreneurial morality and ethics among the young: changing social and cultural relations

1 For Lino, heaven 'must be crowded with noisy children and bigots who've spent their lives repenting in church of their heavy secret sins'.

2 On the same line, he describes as backward behaviour the rituals performed by 'young people, often clever entrepreneurs, who walk barefoot, sweaty, and filthy to the Sanctuary of the Madonna of the Arch. They beg money for the madonna, but throughout the year they show off jewellery and expensive cars.'

3 He added, 'policemen often give part of these "presents" to their relatives and friends to improve their wretched image'.

4 Thus the *popolino* describe the different 'environment' to which hardened

criminals belong as a *whole* and *separate* (culturally and socially, not merely physically) entity.

5 In my relationship with Tony I was probably rewarded with some trust for the trust I had granted him when, on an apparently casual encounter, I accepted his invitation to have lunch with him. Later he said he had appreciated that I had shown no reluctance or concern in following him through notoriously dangerous alleys to a rather sinister trattoria and that I had appeared to enjoy both the food and the conversation.

6 Young Southerners also explain in this way their refusal to emigrate to the North. Economists (e.g. D'Antonio 1995b: 36–7) have raised serious objections to a policy of internal emigration (from South to North) in today's Italy.

7 Similarly, Enzo has established a sense of security by having his motorbike blessed at the sanctuary of the Madonna of the Arch and emblazoned with this madonna's protective image.

8 See, e.g., 'Student Guardian' in the *Guardian* 29 September 1992, p. 23, and *Times Higher Education Supplement*, 26 March 1993, pp. 12 and 14. Instead of dropping out, these phantom students continued to pay their registration fees, hoping that they would eventually graduate.

9 One also thinks of the so-called exam market, for which university departments throughout Italy (*Times Higher Education Supplement*, 11 June 1993, p. 11) are under magistrates' inquiry (for the Naples case, see Di Addea 1987).

10 Whereas Enzo feels morally blackmailed by favouritism and rejects it altogether, Giovanni and Lucia ideally deplore it but describe their practical compromises as realism.

11 Tony added, 'The kids also learn good Italian, but they won't forget Neapolitan. They have friends in the quarter, and in the family we speak Neapolitan.'

12 The media have reported repeatedly on this kind of cooperative (see, e.g., *Il Mattino*, 19 November 1984; Improta 1986).

13 The case-study of this man, born in a poor and illiterate local family, shows his determination to succeed also (unusually for his generation) through acquiring a *titolo di studio*.

14 Andrea's brokership is so lucrative and satisfactory in terms of self-esteem and power that he has lately taken early retirement from his formal job in order to perform this activity full time.

15 Over the years, he has used as resource options both Giovanni's relative (in the workplace) and Giovanni and Lucia.

16 Giovanni said, 'It's good that nowadays you don't have to depend on loan sharks,' adding that he was grateful to Andrea for having used his bank contacts to speed the loan.

17 As is suggested by Mair's discussion of African small entrepreneurs (1984: ch. 7), this may generate conflict.

18 I have recorded how local people, who generally make such a move only when absolutely necessary, tend to behave like Giovanni and Lucia. For instance, Anna and Luigi, now accommodated in a council flat on the periphery, have kept the flat where they moved after the 1980 earthquake had damaged their

original one – they say they feel good there and it is in the quarter that they have their business and many close relations.

4 Acceptance vs. discernment: the morals of family, kinship and neighbourhood as resource options

1 Focusing on Greek ethnography, the volume edited by Loizos and Papataxiarchis (1991b) offers articulate discussion of the difficulties posed by this opposition and, more generally, by stereotypical assumptions on gender (and kinship) roles (see, e.g., Loizos and Papataxiarchis 1991a; Du Boulay 1991; Herzfeld 1991).

2 For detailed discussion of this part of Naples ethnography in a broader context, see Pardo 1995a.

3 Some mentioned 'o Malommo (Antonio Spavone) as an example of these villains of the past (on this figure, see Jouachim 1979; Roberti et al. 1985, vol. I). His best-known predecessors, among them Luigi Campoluongo, have inspired works of art (see, e.g., De Filippo 1973 [1960]). Tore 'e Criscienzo was a typical nineteenth-century Camorrista of a similar kind (Baglivo 1983).

4 The moped was notoriously indispensable to Lino's business, and the financial damage would be aggravated by his having to limit his activities until he could manage to get a replacement.

5 Powerful examples were given in support of this view. Many people referred to the murder by the Camorristi of a policeman who had been investigating leftist terrorism. The links between terrorism (leftist and rightist) and criminality in Naples will have to be discussed elsewhere. It may be useful, however, to recall that leftist terrorists have attempted to politicize 'proletarians' and 'sub-proletarians' in prison, while those of the right have used criminals for their bombing campaigns.

6 In order to stay clear of criminals, local *popolino* may well choose not to recover their stolen goods. However, highlighting the problem of degrees of acceptable illegality, they do not refrain from buying goods of dubious provenance.

7 We know that Andrea's contact with crime through his assistant, though very indirect (and, he says, unwitting), seriously jeopardized his brokership and local business.

8 For example, as expected, Amalia has not asked any form of reciprocation, probably being content with the mitigating effect of her good action on her mid-level criminality. In this she is unlike 'real criminals', whose benefaction is always regarded cynically. This underlines the important issue of differentiating between levels of criminality in the analysis of these processes.

9 According to Belmonte, for example, 'members of families are drawn to one another by too much need. Material and utilitarian elements threaten always to outweigh the emotional' (1989 [1979]: 52). On such a line of argument regarding Southerners more generally, see Banfield (1958). Against such misleading views, see De Spirito (1983), CENSIS (1988).

10 Davis (1977: esp. pp. 174–6) discusses comparatively this issue of the household as a physical and moral entity.

11 This kind of flexibility has been addressed in European settings (see, e.g., Blok

1974; Wallman 1984). Important issues in this field have been recently addressed in a special issue of *L'Uomo* (Minicuci 1994).

12 The new favour-seeker (Ciro) was only a connection of a recent acquaintance (Michele).

13 Quite interestingly, and typically, there is reason to think that Ciro was aware of this.

14 This is particularly true with regard to professional favour-bestowers.

15 His kin accept his invitations, but they still say that they 'prefer to shop elsewhere'.

16 Douglass (1991) provides a historical account of this kind of household.

17 Rare exceptions apart, people tend to marry in their early twenties. In the past, as many have noted, premarital intercourse was the major single cause of early (reparatory) marriages, even in the absence of pregnancy.

18 As is suggested by informants' accounts, my own observation, social workers' reports and background information, this behaviour is widespread in Naples. Interestingly, it also agrees with the basic rules of Italian family law (Arts. 433 and 439, *Codice Civile* new text), of which people are not necessarily aware.

19 Davis (1977: 181 ff.) provides comparative discussion of this issue. The new family law (No. 151, 19 May 1975) has abolished the institution of the *dote* (dowry; cf. Art. 177 *Codice Civile* old text with Art. 177 *Codice Civile* new text).

20 See Art. 177 *Codice Civile* new text and, more generally, Section iii.

21 I have observed that even in the case of death this issue is not disputed.

22 They do the same for an old uncle. This suggests an answer to the question of attitudes towards 'needy relatives' (see, e.g., Kertzer 1983: 13). Again, such behaviour is motivated by the local culture of the family, which happens to agree basically with the new family law.

23 Both before and after marriage, we have found, women contribute to the household's income and then are crucial motors in the construction of successful businesses, as well as in emancipation and embourgeoisement.

24 The material on homosexuality discussed in Chapter 5 brings to light intriguing nuances in this positive role of the biological.

25 The management of gossip is not, however, a prerogative of women, let alone their only alternative to silence. Men and women control different, interconnected areas of gossip, and they express different though equally effective styles of management of this important resource. Complex views on this issue are discussed in Loizos and Papataxiarchis (1991a: esp. pp. 12–13).

26 Ciro and Giovanna's son and Eduardo and Imma's daughter are *fidanzati in casa* (formally engaged to marry).

27 These forms of gratitude compound with those described earlier. On a number of occasions I also observed Michele, Nunzia and their children having to insist on paying for various merchandise.

28 Above all, she was helped by her unmarried younger sister and her sister-in-law. In the universes of Nunzia and other informants such closeness is not strictly geographical.

29 This aspect of individuals' lives in relation to the neighbourhood, the family and the social services could be fruitfully compared with the situation in central London (Wallman 1984; Hobbs 1989).

30 As has been argued (see, e.g., Albera 1988), theoretical narrowness has biased much anthropological work. Strong criticism has, however, also been made of the arbitrary polarization of categories such as 'community' and 'nation', 'micro-' and 'macro-', between which all sorts of agents are said to intervene (see, e.g., Davis 1975: 50; 1977). Dynamic and complex relationships in fact exist between these levels.

31 And yet, of all Italians, Neapolitans are said to be the most hyperbolically theatrical (Barzini 1964: 104–5; De Matteis 1991). Of all the stereotypes about them this is perhaps the most misleadingly close to their self-representation.

5 Transgression, control and exchange: the rationality of the ambiguous and the liminal in life and death

1 An important role is played in popular religiosity by figures and beliefs that are not recognized – or barely tolerated – by the ecclesiastical hierarchy.

2 In the vast debate on taxonomies, basic references are Durkheim and Mauss (1963), Hertz (1960), Van Gennep (1960), Eliade (1959), Douglas (1966, 1970) and the work of Lévi-Strauss. Useful analyses have been developed in Bulmer (1973), Tambiah (1973), Bourdieu (1973), Ortner (1975) and Willis (1975).

3 Places that are isolated or difficult to reach are also thus described. For example, I have heard people use this expression as, on these grounds, they ruled out moving to a new house or explained why they seldom visited a friend or kin. I recall, however, no instance in which there was confusion about its meaning.

4 It is noteworthy that the expression 'ascì for' da grazia 'e Dio' (to get out of God's grace) may be used in (serious) cases of temporary loss of self-control caused by strong emotions (especially anger).

5 According to the *popolino*, 'It's as if God had wanted to mark her.'

6 She was also occasionally described as a 'poor, lonely old widow' who ought to be helped.

7 Parrinder (1980: 225–6) makes stimulating reference to the theology of St Augustine and of St Thomas Aquinas in discussing Christianity's uneasy recognition of the utility of prostitution.

8 Sometimes these women embody a local version of the sex therapist. For example, informants used an ex-prostitute neighbour's wisdom 'to make a man out of their son'. More often, advice is asked on how to cope with a boyfriend or husband who is 'becoming cold'.

9 This extends to other 'unfortunates' such as the physically or psychologically weak and homosexuals.

10 As we have seen, the concept of work includes non-monetary-oriented activities, which accounts for the unobvious importance of workers such as children in the local division of labour. I am suggesting here that the application of this concept to other unobvious (and non-ordinary) categories of labourers and entrepreneurs has complex theoretical implications.

11 'Serious women don't normally go into such clubs,' I was told.

12 At this level, minimum interest is 10 per cent per month, but it can be much higher.

13 While both the *popolino* and the bourgeoisie refer to petty moneylenders simply

by defining their activity ('chill' ca dann' 'e sord' co' 'nderess" (those who lend money at interest)), they qualify usurers by using this term, the unequivocally negative meanings of which they usually stress through voice inflexion and body language. In spite of obvious discomfort (some said 'shame', most 'guilt') about discussing personal debt, people gave examples to substantiate this negative attitude. On a different level, in the case of very small sums (in the order of £1000 or less) interest is usually very high but repayment is supposed to occur within weeks, not months.

14 Serious problems arise when major moneylending involves the criminals' 'protection' of the moneylenders' interests. Not only does violence against borrowers and 'dishonest' mediators inevitably mark missed repayments; but such involvement also allows a degree of criminal control over an important aspect of this economy.

15 This brings stimulatingly to mind the Indian case discussed by Parry (1989). The sums transacted at this level are usually well below £10,000. Depending on the size of the sum, the interest rate varies; 3 per cent per month is the minimum.

16 Now the Church condemns usury more explicitly (see, e.g., *Catechismo della Chiesa Cattolica* 1992: 2411, 2443 and 2838–45). However, its clergy has been traditionally (see, e.g., Weber 1978: 587–8) involved in various forms of moneylending (e.g., the Montes Pietatis). Stressing further the arbitrary boundaries of the concept of usury, in Naples some priests actively oppose it (see, e.g., *Il Mattino*, 15 November 1991; *La Repubblica* 4 and 12 March 1992) while others, informants have reported, lend money at low interest.

17 It may be useful to remind the reader that, according to local wisdom, 'it all depends on how quickly you repay debt'.

18 For Mario as for most locals this means renting a flat for a month or two in a popular summer resort, usually near Naples. Lina's holidays abroad are a new, still uncommon alternative.

19 Even Paolo, in his dark days, managed to celebrate 'properly' his children's christenings, communions and confirmations, which here are almost as expensive as weddings.

20 It is also significant, for instance, that Ciro constructed his professional brokership while occupying a high-ranking position in a religious association, but only after he left the association did he begin lending money at interest.

21 Elsewhere I have questioned the collective value of these religious events (see Pardo 1995b).

22 Offering money and *ex votos* of precious metals, walking long distances and weeping and loudly expressing penitence are some manifestations of the sacrificial aspect of participation in pilgrimages.

23 For example, as a wedding present she has waived the last instalments for the trousseau for some local brides. Thus she also improves her prospects for future business, but I am inclined to think that this instrumental consideration plays a secondary role.

24 St Ciro, having been a doctor in life, is approached for health problems (in this case with the enthusiastic endorsement of the Church). The power of a saint or madonna is rarely believed to be specialized, but each is attributed special

influence in a specific field, thus becoming the protector of a particular category of humans: the blind (St Lucy), drivers (St Christopher), the pregnant (St Anne), carpenters (St Joseph, who also is the protector of 'good death'), and so forth.

25 In Otto's definition, the numinous includes the sacred but is not exhausted by it.

26 Many informants of different ages and sexual identities have associated such sensual experiences with the presence of spirits (Pardo 1989). The case of Lina has provided another example of the strong sexual symbolism associated with these spirits.

27 Was this a very unusual (and worrying) foreboding of her grandfather's impending inappropriate death? Or was there an even more dangerous message in such coincidence that she could not grasp?

28 Only certain recognized loci of ambiguity (for example, homosexuals, see later) can interact with spirits.

29 This introduces a complication in the role that certain dead are believed to play in the existence of certain living, emphasizing the difficulty of distinguishing accurately between sacred and non-sacred (and good and evil) forms of liminality.

30 This sacrament is now formally called Unction for the ill (*Rituale Romano* 1974; *Catechismo della Chiesa Cattolica* 1992: 1499–1532). However, the old definition remains predominant and people tend to call the priest to impart this sacrament only when there is no longer hope – among the *popolino* this remains a sacrament for the dying.

31 In the lottery (lotto) each number, from 1 to 90, has one or more meanings. These meanings are reported in a book, called *Smorfia*, similar to that recently published in Britain in connection with the National Lottery.

32 This is a complicated affair even in cases as simple as 'Antonio and Giuseppe are in purgatory', which can be straightforwardly transformed into 13 (for Antonio, because St Anthony's day is 13 June), 19 (for Giuseppe, because St Joseph's day is 19 March), and 85 (for souls in purgatory, by convention). Additional possibilities are 32 (13 + 19: Antonio and Giuseppe are *together*), and 6 and 3 (the months relating to St Anthony's and St Joseph's days). Since the lottery allows combinations of up to five numbers, wins are proportional to the size of the bet and of the combination. The numbers of the day, month and year of the meeting with the *assistito* can also be used and numbers can be inferred from the *assistito*'s behaviour and body language, the incidents surrounding the meeting, and the weather. Informants stress that interpretation is made particularly difficult by the fact that some numbers have secondary meanings that may be judged prominent.

33 However, despite such 'faculties' (Mario, we know, also claims to feel the presence of spirits), he was not believed to be able to provide winning numbers, or described as an *assistito*.

34 This 'peculiarity' of monks recalls the behaviour of spirits such as the Monacello (see n. 26).

35 Lino left saying: 'Pur' 'e pullast' ha vinciut', chella sament'' (That despicable man won chickens, too).

36 Serao's romanticism (and realism) and disputed position in nineteenth-century Italian literature suggest caution (see Palermo 1981: esp. ch. 3), but she has described the Neapolitan *popolino* and petty bourgeoisie extensively.

37 This also explains why, usually sociable, some of them became so secretive and concerned when they performed the apparently innocent and pious task of arranging visits to the 'holy monk'.

38 Of course, his faculties also serve the Church's interest by attracting to it various persons who would not otherwise attend.

39 The 'miracle of St Gennaro' happens every year in May and September. According to belief, the blood shed by the saint on his beheading has been preserved since that time and is now kept in an ampulla in the Naples cathedral.

40 Should liquefaction fail to occur, people would expect catastrophe to befall their city.

41 This is the case, for example, of the *tombola figurata*. This version of *tombola* (a traditional game similar to bingo) is usually organized in private houses. The hostess receives 10 per cent on the bets 'to pay for electricity, heating and drinks'. The adjective *figurata* refers to the illustrative stories made up by combining the meanings of the numbers extracted in sequence. The stories may be completely invented, may refer to current affairs, or they may refer to events (rarely current) involving the participants and 'rephrase' such events to the teller's taste. Virtually anything can be said as long as it is not too direct. The audience does not normally interrupt. Should a new number's meaning(s) be inconsistent with the story, a new story is started. The stories are often complex and 'dirty' as well-known sexual meanings attached to numbers are used. These stories, acts of popular creation, deserve extended comparative analysis, particularly considering that 'less dirty' versions are becoming widespread across the social spectrum.

42 See Deuteronomy 30: 17; Leviticus 18: 22, 20: 13; Romans 1: 27; I Corinthians 6: 9.

43 This quality, which grants homosexuals the status of special resources, indicates a further possible explanation – apart from the improvement of personal sense of self-worth – for some people's (e.g., Lina's) goodness towards the sexually ambiguous.

44 The female equivalent is (*vecchia*) *zita*, (old) spinster.

45 My observations suggest that his kind of junction is becoming predominant.

6 The mass diffusion of contacts: redefined power relations, values of representation

1 Lukes (1991a: ch. 1) offers a sophisticate discussion of the complexity of (the forms and nature of) moral conflict, especially in the political arena, and of the role of different agents.

2 The origin and the true amount of government money periodically 'bestowed' on the city – and indeed the South – and the use that is made of it are contentious (see, e.g., D'Antonio 1995b).

3 Gellner addresses this point in some detail (see 1969: 77).

4 To observers who believe that patronage is much too reductive (or fictitious) a category to explain relations of power in contemporary Europe this may appear an idle question. Various ethnographers have recently addressed this

question, coming to different conclusions (see, e.g., Holmes 1989; Herzfeld 1992: 51–62; Korovkin 1988).

5 Lengthy negotiations among the various politicians affect the distribution of posts also at this level.

6 Papele draws also satisfaction from this job, for, he says, it shows that he is clever, well connected, and useful to many.

7 This kind of problem, typical of public-sector employment, has been addressed only occasionally and indecisively. An informant gave a telling description when he said, 'Workers are rarely prosecuted, because all the corruption would emerge and lots of people would be unhappy.' He was referring to embezzlement of money formally spent on improving the administrative process and services (see, e.g., Palombo 1986; D'Urso 1986), and to the fact that judicial inquiries inevitably lead to administrative and political crises.

8 Lino applies this kind of strategy on behalf of others. He has helped a nephew, who is doing statutory military service, to be transferred near Naples, mobilizing for the purpose an acquaintance who has contacts in the army through the subcontracting firm for which he works. The favour, obtainable in the past almost exclusively through politicians, has cost his nephew one million lire instead of the customary four or five. 'This,' the young man says, 'is a price I'm happy to pay to be near my family, my girlfriend and my business.'

9 Boissevain (1977) argues that people vote according to class interests unless they are led to behave differently by false consciousness. Davis (1977: 31) addresses this issue from a quite different perspective, having argued elsewhere (1970) that even the most isolated peasant is quite aware of his electoral choices.

10 Prato (1995) makes a similar point drawing on ethnographic evidence from contemporary South Italy.

11 While my *popolino* informants use Italian mainly in formal situations, Patrizia and Flora speak only Italian, though they do understand Neapolitan.

12 These associations must be distinguished from those to which, say, Ciro and Michele belong. Part of a national network institutionally linked to the Church, Associazioni Cattoliche run all sorts of leisure, educational and charitable initiatives on its behalf. In fact, Associazioni Cattoliche have long been the backbone of religious and electoral proselytism.

13 They say, with admiration, that 'the *popolino* take the bull by the horns throughout their lives'.

14 When Umberto says that 'of course' this does not make him 'less moral', he raises not only one of the most problematic issues in the relationship between the *popolino* and their leftist rulers but also, on a different level, a question hotly debated throughout Europe.

15 The élites, briefly considered in recent essays (Pardo 1993, 1994b, 1995b), are the object of extensive field research on power, thought, morality and voluntary action in this changing democracy. Here it is worth noting that, predictably, I have recorded various instances of their sophisticated, if unorthodox, strategies in various goal-pursuits.

16 In the mid-1970s the Communists obtained an unprecedented electoral success, coming to power in most of the large Italian cities, even traditional Christian

Democrat strongholds such as Naples, at the time in the midst of a grave crisis (Pardo 1993: 78–9). Something similar has happened again recently (1993) in favour of leftist coalitions. However, serious problems remain unresolved (Pardo 1995b).

17 It is widespread opinion, among my informants, that the left is doomed to such an attitude.

18 An article now in preparation addresses in detail the significance of the urban grassroots of local criminals (particularly the Camorristi). For historical accounts, see Alongi (1890), De Blasio (1973 [1901]), Monnier (1965 [1863]), Garofalo (1984).

19 The Neapolitan historian Aurelio Lepre (1963) has suggested that, in accord with a general pattern in the modern state, there was a tendency under the Bourbons to limit the power of these agencies. Again, I would point to the difficulty of opposing the categories of the local level and the centre (see Chapter 4: n.30).

20 Because the local rulers needed to show that they enjoyed popular consent, they had been involved in this kind of alliance even before 1882 with effects which have been powerfully described by the contemporary historian Pasquale Villari (1979 [1885]).

21 The experience of senior magistrates with the Neapolitan Camorra would confirm this view. Local specialists seem to have reached the same conclusion from a different perspective (see, e.g., Lamberti 1988). Bearing in mind the contemporary and historical differences between Mafia and Camorra, the case of 'identification' may perhaps be made regarding the modern Mafia (Alinovi et al. 1985; Arlacchi 1982, 1983; Falcone 1992) and the rural Camorra (De Gregorio 1983; Marrazzo 1984). On a different line, Hobsbawm stresses this aspect as one of the historical differences between the two criminal phenomena (1959: ch. 3).

22 In today's mood of careful reappraisal of the relationship between ordinary people and their rulers, this claim is by no means undisputed. Fresh historical and contemporary research may well help to bring new light on this complex issue.

23 This possibility is broadly in line with the analysis of many observers of the rural South after Unification (see esp. Molfese 1964).

24 Luigi Pirandello (1925) has immortalized significant aspects of such tactics.

25 This recalls the situation elsewhere in the South (e.g., North Apulia (Snowden 1986)), but is remarkably different from the Sicilian case, where the regime conducted a strong anti-Mafia campaign.

26 Unlike the Mafiosi, however, they did not become directly involved in local government.

27 Franco Rosi's film *Le mani sulla città* shot in the 1960s, and the books of Caprara (1975) and Allum (1973) give a description of this period.

28 Ordinary people express a similar belief. For example, Lino, describing his relationship with the lawyer and influential politician who had helped him out of jail, said one must be careful because 'they're very cunning and greedy'. But, as I have indicated, people like Lino do not normally engage in joint activities with criminals, nor do they share their culture.

29 The national and international dimension of this level of criminality is the

object of much speculation (see, e.g., Commissione Parlamentare Antimafia 1994; see also Baglivo's (1983) case-study of Michele Zaza, the leader of a Camorra clan; Figurato and Marolda 1981; Roberti et al. 1985, vol. II). It should be noted, however, that the Camorristi seem to have exported their organizational experience and technique rather than their culture. It is significant that Villari (1979 [1885]), writing in the last century, stressed the Neapolitan specificity of the Camorra and the necessity of studying it not abstractly but in its context.

30 Boissevain (1977) hypothesized this kind of brokership for Malta.

7 The relation of agency to organization and structure: deconstructed polarizations at the grassroots of democracy

1 Beetham suggests that it is a mistake to view the terms of this relationship (bureaucracy, the market and democracy) as antithetical (1987: esp. pp. 101 and 111).

2 A separate essay (Pardo 1995b) expands further on this point. The situation of Naples contrasts intriguingly with the processes observed elsewhere in Catholic – and peasant – Italy (Holmes 1989).

3 This issue is central to today's debate on nation-state formations and on their continuing existence (on the Italian case, see Rusconi 1993). It is, of course, useful to refer to the different perspectives developed by Salvatorelli (1943), Gellner (1969: ch. 7 and 1979: pt 3), and Giddens (1985) and to the methodological issues raised earlier.

4 We know (see, e.g., Chapter 5) that a proportion of local people's debt is also thus explained, and that the morality linked to debt and the processes through which debt is repaid may contribute positively to capitalist enterprise.

5 That supramundane powers are rarely unknown or unknowable, in an ontological sense, to the *popolino* only underlines this point. Davis has developed a similar argument from a different perspective (1977: 148–58).

6 Although the dead are believed to need the attention and care of the living, the living know that they have limited control (sometimes no control at all) over them or the supramundane in general. We have studied how obtaining supramundane protection is a personal spiritual and cognitive enterprise that can only in certain cases be supported (in a limited way) by the actor's significant group.

7 The issues of power involved (see Chapters 2 and 5) refer to a point made quite persuasively by Stankiewicz (1980: 105), for it may well be that what we observe is 'toleration', not 'tolerance'.

8 Such expediency rings a familiar bell to anthropologists. See, e.g., Herzfeld (1992: esp. ch. 5) and, from a politically committed perspective, Lanternari (1982).

9 It may perhaps retain some control over part of the 'bourgeoisie', particularly the petty bourgeoisie (Chapters 5 and 6).

10 Equally significant although superficially opposite results are observable elsewhere in northern Europe. In Holland, for example, the state's bureaucracy has taken the concepts of equal rights and freedom to their logical, institutionalized and notoriously problematic extremes.

11 I borrow this metaphor from Herzfeld (1992: esp. ch. 1 and pp. 51–7), who draws on the work of Mary Douglas in his analysis of bureaucracy.

12 Stankiewicz (1980) argues this point quite radically; see, e.g., pp. 9–17 and, most significantly, p. 96, where, having observed the inability of democratic theory to define equality and the limits to freedom, or to adopt an arbitrary 'solution', he provocatively states: 'Since the definition of democracy's norms seems arbitrary, let us cut the Gordian Knot and let the operating system which calls itself "democracy" define all its terms. "Equality", "freedom" and "authority" are what the system says they are, and the result is "democracy" if the members have been socialized to call it that' (see also Postscript).

13 Beetham reminds us that for Weber 'bureaucracy had an inherent tendency to exceed its instrumental function, and to become a separate force within society, capable of influencing the goals and character of that society' (1974: 65). More recently (1987: ch. 3), he has addressed the various aspects of the relationship between administrative efficiency and democracy and the nature and sources of bureaucratic power and forms of control over such power.

14 During recent fieldwork among local politicians I was repeatedly told that it is precisely the bureaucrats' sophisticated knowledge of the system and its procedures that explains their success in operating well beyond the boundaries of the permissible.

15 For example, Bobbio's (1987) critique of participatory democracy in favour of representative democracy does not seem to account for the danger of an increment in the – already overwhelming – permeation of Italian society by political parties and politics in general. Prato (1995) has given a detailed analysis of these processes. Cotta (1992) provides a view of democratic process in Italy which could be usefully assessed in the light of recent changes in the electoral system and of the electorate's response. It is, indeed, most significant that in recent elections Neapolitans have consistently voted the corrupt out of power, both at local level and at national level. A similar pattern has been repeated elsewhere in Southern and Central urban Italy.

16 Beetham discusses this thesis and the opposite one that such knowledge is attainable only by the élites (1987: esp. pp. 104 ff.).

17 There is a rough Cartesianism to the interpretation of the Kantian concept of a priori categories that characterizes such notions as that of 'objective class' (in the sense of Marx 1965). Craib (1985: esp. ch. 8) points to the confusing circularity of the view that individuals, overwhelmed by society in both action and thought, are manipulated in an 'objective structure' which exists above and beyond them and is imposed upon them whether they are aware of it or not.

18 This kind of strategy has proved effective as far back as the revolt against the Spanish in 1647 (Burke 1983). Notoriously, Masaniello, the legendary fisherman who led that revolt, was lured into becoming part of the establishment and then eliminated.

19 On these grounds, arguments are also made for regulation and organization of their activities.

20 In more recent years, other small groups of 'unemployed' have formed at critical moments in local political life and, after brief but heated activity, dis-

appeared. They have acted under different names and with different political allegiances, cutting across the political spectrum.

21 E. P. Thompson drafted what has been called a 'culturalist manifesto' (Moss 1993: 394) in the preface to *The Making of the English Working Class* (1963; but see also 1978). Moss criticizes this approach from a perspective very different from that argued here.

22 Historians such as Cannadine (1991) argue that this model is largely discredited (see also Furbank 1985: 60). Along with others (McCord 1985; F. M. L. Thompson 1989), he appears to be quite disinclined to grant a primary role to the concept of class.

23 The influential concept of housing classes – originally debated by Rex and Moore (1967) and Pahl (1975) with reference to the British Midlands, and criticized by Saunders (1981, 1984) – focuses on social divisions related to production and consumption which in fact appear to be increasingly indefinable in contemporary Europe. Its main aim is to account for the role of culture in the competition over desirable housing. Saunders (1981) has rightly argued that this concept of housing classes misinterprets in terms of class formation Weber's theory of the conjunctural crystallization of individual positions (in the market) into 'status groups'.

24 The idea that class is an increasingly outmoded concept (Clark and Lipset 1991) continues to be the object of debate (see, e.g., Pahl 1989; Goldthorpe and Marshall 1992; Pahl 1993).

References

AA.VV. 1983 *Cos'è la Camorra*. Naples: Sintesi.

1991. *Contributo per l'intesa di programma per il risanamento e lo sviluppo dell'area metropolitana di Napoli (lavori preparatori)*. Ministero del Bilancio e della Programmazione Economica, Ministero dell'Interno, Dipartimento per gli Interventi Straordinari nel Mezzogiorno-Presidenza del Consiglio, Dipartimento per i Problemi delle Aree Urbane-Presidenza del Consiglio. Rome: Istituto Poligrafico e Zecca dello Stato.

Abrams, P. 1982. *Historical Sociology*. Shepton Mallet: Open Books.

Acciari, S. and Calderoni, P. 1984. Gava e Scotti ci offrirono. *L'Espresso*, 19 February.

Adams Brown, W. 1920. Expiation and atonement: Christian. In J. Hastings (ed.), *Encyclopaedia of Religion and Ethics*, vol. V. Edinburgh: T. & T. Clark, pp. 41–50.

Albera, D. 1988. Open systems and closed minds: the limitations of naïvety in social anthropology – a native's view. *Man* 23: 435–52.

Aliberti, G. 1976. La 'Questione di Napoli'nell'età liberale (1861–1904). In *Storia di Napoli*, vol. V. Naples: Edizioni Scientifiche Italiane, pp. 517–62.

1987. *Potere e società locale nel Mezzogiorno dell'800*. Bari: Laterza.

Alinovi, A. 1985. *Relazione della Commissione Parlamentare sul fenomeno della Mafia*. Rome: Camera dei Deputati. Senato della Repubblica. Stabilimenti Tipografici Carlo Colombo.

Allum, P. 1973. *Politics and Society in Post-War Naples*. Cambridge: Cambridge University Press.

Alongi, G. 1890. *La camorra*. Turin: Bocca.

Altan, T. 1986. *La nostra Italia*. Milan: Feltrinelli.

Anthropological Quarterly 1967. *Appearance and Reality: Status and Roles of Women in Mediterranean Societies*. Washington, DC: Catholic University of America Press.

Ambrasi, D. 1980. Il Cristianesimo e la chiesa napoletana dei primi secoli. In *Storia di Napoli*, vol. VI. Edizioni Scientifiche Italiane, pp. 133–239.

Apolito, P. 1987. L'antropologia del 'ritorno'. *L'Informazione Bibliografica* 4: 565–80.

Aristotle. 1962. *The Politics*. London: Penguin.

Arlacchi, P. 1980. Mafia e Tipi di Società. *Rassegna Italiana di Sociologia* 1: 3–49.

1982. Il capitalismo mafioso (la 'ndrangheta calabrese). In E. Nocifora (ed.), *Mafia, 'ndragheta e camorra*. Rome: Lavoro, pp. 37–55.

1983. *La Mafia imprenditrice*. Bologna: Il Mulino.

1987. Stato e mercati illegali. *La Voce della Campania* 1: 26–9.

Baglivo, A. 1983. *Camorra SpA*. Milan: Rizzoli.

Bailey, F. G. 1969. *Stratagems and Spoils*. Oxford: Basil Blackwell.

Banfield, E. C. 1958. *The Moral Basis of a Backward Society*. Glencoe: Free Press.

Barth, F. 1963. *The Role of the Entrepreneur in Social Change in Northern Norway*. Oslo: Scandinavian University Books.

1966. *Models of Social Organization. Royal Anthropological Institute*. Occasional Paper 23.

Barzini, L. 1964. *The Italians*. London: Penguin.

Becchi-Collidà, A. 1984a. La città ambigua: economia e territorio a Napoli. In A. Becchi-Collidà (ed.), *Napoli miliardaria*. Milan: Franco Angeli, pp. 9–35.

Becchi-Collidà, A. (ed.) 1984b. *Napoli miliardaria*. Milan: Franco Angeli.

Beetham, D. 1974. *Max Weber and the Theory of Modern Politics*. London: Allen & Unwin.

1987. *Bureaucracy*. Milton Keynes: Open University Press.

Bellacci, M. and Rea, S. (eds.). 1989. *Napoli a confronto sul centro storico*. Studi Centro Storico Napoli. Milan: Edizioni del Sole 24 Ore.

Belmonte, T. 1989 [1979]. *The Broken Fountain*. New York: Columbia University Press.

Bemporad, J. 1987. Suffering. In M. Eliade (ed.), *Encyclopedia of Religion*, vol. XIV. New York: Macmillan & Free Press, pp. 99–103.

Bentham, J. 1787. *Defence of Usury*. London.

Blau, P. M. 1972. *The Dynamics of Bureaucracy*. Chicago: University of Chicago Press.

Bloch, M. 1949. *La société féodale*. Paris: Albin Michel.

Bloch, M. and Houtman, G. 1988. Interview with Maurice Bloch. *Anthropology Today* 4 (1): 18–21.

Blok, A. 1974. *The Mafia of a Sicilian Village*. Oxford: Basil Blackwell.

1981. Rams and billy-goats: a key to the Mediterranean code of honour. *Man* 16: 427–40.

Bobbio, N. 1983. Italy's permanent crisis. *Telos* 54: 123–33.

1987. *The Future of Democracy*. Cambridge: Polity Press.

Bobbio, N. and Matteucci, N. (eds.) 1976. *Dizionario di Politica*. Turin: Utet.

Boissevain, J. 1966. Patronage in Sicily. *Man* 1: 18–63.

1974. *Friends of Friends: Networks, Manipulators, and Coalitions*. Oxford: Basil Blackwell.

1975. Introduction: Towards a social anthropology of Europe. In J. Boissevain and J. Friedl (eds.), *Beyond the Community: Social Process in Europe*. The Hague: Department of Educational Science of the Netherlands, pp. 9–17.

1977. When the saints go marching out: reflections on the decline of patronage in Malta. In E. Gellner and J. Waterbury (eds.), *Patrons and Clients in Mediterranean Societies*. London: Duckworth, pp. 81–96.

1983. Foreword. In M. Kenny and D. J. Kertzer (eds.), *Urban Life in Mediterranean Europe. Anthropological Perspectives*. Chicago: University of Illinois Press, pp. vii–x.

Bolle, K. W. 1967. Expiation. In *New Catholic Encyclopedia*, vol. V. Washington DC: McGraw-Hill, pp. 758–9.

Bourdieu, P. 1973. The Berber house. In M. Douglas (ed.), *Rules and Meanings*. Harmondsworth: Penguin, pp. 98–110.

1977. *Outline of a Theory of Practice*. Cambridge: Cambridge University Press.

1984. *Distinction: A Social Critique of the Judgement of Taste*. Cambridge, Mass.: Harvard University Press.

1991. *Language and Symbolic Power*. Cambridge: Polity Press.

1993. *La misère du monde*. Paris: Editions du Seuil.

Brubaker, R. 1991. *The Limits of Rationality: An Essay on the Social and Moral Thought of Max Weber*. London: Routledge.

Bulmer, M. (ed.) 1986. *Sociological Research Methods: An Introduction*. London: Macmillan.

Bulmer, R. 1973. Why the cassowary is not a bird. In M. Douglas (ed.), *Rules and Meanings*. Harmondsworth: Penguin, pp. 167–93.

Burke, P. 1983. The Virgin of the Carmine and the revolt of Masaniello. *Past and Present* 99: 3–21.

Burns, J. H. 1948. *The Gallery*. New York and London: Harper.

Calderoni, P. 1985. Una bomba, un boss. *L'Espresso* 13 October.

1986. Camorra nera. *L'Espresso*, 21 December.

Calvert, P. 1982. *The Concept of Class*. London: Hutchinson.

Campbell, J. K. 1964. *Honour, Family and Patronage: A Study of Institutions and Moral Values in a Greek Mountain Community*. Oxford: Clarendon Press.

Cannadine, D. 1991. Through the key hole. *New York Review of Books* 21 November.

Cappelli, O. 1978. *Governare Napoli*. Bari: De Donato.

Caprara, M. 1975. *I Gava*. Milan: Feltrinelli.

Castells, M. 1977. *The Urban Question*. London: Edward Arnold.

1983. *The City and the Grassroots: A Cross-Cultural Theory of Urban Social Movements*. London: Edward Arnold.

Catechismo della Chiesa Cattolica 1992. Rome: Libreria Editrice Vaticana.

CENSIS (Centro Studi Investimenti Sociali) 1984. *Evoluzione e governo dell'area napoletana: Società, economia e comportamenti familiari*. Naples: Società Editrice Napoletana.

1988. *La nuova antropologia del mezzogiorno. I comportamenti famigliari*. Rome: CENSIS.

Cetro, R. 1984. Il lavoro a domicilio. In A. Becchi-Collidà (ed.), *Napoli miliardaria*. Milan: Franco Angeli, pp. 120–32.

Chubb, J. A. 1981. Naples under the left: the limits of social change. In S. N. Eisenstadt and R. Lemarchard (eds.), *Political Clientism, Patronage and Development*. London: Sage, pp. 91–124.

Clark, T. N. and Lipset, S. M. 1991. Are social classes dying? *International Sociology* 6: 397–410.

Codice Civile (il) e le Leggi Complementari 1990. 12th edn, ed. M. Abate. Piacenza: La Tribuna.

Cohn, N. 1957. *The Pursuit of the Millennium*. London: Secker & Warburg.

Collmann, J. 1981. Postscript: the significance of clients. *Social Analysis* 9: 103–12.

Colombis, A. 1975. Organizzazione sociale e familismo amorale a Chiaromonte: critica della tesi di E. C. Banfield da parte di un familista. *Sociologia dell'Organizzazione* 4: 437–88.

Commissione Parlamentare Antimafia. 1994. *Camorra e Politica*. Bari: Laterza

Comune di Napoli 1981. *Annuario Statistico*.

  1991. *Annuario Statistico*.

Cortellazzo, M. and Zolli, P. 1983. *Dizionario etimologico della lingua italiana*. Bologna: Zanichelli.

Costagliola, G. 1981. Sentenza processo Cimiteri. Naples: Tribunale di Napoli, ms.

Costituzione della Repubblica Italiana. 1948. Rome.

Cotta, M. 1976. Rappresentanza Politica. In N. Bobbio and N. Matteucci (eds.), *Dizionario di Politica*. Turin: Utet, pp. 840–5.

  1992. Elite unification and democratic consolidation in Italy: a historical overview. In J. Higley and R. Gunther (eds.), *Elites and Democratic Consolidation in Latin America and Southern Europe*. Cambridge: Cambridge University Press, pp. 146–77.

Craib, I. 1985. *Modern Social Theory: From Parsons to Habermas*. Brighton: Wheatsheaf.

CRESM (Centro Ricerche Economiche e Sociali del Mezzogiorno) 1986. *Vivere e cambiare nella 167 di Secondigliano: Trasformazioni urbane soeiali nell'area napoletana*. Naples.

Croce, B. 1967 [1944]. *Storia del Regno di Napoli*. Bari: Laterza.

Crompton, R. 1993. *Class and Stratification*. Cambridge: Polity Press.

Crump, T. 1975. The context of European anthropology: the lesson from Italy. In J. Boissevain and J. Friedl (eds.), *Beyond the Community: Social Process in Europe*. The Hague: Department of Educational Science of the Netherlands, pp. 18–28.

Cuoco, V. 1966 [1806]. *Saggio storico sulla rivoluzione di Napoli* (2nd edn with amendments). Milan: Rizzoli.

Curi, U. 1982. Alcune riflessioni su mafia, camorra e sistema politico. *Questione Giustizia* 4: 793–8.

D'Antonio, M. 1995a. Prefazione. In M. D'Antonio, M. Scarlato and G. Zezza, *Commercio estero e sviluppo economico: Il mezzogiorno nel mercato internazionale*. Naples: Edizioni Scientifiche Italiane, pp. 7–9.

  1995b. La questione meridionale: quale prospettiva? In M. D'Antonio, M. Scarlato and G. Zezza, *Commercio estero e sviluppo economico: Il mezzogiorno nel mercato internazionale*. Naples: Edizioni Scientifiche Italiane, pp. 11–43.

  1995c. Il mezzogiorno nel mercato estero: un percorso difficile. In M. D'Antonio, M. Scarlato and G. Zezza, *Commercio estero e sviluppo economico: Il mezzogiorno nel mercato internazionale*. Naples: Edizioni Scientifiche Italiene, pp. 45–113.

D'Ascoli, F. 1979. *Dizionario etimologico napoletano*. Naples: Edizioni del Delfino.

Davis, J. 1970. Morals and backwardness. *Comparative Studies in Society and History* 12: 340–53.

1975. Beyond the hyphen: some notes and documents on community-state relations in South Italy. In J. Boissevain and J. Friedl (eds.), *Beyond the Community: Social Process in Europe.* The Hague: Department of Educational Science of the Netherlands, pp. 49–55.

1977. *People of the Mediterranean: An Essay in Comparative Social Anthropology.* London: Routledge & Kegan Paul.

1992. *Exchange.* Buckingham: Open University Press.

De Blasio, A. 1973 [1901]. *Nel paese della camorra.* Naples: Pierro.

De Filippo, E. 1973 [1945]. *Napoli milionaria.* In *I capolavori di Eduardo*, vol. I. Turin: Einaudi.

1973 [1960]. *Il Sindaco del Rione Sanità.* In *I capolavori di Eduardo*, vol. II. Turin: Einaudi.

De Giovanni, B. 1983. Introduzione. In AA. VV. *Cos'è la camorra.* Naples: Sintesi.

1990. *Dopo il Comunismo.* Naples: Cronopio.

De Gregorio, S. 1983. *I nemici di Cutolo.* Naples: Pironti.

De Marco, C. and Talamo, M. 1976. *Lavoro nero: Decentramento produttivo e lavoro a domicilio.* Milan: Mazzotta.

De Martino, E. 1952. Gramsci e il Folklore. *Il Calendario del Popolo* 91 (8): 1109.

1977. *Sud e magia.* Milan: Feltrinelli.

De Matteis, S. 1991. *Lo specchio della vita, Napoli: Antropologia della città del teatro.* Bologna: Il Mulino.

De Mauro, T. 1993. *Lessico di frequenza dell'italiano parlato.* Milan: Etas.

De Rosa, G. 1987. S. Alfonso e il secolo dei lumi. *Rassegna Italiana di Teologia* 1: 13–31.

De Seta, C. 1969. *Cartografia della città di Napoli*, 3 vols. Naples: Edizioni Scientifiche Italiane.

1988. *Napoli.* Rome and Bari: Laterza.

De Spirito, A. 1983. *Antropologia della famiglia meridionale.* Rome: Officina.

Di Addea, M. 1987. Procedimento a carico di Strianese Oreste ed altri. Naples: Tribunale di Napoli, ms.

Diamantini, C. 1984. L'artigianato manifatturiero nel Centro di Napoli. In A. Becchi-Collidà (ed.), *Napoli miliardaria.* Milan: Franco Angeli, pp. 150–80.

Dini, V. 1990. Che cosa è la napoletanità. *Micromega* 4: 161–70.

Douglas, M. 1966. *Purity and Danger.* London: Routledge & Kegan Paul.

1970. *Natural Symbols.* London: Cresset Press.

Douglas, M. (ed.) 1973. *Rules and Meanings.* Harmondsworth: Penguin.

Douglass, W. A. 1991. The joint-family household in eighteenth-century Southern Italian society. In D. J. Kertzer and P. Saller (eds.), *The Family in Italy: From Antiquity to the Present.* New Haven and London: Yale University Press, pp. 286–303.

Dow, J. 1921. Usury (Christian). In J. Hastings (ed.), *Encyclopaedia of Religion and Ethics.* Edinburgh: T. & T. Clark, vol. XII, 551–5.

Du Boulay, J. 1991. Cosmos and gender in village Greece. In P. Loizos and E. Papataxiarchis (eds.), *Contested Identities: Gender and Kinship in Modern Greece.* Princeton: Princeton University Press, pp. 47–78.

Durkheim, E. and Mauss, M. 1963. *Primitive Classification*. Chicago: University of Chicago Press.

D'Urso, G. 1986. Procedimento pendente in formale istruttoria. Naples: Tribunale di Napoli, ms.

Eder, K. 1993. *The New Politics of Class: Social Movements and Cultural Dynamics in Advanced Societies*. London: Sage.

Eisen, A. 1978. The meanings and confusions of Weberian 'rationality'. *British Journal of Sociology* 29 (1): 57–70.

Eisenstadt, S. N. and Roninger, L. 1984. *Patrons, Clients, and Friends: Interpersonal Relations and the Structure of Trust in Society*. Cambridge: Cambridge University Press.

Eliade, M. 1959. *The Sacred and the Profane: The Nature of Religion*. New York: Harcourt Brace Jovanovich.

Eliade, M. (ed.) 1987. *Encyclopedia of Religion*. New York: Macmillan & Free Press.

Ellen, R. (ed.) 1984. *Ethnographic Research*. London: Academic Press.

Elliott, B. and McCrone, D. 1982. *The City: Patterns of Domination and Conflict*. London: Macmillan.

Epstein, A. L. (ed.) 1967. *The Craft of Social Anthropology*. London: Tavistock.

Esposito, L. and Persico, P. 1978. *Artigianato e lavoro a domicilio in Campania*. Milan: Franco Angeli.

Falcone, G. 1992. *Men of Honour: The Truth about the Mafia*. London: Fourth Estate.

Ferraresi, F. 1980. *Burocrazia e politica in Italia*. Bologna: Il Mulino.

Figurato, M. and Marolda, F. 1981. *Storia di contrabbando. Napoli, 1945–1981*. Naples: Pironti.

Firth, R. 1979. Work and value: reflections on ideas of Karl Marx. In S. Wallman (ed.), *Social Anthropology of Work*. London: Academic Press, pp. 177–204.

   1984. Foreword. In R. F. Ellen (ed.), *Ethnographic Research*. London: Academic Press, pp. vii–ix.

   1985. Degrees of intelligibility. In J. Overing (ed.), *Reason and Morality*. London: Tavistock, pp. 29–46.

Fred, M. 1979. How Sweden works: a case from the bureaucracy. In S. Wallman (ed.), *Social Anthropology of Work*. London: Academic Press, pp. 159–76.

   1984. Democracy at work in the Swedish bureaucracy. *Kroeber Anthropological Society Papers* 63–4: 117–25.

Frey, L. (ed.) 1975. *Lavoro a domicilio e decentramento dell'attività produttiva nei settori tessile e dell'abbigliamento in Italia*. Milan: Franco Angeli.

Frykman, J. 1981. Pure and rational. The hygienic vision: a study of cultural transformation in the 1930s' The New Man. *Ethnologia Scandinavica* 36–62.

Frykman, J. and Löfgren, O. 1987. *Culture Builders: A Historical Anthropology of Middle-Class Life*. London: Rutgers University Press.

Furbank, P. N. 1985. *Unholy Pleasure, or The Idea of Social Class*. London: Oxford University Press.

Fustel de Coulanges, N. D. 1980 [1864]. *The Ancient City*. Baltimore and London: Johns Hopkins University Press.

Galasso, G. 1978. *Intervista [with P. Allum] sulla storia di Napoli*. Bari: Laterza.

Gambetta, D. 1988. Fragments of an economic theory of the Mafia. *European Journal of Sociology* 29: 127–45.

1991. 'In the beginning was the Word . . .': the symbols of the Mafia. *European Journal of Sociology* 32: 53–77.

Gambino, N. 1985. Sono servizi di camorra. *La Voce della Campania* 9: 12–4.

Gans, H. J. 1968. The participant observer as a human being: observation on the personal aspect of fieldwork. In H. S. Becker, B. Greer, D. Riesman and R. S. Weiss (eds.) *Institutions and the Person: Papers Presented to Everett C. Huges.* Chicago: Aldine, pp. 300–17.

Garofalo, G. 1984. *La seconda guerra napoletana.* Naples: Società Editrice Napoletana.

Gellner, E. 1969. *Thought and Change.* London: Weidenfeld & Nicolson.

1977. Patrons and clients. In E. Gellner and J. Waterbury (eds.), *Patrons and Clients in Mediterranean Societies.* London: Duckworth: pp. 1–6.

1979. *Spectacles and Predicaments.* Cambridge: Cambridge University Press.

Gellner, E. and Waterbury, J. (eds.) 1977. *Patrons and Clients in Mediterranean Societies.* London: Duckworth.

Gershuny, J. I. and Pahl, R. 1979. Work outside employment: some preliminary speculations. *New Universities Quarterly* Winter, 120–35.

Gerth, H. H. and Wright Mills, C. (eds.) 1970. *From Max Weber: Essays in Sociology.* London: Routledge & Kegan Paul.

Giddens, A. 1979. *Central Problems in Social Theory: Action, Structure, and Contradiction in Social Analysis.* London: Macmillan.

1985. *A Contemporary Critique of Historical Materialism.* Vol. II, *The Nation-State and Violence.* Cambridge: Polity Press.

Giovannini, M. J. 1981. Women: a dominant symbol within the cultural system of a Sicilian town. *Man* 16: 408–26.

Gluckman, M. 1967. Introduction. In A. L. Epstein (ed.), *The Craft of Social Anthropology.* London: Tavistock, pp. xi–xx.

Goddard, V. 1977. Domestic industry in Naples. *Critique of Anthropology* 3: 139–50.

Goffman, E. 1959. *The Presentation of Self in Everyday Life.* New York: Doubleday.

Goldthorpe, J. H. and Marshall, G. 1992. The promising future of class analysis: a response to recent critiques. *Sociology* 26: 381–400.

Gouldner, A. W. 1954. *Patterns of Industrial Bureaucracy.* New York: Free Press.

Gramsci, A. 1950. Osservazioni sul folklore. In *Letteratura e vita nazionale.* Turin: Einaudi. (English translation In D. Forgacs and G. Nowell (eds.), *Antonio Gramsci: Selections from Cultural Writings.* London: Lawrence & Wishart, 1985, pp. 188–95.)

1971. *Selections from the Prison Notebooks.* London: Lawrence & Wishart.

1975. La religione, il lotto e l'oppio della miseria. In *Note sul Machiavelli.* Rome: Editori Riuniti.

Graziano, L. 1980. *Clientelismo e sistema politico: Il caso dell'Italia.* Milan: Franco Angeli.

Graziani, A. and Pugliese, E. (eds.) 1979. *Investimenti e disoccupazione nel Mezzogiorno.* Bologna: Il Mulino.

Gribaudi, G. 1980. *Mediatori: Antropologia del potere democristiano nel Mezzogiorno*. Turin: Rosenberg & Seller.

Groethuysen, B. 1927. *Origines de l'ésprit bourgeois en France*. Paris: Beauchesne.

Gruerber, J. 1973. *Le ralliement du clergé français a la morale liguorienne: L'abbé Gousset et ses précurseurs (1785–1832)*. Rome: PUG.

Gründel, J. 1975. Sex. In K. Rahner (ed.), *Encyclopedia of Theology: A Concise Sacramentum Mundi*. London: Burns & Oates, pp. 1563–79.

Guadagno G. and De Masi, D. 1969. Trasformazioni socio-economiche e criminalità nell'area di Napoli. Naples.

Gulliver, P. H. 1977. On mediators. In I. Hamnett (ed.), *Social Anthropology and Law*. London: Academic Press, pp. 15–52.

Hamnett, I. 1977. Introduction. In I. Hamnett (ed.), *Social Anthropology and Law*. London: Academic Press, pp. 1–13.

Hann, C. M. (ed.) 1996. *Civil Society: Challenging Western Models*. London: Routledge.

Hannerz, U. 1980. *Exploring the City: Inquiries Toward an Urban Anthropology*. New York: Columbia University Press.

Harris, R. 1986. *Power and Powerlessness in Industry*. London: Tavistock.

Hastings, J. (ed.) 1920. *Encyclopaedia of Religion and Ethics*. Edinburgh: T. & T. Clark.

Heath, A. 1976. *Rational Choice and Social Exchange*. Cambridge: Cambridge University Press.

Herbermann, C. G., Pace, E. A., Pallen, C. B., Shahan, T. J. and Wynne, J. J. (eds.) 1912. *The Catholic Encyclopedia*. London: Caxton.

Hertz, R. 1922. Le peché et l'expiation dans le sociétés primitives. *Revue de l'Histoire des Religions* 86: 5–60.

1960. *Death and the Right Hand*. New York: Free Press.

Herzfeld, M. 1987. *Anthropology Through the Looking Glass: Critical Ethnography in the Margins of Europe*. Cambridge: Cambridge University Press.

1991. Silence, submission and subversion: towards a poetics of womanhood. In P. Loizos and E. Papataxiarchis (eds.), *Contested Identities: Gender and Kinship in Modern Greece*. Princeton: Princeton University Press, pp. 79–97.

1992. *The Social Production of Indifference: Exploring the Symbolic Roots of Western Bureaucracy*. Oxford: Berg.

Higley, J. and Gunther, R. (eds.) 1992. *Elites and Democratic Consolidation in Latin America and Southern Europe*. Cambridge: Cambridge University Press.

Hobbs, D. 1989. *Doing the Business: Entrepreneurship, the Working Class, and Detectives in the East End of London*. Oxford: Oxford University Press.

Hobsbawm, E. J. 1959. *Primitive Rebels*. Manchester: Manchester University Press.

Hollis, M. and Lukes, S. (eds.) 1982. *Rationality and Relativism*. Oxford: Basil Blackwell.

Holmes, D. R. 1989. *Cultural Disenchantments: Worker Peasantries in Northeast Italy*. Princeton: Princeton University Press.

Horton, R. 1982. Tradition and modernity revisited. In M. Hollis and S. Lukes (eds.), *Rationality and Relativism*. Oxford: Basil Blackwell, pp. 201–60.

Improta, G. 1986. Dentro la Lega. *La Voce della Campania* 7: 14–17.

Ingram, D. 1987. *Habermas and the Dialectic of Reason.* New Haven: Yale University Press.

IRSES (Istituto Ricerche Studi Economici e Sociali) 1987. *Napoli dati: Statistiche sociali, documentazioni e fonti.* Milan: Franco Angeli.

ISTAT (Istituto Nazionale di Statistica) 1994a. *Popolazione e Abitazioni: Fascicolo Provinciale, Napoli.* Rome: Istituto Poligrafico dello Stato.

   1994b. *Imprese, Istituzioni e Unità Locali: Fascicolo Provinciale, Napoli.* Rome: Istituto Poligrafico dello Stato.

   1995. *I grandi comuni: Napoli.* Rome: Istituto Poligrafico dello Stato.

Jackson, A. 1987. Reflections on ethnography at home and the ASA. In A. Jackson (ed.), *Anthropology at Home.* London: Tavistock, pp. 1–15.

Jarvie, I. C. 1969. The problem of ethical integrity in participant observation. *Current Anthropology* 10: 505–8.

Jouachim, M. 1979. *'O Malommo.* Naples: Pironti.

Kapferer, B. 1976. Introduction: transactional models reconsidered. In B. Kapferer (ed.), *Transaction and Meaning.* Philadelphia: Institute for the Study of Human Issues, pp. 1–22.

Kenny, M. and Kertzer, D. J. 1983. Introduction. In M. Kenny and D. J. Kertzer (eds.), *Urban Life in Mediterranean Europe. Anthropological Perspectives.* Chicago: University of Illinois Press, pp. 3–21.

Kertzer, D. J. 1980. *Comrades and Christians: Religion and Political Struggle in Communist Italy.* New York: Cambridge University Press.

   1983. Urban research in Italy. In M. Kenny and D. J. Kertzer (eds.), *Urban Life in Mediterranean Europe. Anthropological Perspectives.* Chicago: University of Chicago Press, pp. 53–75.

   1988. *Ritual, Politics and Power.* New Haven and London: Yale University Press.

Kertzer, D. J. and Saller, P. 1991. *The Family in Italy: From Antiquity to the Present.* New Haven and London: Yale University Press.

Kilpatrick, T. B. 1921. Suffering. In J. Hastings (ed.), *Encyclopaedia of Religion and Ethics*, vol. XII. Edinburgh: T. & T. Clark, pp. 1–10.

Korovkin, M. 1988. Exploitation, cooperation, collusion: an enquiry into patronage. *European Journal of Sociology* 29: 105–26.

LaCocque, A. 1987. Sin and guilt. In M. Eliade (ed.). *Encyclopedia of Religion*, vol. XIII. New York: Macmillan & Free Press, pp. 325–31.

Laino, G. 1984. *Il cavallo di Napoli: i Quartieri Spagnoli.* Milan: Franco Angeli.

Lamberti, A. 1982. Le facilitazioni ambientali, culturali, economiche e politiche del fenomeno camorra. In E. Nocifora (ed.), *Mafia, 'ndrangheta e camorra.* Rome: Lavoro, pp. 57–71.

   1988. Mercato politico e mercato criminale. *La Città Nuova* 5: 43–8.

Landsberg, P. L. 1953. *The Experience of Death: The Moral Problem of Suicide.* New York: Arno Press.

Lanternari, V. 1982. *L' 'incivilimento' dei barbari.* Bari: Dedalo.

La Palombara, J. 1987. *Democracy Italian Style.* New Haven and London: Yale University Press.

Lay, C. 1981. *Napoli. Il terremoto quotidiano.* Naples: Loffredo.

Leach, E. R. 1977. *Political Systems of Highland Burma.* London: Bell.

Le Goff, J. 1980. *Time, Work and Culture in the Middle Ages*. Chicago: University of Chicago Press.
1984. *The Birth of Purgatory*. London: Scolar Press.
Lenski, G. 1987. Power and privilege. In S. Lukes (ed.), *Power*. Oxford: Basil Blackwell, pp. 243–52.
Leone, U. 1980. L'evoluzione del tessuto urbano napoletano. *Orizzonti Economici* 25: 5–10.
Lepre, A. 1963. *Contadini, borghesi ed operai nel tramonto del feudalesimo napoletano*. Milan: Feltrinelli.
1979. *Il Mezzogiorno dal feudalesimo al capitalismo*. Naples: Società Editrice Napoletana.
Lévi-Strauss, C. 1969. *The Elementary Structures of Kinship*. Boston: Beacon Press.
Levis, R. J. 1967. Theology of marriage: ends of marriage. In *New Catholic Encyclopedia*, vol. IX. Washington, DC: McGraw-Hill, pp. 267–70.
Lewis, N. 1978. *Naples '44*. London: Collins.
Li Causi, L. 1975. Anthropology and ideology: the case of patronage in Mediterranean societies. *Critique of Anthropology* 4–5: 90–109.
Liguori, M. and Veneziano, S. 1982. *Disoccupati a Napoli*. Rome: Edizioni Scientifiche Italiane.
1984. Disoccupazione e politiche del lavoro. In A. Becchi-Collidà (ed.), *Napoli miliardaria*. Milan: Franco Angeli, pp. 75–101.
Littlewood, P. 1977. Patronage, ideology, and reproduction. *Critique of Anthropology* 15: 29–48.
Lively, J. 1975. *Democracy*. Oxford: Oxford University Press.
Loizos, P. and Papataxiarchis, E. 1991a. Introduction. In P. Loizos and E. Papataxiarchis (eds.), *Contested Identities: Gender and Kinship in Modern Greece*. Princeton: Princeton University Press, pp. 3–25.
1991b (eds.). *Contested Identities: Gender and Kinship in Modern Greece*. Princeton: Princeton University Press.
Lombardi-Satriani, L. M. 1974. *Antropologia culturale e analisi dell cultura subalterna*. Florence: Guaraldi.
Lukes, S. 1974. *Power: A Radical View*, London: Macmillan.
1982. Relativism in its place. In M. Hollis and S. Lukes (eds), *Rationality and Relativism*. Oxford: Basil Blackwell, pp. 261–305
1987. Introduction. In S. Lukes (ed.), *Power*. Oxford: Basil Blackwell, pp. 1–18.
1991a. *Moral Conflict and Politics*. Oxford: Clarendon Press.
1991b. The rationality of norms. *European Journal of Sociology* 1: 142–9.
Luongo, E. and Oliva, A. 1959. *Napoli come è*. Milan: Feltrinelli.
MacKintosh, H. R. 1920. Sin. In J. Hastings (ed.), *Encyclopaedia of Religion and Ethics*, vol. XI. Edinburgh: T. & T. Clark, pp. 538–44.
Maffei, S. 1973. Sono sessanta le giovani operaie paralizzate dalla colla al benzolo. *La Gazzetta Popolare* 20 May.
Mair, L. 1984. *Anthropology and Development*. London: Macmillan.
Malaparte, C. 1952. *The Skin*. London: Alvin Redman.
Marotta, G. 1991. Ideali etici e politici e primato della cultura nella storia

del Mezzogiorno. *Mezzogiorno d'Europa: Journal of Regional Policy* 3–4: 673–710.

Marrazzo, G. 1984. *Il Camorrista*. Naples: Pironti.

Marselli, G. A. 1962. Sociologi nordamericani e società contadina italiana: a proposito del libro di Banfield. *Quaderni di Sociologia Rurale* 1: 109–30.

Martin, R. 1977. *The Sociology of Power*. London: Routledge & Kegan Paul.

Marx, K. 1965. *The German Ideology*. London: Lawrence & Wishart.

Massa, S. and Raffa, M. 1975. Napoli: il movimento dei disoccupati organizzati. *Fabbrica e Stato*, 15–16: 55–75.

Mauss, M. 1966. *The Gift*. London: Cohen & West.

Mazzacane, L. (ed.) 1978. *I 'bassi' a Napoli*. Naples: Guida.

McCord, N. 1985. Adding a touch of class. *History* 70: 410–19.

Meyer, B. F. 1967. Expiation (in the Bible). In *New Catholic Encyclopedia*, vol. V. Washington, DC: McGraw-Hill, pp. 759–61.

Michel, A. 1939. Purgatoire. In *Dictionnaire de theologie catholique*. Paris: Alcan, vol. 12, 1163–326.

Miller, A. 1981a. Istruttoria processo cimiteri. Naples: Tribunale di Napoli, ms.
    1981b. Attardi Vincenzo ed altri: Processo penale relativo a truffa in materia di collocamento. Naples: Tribunale di Napoli, ms.
    1985. Misure di prevenzione patrimoniale ed esercizio del credito. *Banca, Borsa e Titoli di Credito* 38 (3): 399–407.

Milton, K. (ed.) 1993. *Environmentalism: The View from Anthropology*. London: Routledge.

Mingione, E. 1985. Social reproduction of the surplus labour force: the case of Southern Italy. In N. Redclift and E. Mingione (eds.), *Beyond Employment: Household, Gender, and Subsistence*. Oxford: Basil Blackwell, pp. 14–54.

Minicuci, M. (ed.) 1994. *Riunirsi, riconoscersi, rappresentarsi*. Special issue, *L'Uomo* 7 n.s. (1/2).

Mitchell, C. 1983. Case and situation analysis. *British Sociological Review* 31 (2): 187–211.

Moberly, E. Q. 1983. *Homosexuality: A New Christian Ethic*. Cambridge: Clarke.

Molfese, F. 1964. *Storia del brigantaggio dopo l'Unità*. Milan: Feltrinelli.

Molinski, W. 1975. Marriage: Institution and sacrament. Parents. In K. Rahner (ed.), *Encyclopedia of Theology: A Concise Sacramentum Mundi*. London: Burns & Oates, pp. 905–31.

MondOperaio. 1985. Dossier Napoli. 4: 481–503.

Monnier, M. 1965 [1863]. *La camorra: Notizie storiche raccolte e documentate*. Naples: Berisio.

Moore, S. F. 1978. *Law as Process*. London: Routledge & Kegan Paul.

Moss, B. H. 1993. Republican socialism and the making of the working class in Britain, France, and the United States: a critique of Thompsonian culturalism. *Comparative Studies in Society and History* 35: 390–413.

Muraskin, W. 1974. The moral basis of a backward sociologist: Edward Banfield, the Italians, and the Italian-Americans. *American Journal of Sociology* 79: 1484–96.

Nelson, B. 1949. *The Idea of Usury: From Tribal Brotherhood to Universal Otherhood*. Princeton: Princeton University Press.

New Catholic Encyclopedia. 1967. Washington, DC: McGraw-Hill.

Nietzsche, F. 1966. *Thus Spoke Zarathustra*. New York: Viking Books.
 1968. *Will to Power*. New York: Viking Books.
 1973. *Beyond Good and Evil*. Harmondsworth: Penguin.
Nocifora, E. (ed.) 1982. *Mafia, 'ndrangheta e camorra*. Rome: Lavoro.
Offe, C. 1991. Introduction: the puzzling scope of rationality. *European Journal of Sociology* 32 (1): 81–3.
O'Neil, A. C. 1912. Sin. In C. G. Herbermann et al. (eds.), *The Catholic Encyclopedia*, vol. XIV. London: Caxton, pp. 4–11.
Ortner, S. 1975. Gods' bodies, gods' food: a symbolic analysis of a Sherpa ritual. In R. Willis (ed.), *The Interpretation of Symbolism*. London: Malaby Press, pp. 133–69.
 1984. Theory in anthropology since the sixties. *Comparative Studies in Society and History* 26: 126–66.
Otto, R. 1950. *The Idea of the Holy*. Oxford: Oxford University Press.
Overing, J. (ed.) 1985. *Reason and Morality*. London: Tavistock.
Pacifico, M. 1982. *Casalinghe in fabbrica: Una ricerca tra le donne della Cirio*. Naples: Sintesi.
Pahl, R. 1975. *Whose City?* Harmondsworth: Penguin.
 1980. Employment, work, and domestic division of labour. *International Journal of Urban and Regional Research* 4 (1): 1–20.
 1984. *Divisions of Labour*. Oxford: Basil Blackwell.
 1989. Is the emperor naked? Some questions on the adequacy of sociological theory in urban and regional research. *International Journal of Urban and Regional Research* 13: 709–20.
 1993. Does class analysis without class theory have a promising future? A reply to Goldthorpe and Marshall. *Sociology* 27: 253–8.
Paine, R. 1976. Two modes of exchange and mediation. In B. Kapferer (ed.), *Transaction and Meaning*. Philadelphia: Institute for the Study of Human Issues, pp. 63–86.
Palermo, A. 1981. La letteratura 1860–1930. In *Storia di Napoli*, vol. X, 285–362.
Palombo, G. 1986. Relazione relativa a un'ispezione sul Comune di Napoli disposta dalla Presidenza del Consiglio dei Ministri. Rome, ms.
Pálsson, G. 1992. Introduction: beyond boundaries. In G. Palsson (ed.), *Beyond Boundaries: Understanding, Translation and Anthropological Discourse*. Oxford: Berg, pp. 1–40.
Pardo, I. 1985. Sullo studio antropologico della morte: linee metodologiche. Introduction to R. Huntington and P. Metcalf, *Celebrazioni della morte*. Bologna: Il Mulino, pp. 5–41.
 1989. Life, death and ambiguity in the social dynamics of inner Naples. *Man* 24: 103–22.
 1992. 'Living' the house, 'feeling' the house: Neapolitan issues in thought, organization, and structure. *European Journal of Sociology* 33 (2): 251–79.
 1993. Socialist visions, Naples, and the Neapolitans: value, control and representation in the agency/structure relationship. *Journal of Mediterranean Studies* 1: 77–92.
 1994a. On the Neapolitan way of death: representations of mourning and the hereafter. *Journal of Mediterranean Studies* 1: 143–6.
 1994b. Spurious alliances in Naples: issues of jurisprudence and ethics of

power. Paper presented at the University of Kent, ms. in preparation for publication.

1995a. Morals of legitimacy in Naples: streetwise about legality, semi-legality and criminality. *European Journal of Sociology* 36 (1): 44–71.

1995b. Representations of belief: individual morality and action vs. collective performances in Italy. ASA Conference, University of Hull. In preparation for publication.

Pareto, V. 1935. *The Mind and Society*. New York: Harcourt Brace & World.

Park, R. E., Burgess, E. W. and McKenzie, R. D. 1967 [1925]. *The City*. Chicago: University of Chicago Press.

Parkin, F. 1979. *Marxism and Class Theory: A Bourgeois Critique*. London: Tavistock.

Parrinder, G. 1980. *Sex in the World's Religions*. London: Sheldon.

Parry, J. P. 1986. The gift, the Indian gift and the 'Indian gift'. *Man* 21 (3): 453–73.

1989. On the moral perils of exchange. In J. Parry and M. Bloch (eds.), *Money and the Morality of Exchange*. Cambridge: Cambridge University Press, pp. 64–93.

Parry, J. P. and Bloch, M. 1989. Introduction: money and the morality of exchange. In J. Parry and M. Bloch (eds.), *Money and the morality of exchange*. Cambridge: Cambridge University Press, pp. 1–32.

Parsons, A. 1962. Autorità patriarcale e autorità matriarcale nella famiglia napoletana. *Quaderni di Sociologia* 4: 416–52.

Paul VI. 1968. Humanae Vitae. Litterae Encyclicae. De Propagatione Humanae Prolis Recte Ordinanda. *Acta Apostolicae Sedis* LX (9): 481–503.

Peristiany, J. G. 1968. *Contributions to Mediterranean Sociology*. The Hague: Mouton.

Pinnarò, G. and Pugliese, E. 1985. Informalization and social resistance: the case of Naples. In N. Redclift and E. Mingione (eds.), *Beyond Employment: Household, Gender, and Subsistence*. Oxford: Basil Blackwell, pp. 228–47.

Pirandello, L. 1925. *L'altro figlio*. Firenze: R. Bemporad & F.

Pizzorno, A. 1967. Familismo amorale e marginalità storica, ovvero perchè non c'è niente da fare a Montegrano. *Quaderni di Sociologia* 27 (3): 247–61.

Prato, G. B. 1987. La morte nella società moderna. *Rassegna Italiana di Teologia* 1: 94–8.

1993. Political decision making: environmentalism, ethics, and popular participation in Italy. In K. Milton (ed.), *Environmentalism: The View from Anthropology*. London: Routledge, pp. 174–88.

1995. Political representation and new forms of political action in Italy: the case of Brindisi. Ph.D. thesis, University of London.

Ragone, G. and Clarizia, P. 1985. Il vero e il falso della disoccupazione. *MondOperaio* 4: 40–3.

Rahner, K. (ed.) 1975. *Encyclopedia of Theology: A Concise Sacramentum Mundi*. London: Burns & Oates.

Ramondino, F. 1977. *Napoli, i disoccupati organizzati: I protagonisti raccontano*. Milan: Feltrinelli.

Redclift, N. and Mingione, E. (eds.) 1985. *Beyond Employment: Household, Gender, and Subsistence*. Oxford: Basil Blackwell.

Rex, J. and Moore, R. 1967. *Race, Community, and Conflict.* Oxford: Oxford University Press.

Ricci, S. and Scarano, C. 1990. *Silvio Spaventa. Politico e statista dell'Italia unita nei documenti della Biblioteca Civica 'A. Mai'.* No. I. Bergamo: Bergomum.

Ricoeur, P. 1969. *The Symbolism of Evil.* Boston: Beacon Press.

1987. Evil. In M. Eliade (ed.), *Encyclopedia of Religion,* vol. V. New York: Macmillan & Free Press, pp. 199–206.

Rituale Romano, 1974. Rome: Conferenza Episcopale.

Roberti, F., Iervolino, A., Gay, L. and Pagano, A. 1985 Requisitoria contro l'organizzazione 'Nuova Famiglia', 4 vols. Naples: Tribunale di Napoli. ms.

Runciman, W. G. 1991. Are there any irrational beliefs? *European Journal of Sociology* 32 (2): 215–28.

Rusconi, G. E. 1993. Will Italy remain a nation? *European Journal of Sociology* 34 (2): 309–21.

Salin, E. 1949. Usury. In E. R. A. Seligman (ed.), *Encyclopaedia of the Social Sciences,* vol. XV. New York: Macmillan, pp. 193–7.

Saltman, M. 1985. 'The law is a ass': an anthropological appraisal. In J. Overing (ed.), *Reason and Morality.* London: Tavistock, pp. 226–39.

Salvatorelli, L. 1943. *Pensiero e azione del Risorgimento.* Turin: Einaudi.

Sanga, G. (ed.) 1980. *La cultura popolare: Questioni teoriche. (La Ricerca Folklorica* 1) Milan: Grafo.

Sanjek, R. 1990. Urban anthropology in the 1980s: a world view. *Annual Review of Anthropology* 19: 151–86.

Saredo, G. 1901. *Regia Commissione d'Inchiesta per Napoli.* Relazione sull'Amministrazione Comunale. 2 vols. Rome.

Sartori, G. 1987. *The Theory of Democracy Revisited,* 2 vols. Chatham, N.J.: Chatham House.

Sattler, H. V. 1967. Theology of marriage: marriage as a vocation. In *New Catholic Encyclopedia,* vol. IX. Washington, DC: Mcgraw-Hill, pp. 265–7.

Saunders, P. 1981. *Social Theory and the Urban Question.* London: Hutchinson

1984. Beyond housing classes: the sociological significance of private property rights in means of consumption. *Journal of Urban and Regional Research* 8: 202–27.

Schneider, J. 1971. Of vigilance and virgins: honour, shame, and access to resources in Mediterranean societies. *Ethnology* 9: 1–24.

Schneider, J. and Schneider, P. 1976. *Culture and Political Economy in Western Sicily.* New York: Academic Press.

Schneider, P., Schneider, J. and Hansen, E. 1972. Modernization and development: the role of regional elites and non-corporate groups in the European Mediterranean. *Comparative Studies in Society and History* 14: 328–50.

Scott, J. 1977. Patronage or exploitation? In E. Gellner and J. Waterbury (eds.), *Patrons and Clients in Mediterranean Societies.* London: Duckworth, pp. 21–39.

SCSN (Società Studi Centro Storico) 1986. *Il Regno del Possibile.* Milan: Edizioni del Sole 24 Ore.

1992. *L'artigianato produttivo nel centro storico di Napoli.* Rome: Servizio Italiano Pubblicazioni Internazionali.

224   *References*

Seligman, E. R. A. (ed.) 1949. *Encyclopaedia of the Social Sciences*. New York: Macmillan.
Serao, M. 1902. *Il paese di cuccagna: Romanzo napoletano*. Naples: Angelo Trani 1973 [1884]. *Il ventre di Napoli*. Milan: Treves.
Silver, A. 1989. Friendship and trust as moral ideas: an historical approach. *European Journal of Sociology* 30 (2): 274–97.
Silverman, S. F. 1965. Patronage and community–nation relationships in Central Italy. *Ethnology* 4: 172–89.
   1977. Patronage as a myth. In E. Gellner and J. Waterbury (eds.), *Patrons and Clients in Mediterranean Societies*. London: Duckworth, pp. 7–19.
Simmel, G. 1964. *The Sociology of Georg Simmel*, ed. R. K. Wolff. New York: Free Press of Glencoe.
Smith, B. C. 1987. *Bureaucracy and Political Power*. Brighton: Wheatsheaf.
Snowden, F. M. 1986. *Violence and Great Estates in the South of Italy: Apulia 1900–1922*. Cambridge: Cambridge University Press.
Stankiewicz, W. J. 1980. *Approaches to Democracy: Philosophy of Government at the Close of the Twentieth Century*. London: Arnold.
Starr, J. and Collier, J. F. 1989. Introduction. In J. Starr and J. F. Collier (eds.), *History and Power in the Study of Law: New Directions in Legal Anthropology*. New York: Cornell University Press, pp. 1–28.
Stauth, G. 1992. Nietzsche, Weber, and the affirmative sociology of culture. *European Journal of Sociology* 33 (2): 219–47.
Stirling, P. 1968. Impartiality and personal morality. In J. G. Peristiany (ed.), *Contributions to Mediterranean Sociology*. The Hague: Mouton, pp. 49–64.
Strathern, M. 1985. Discovering 'social control'. *Journal of Law and Society* 12 (2): 111–34.
   1987. The limits of auto-anthropology. In A. Jackson (ed.), *Anthropology at Home*. London: Tavistock, pp. 16–37.
Tambiah, S. J. 1973. Classification of animals in Thailand. In M. Douglas (ed.), *Rules and Meanings*. Harmondsworth: Penguin, pp. 127–66.
Thomas, J. L. 1967. Theology of marriage: use of marriage. *New Catholic Encyclopedia*, vol. IX. Washington, DC: McGraw-Hill, pp. 293–4.
Thompson, E. P. 1963. *The Making of the English Working Class*. London: Gollancz.
   1978. *The Poverty of Theory and Other Essays*. London: Merlin Press.
Thompson, F. M. L. 1989. *The Rise of Respectable Society: A Social History of Victorian Britain (1830–1890)*. London: Collins.
Tocqueville, A. de. 1945. *Democracy in America*. New York: Alfred Knopf.
Tonkin, E. 1984. Participant observation. In R. F. Ellen (ed.), *Ethnographic Research*. London: Academic Press, pp. 216–23.
Tönnies, F. 1955. *Community and Association*. London: Routledge & Kegan Paul.
Valenzi, M. 1987. L'esperienza della giunta di sinistra. *La Città Nuova* 1: 29–33.
Valenzi, M. and Ghiara, M. 1978. *Sindaco a Napoli*. Rome: Editori Riuniti.
Van Gennep, A. 1960. *The Rites of Passage*. London: Routledge & Kegan Paul.
Vermeersch, A. 1912. Usury. In C. G. Herbermann et al. (eds.), *The Catholic Encyclopedia*, vol. XV. London: Caxton, pp. 235–8.
Viazzo, P. 1989. *Upland Communities: Environment, Population, and Social*

Structure in the Alps since the Sixteenth Century. Cambridge: Cambridge University Press.

Villari, P. 1979 [1885]. *Lettere meridionali e altri scritti sulla questione meridionale sociale in Italia*. Naples: Guida.

Von Hildebrand, D. 1967. Sex. In *New Catholic Encyclopedia*, vol. XIII. Washington, DC: McGraw-Hill, pp. 147–50.

Wallace, C. and Pahl, R. E. 1985. Household work strategies in economic recession. In N. Redclift and E. Mingione (eds.), *Beyond Employment: Household, Gender, and Subsistence*. Oxford: Basil Blackwell, pp. 189–227.

Wallman, S. 1979a. Introduction. In S. Wallman (ed.), *Social Anthropology of Work*. London: Academic Press, pp. 1–24.

1979b (ed.). *Social Anthropology of Work*. London: Academic Press.

1984. *Eight London Households*. London: Tavistock.

Weber, M. 1948. *The Protestant Ethic and the Spirit of Capitalism*. London: Allen & Unwin.

1949. *The Methodology of the Social Sciences*. New York: Free Press.

1970. Politics as a vocation. In H. H. Gerth and C. Wright Mills (eds.), *From Max Weber: Essays in Sociology*. London: Routledge & Kegan Paul, pp. 77–156.

1978. *Economy and Society: An Outline of Interpretive Sociology*, ed. G. Roth and C. Wittich. 2 vols. Berkeley: University of California Press.

White-Mario, J. 1978 [1876]. *La miseria in Napoli*. Naples: Quarto Potere.

Whyte, W. F. 1955. *Street Corner Society: The Social Structure of an Italian Slum*. Chicago: University of Chicago Press.

Willis, R. (ed.) 1975. *The Interpretation of Symbolism*. London: Malaby Press.

Wilson, B. (ed.) 1970. *Rationality*. Oxford: Basil Blackwell.

Zorbaugh, H. W. 1929. *The Gold Coast and the Slum*. Chicago: University of Chicago Press.

Zuckerman, A. 1977. Clientelist politics in Italy. In E. Gellner and J. Waterbury (eds.), *Patrons and Clients in Mediterranean Societies*. London: Duckworth, pp. 63–80.

1979. *The Politics of Faction. Christian Democratic Rule in Italy*. New Haven: Yale University Press.

Index

AA. VV., 191

Abrams, Ph., 4, 9, 167

action: collective, and individual goal pursuit, 28–9, 178–80; morality of, 180, 181–2; individual vs. collective, 154, 178, 182; vs. individualism, 13, 168, 178–82: *see also* agency/structure relationship

Adams Brown, W., 51

agency/structure relationship, 16–17; action from below, 17–18, 29, 134, 137, 158–9, 161–2, 165–6, 174–5, 181; constraints, 144, 152, 153, 156, 158, 161, 163, 164, 173, 176, 183; historical, 161–2

Albera, D., 189, 201

Aliberti, G., 140, 161

Alinovi, A., 206

Allies, 162

Allum, P., 2, 19, 31, 75, 135, 137, 141, 157, 192, 206

Alongi, G., 206

Alphonsus Liguori, Saint, 172

Altan, T., 137, 192

ambiguity: and liminality, 13, 105, 119; of children, 111; of moneylenders, 112; of prostitutes, 107; sexual, 130–2: *see also* work

Ambrasi, D., 139

Anthropological Quarterly, 196

Apolito, P., 189

appearance: relationship with reality, 3–4, 7–9, 103, 144, 148

Aristotle, 115

Arlacchi, P., 21, 23, 206

assistance: people's attitudes to, 136; policy of, 14, 17, 137, 160, 161, 178, 179

assistiti: and symbolism of gender, 125–6; as resources, 13, 125, 126; monks as, 126–9;

moral and spiritual identity of, 126: *see also* liminality; lotteries; rational(ity); work, and liminality

associations, religious: and favour-bestowing, 31, 79, 100, 150; and political canvassing, 79

Augustine, Saint, 201

Baglivo, A., 197, 207

Bailey, F., 12

Banfield, E. C., 2, 189, 199

Barth, F., 12

Barzini, L., 201

Becchi-Collidà, A., 19, 192

Beetham, D., 17, 139, 140, 146, 158, 165, 168, 169, 173, 175, 207, 208

Bella 'Mbriana, 53, 54, 71, 111, 122: *see also* house, culture of

Bellacci, M., 191

Belmonte, T., 2–3, 44, 189, 192, 196, 199

Bemporad, J., 106

Bentham, J., 112

betterment: idea of, 41, 72, 148, 150; identity choices, 58, 80, 144–5; morality of, 37, 49, 168, 185; pursuit of, 39, 81, 96

Blau, P. M., 139, 156, 173

Bloch, Marc, 138

Bloch, Maurice, 12, 49, 190

Blok, A., 133, 138, 161, 196, 199

Bobbio, N., 146, 180, 192, 208

Boissevain, J., 4, 12, 14, 133, 138, 159, 170, 205, 207

Bolle, K. W., 51

Bourbons, 161, 162

Bourdieu, P., 11, 16, 168, 186, 191, 192, 201

bourgeois(ie): as a general category, 5; as favour-seekers, 148, 150, 151–2; French, 116, 172; Northern Italian, 161; *popolino*'s

Cambridge Studies in Social and Cultural Anthropology

Printed in the United Kingdom
by Lightning Source UK Ltd.
102304UKS00001B/75